CHEECH
IS NOT MY REAL NAME

CHEECH

IS NOT MY REAL NAME
But Don't Call Me Chong!

Cheech Marin

With John Hassan

GRAND CENTRAL
PUBLISHING

NEW YORK BOSTON

Grand Central Publishing
Hachette Book Group
1290 Avenue of the Americas, New York, NY 10104
grandcentralpublishing.com
twitter.com/grandcentralpub

First edition: March 2017

Grand Central Publishing is a division of Hachette Book Group, Inc. The Grand Central Publishing name and logo is a trademark of Hachette Book Group, Inc.

The publisher is not responsible for websites (or their content) that are not owned by the publisher.

The Hachette Speakers Bureau provides a wide range of authors for speaking events. To find out more, go to www.hachettespeakersbureau.com or call (866) 376-6591.

Library of Congress Cataloging-in-Publication Data

Names: Marin, Cheech author. | Hassan, John author.
Title: Cheech is not my real name : but don't call me Chong! / Cheech Marin With John Hassan.
Description: First edition. | New York : Grand Central Publishing, 2017
Identifiers: LCCN 2016030657| ISBN 9781455592340 (hardcover) | ISBN 9781478934844 (audio download) | ISBN 9781478934851 (audio cd) | ISBN 9781455592326 (e-book)
Subjects: LCSH: Marin, Cheech. | Comedians—United States—Biography. | Motion picture actors and actresses—United States—Biography. | Hispanic American motion picture actors and actresses—Biography
Classification: LCC PN2287.M483 A3 2016 | DDC 791.4302/8092 [B]—dc23 LC record available at https://lccn.loc.gov/2016030657

Printed in the United States of America

LSC-C

10 9 8 7 6 5 4 3 2 1

To my cousin Louis Robles,
who taught me the love of
learning

CONTENTS

Contents

CHAPTER 1

What are you?

I had never seen a sky so blue in my whole life. Of course, I had never been to Canada before, either. It was mid-September 1968, and I was hitchhiking on a country road outside of Calgary, Alberta. Way off in the distance, the Canadian Rockies rose up like the picture in my mind of what the Rocky Mountains were supposed to look like: tall, majestic, snow-capped, big-assed mountains.

And damn, the sky was blue! It went on and on without a single cloud to give contrast to "infinity and beyond."

What was I doing here?

Good question.

How does a South Central Los Angeles–born, San Fernando Valley–raised Chicano end up walking down a country road like he's in a James Taylor song?

Well, why not?

After all, I had on the youth uniform of the time: blue chambray shirt, faded Levi's, cowboy boots, and a peace sign necklace. I was filled with all the contemporary counterculture ideals and slogans. I was on the leading edge of the "baby boom," the picture of American youth. I was young, dumb, and full of come. So what the hell was I doing here?

I was on the lam.

Well, sort of.

No, actually, I *was* on the lam; I just hadn't realized all the complications yet. I was in Canada because I had made a decision that totally changed my life. I had made it quickly but without fear. I had made it without consulting my family or friends. It was the kind of decision that I have made several times in my life. A door of opportunity opens, and you either go through it or you don't. I trusted my instincts most of the time, but that didn't mean it always worked out.

I had turned in my draft card, philosophically denying the government's authority over me and at the same time choosing to go to Canada to pursue my artistic calling as a potter. It was a philosophical twofer.

That decision placed me in the perfect Chicano existential quandary. Was I running away from something or was I running toward something? Was I an artist or was I a draft resister? Was I a Chicano or a Mexican or a Mexican-American or just an American? Or was I just hungry?

"I don't know. I don't know. I don't know. Leave me alone."

So, with fifty dollars in my pocket I rode "the Dog" (Greyhound bus) up to Calgary. As soon as I crossed the border I felt like a giant weight had been lifted off my shoulders. There was nobody after me here. I wasn't going to be shot or imprisoned. Everybody I saw looked…happy. *How weird—don't they know what's going on?* That was maybe because there was nothing going on here in Canada, the "Land of the Polite." At least there was nothing going on that was politically horrendous. Maybe I was the one who was weird.

Calgary was nothing like I'd pictured it in my imagination. I thought I was going to be met by Sergeant Preston of the Yukon with a dogsled and smiling Eskimos.

But Calgary looked like Bakersfield.

It was actually a cattle and oil town, and many people wore cowboy hats. It was Northern Montana. It was the home of the Calgary

Stampede, the world's biggest rodeo. The Stampede was actually happening when I arrived.

I called Jerry Kaufman (a fellow potter I'd hoped to work with) when I arrived at the bus station. He was very surprised to hear from me. As a matter of fact, he didn't even know that I was really coming. He just remembered that a mutual friend of ours had said that I might be coming...someday...maybe. Whatever. He said he'd be down in a half hour to pick me up. I really miss those innocent days when strangers would take you in and treat you like family. They didn't know any better.

Jerry picked me up, and on the way home he mentioned that since he didn't know I was coming, he and his wife and young son had planned a trip. They were leaving for Seattle in the morning for two weeks, but I was welcome to stay.

When we all got up in the morning, I met the family. They seemed like nice hippies. Not Charles Manson types or anything. Jerry showed me how to work the water pump and the intricacies of the outhouse and which way town was, and then they split.

So there I was, an inner-city Chicano from Hollywood and Vine standing in the middle of miles and miles of farmland with not a single person or building in sight.

A man out standing in his field. Cool!

I loved it. It was a brand-new start in a brand-new country. A country that wasn't at war. A country that didn't care where you came from. A country that would give an honest fella an honest break. I could be a brand-new person here judged only by the content of my character.

Before all that would happen, though, I figured I'd check out this big rodeo. So I started walking with my thumb out. After a while, a truck approached. A big trail of honest Canadian dust swirled behind it. It slowed down as it approached me and then pulled to a stop.

The passenger door flew open and a cowboy that looked like Kenny Chesney's inbred third cousin smiled and shouted out "Hop in, chief!"

"Hop in, chief?" What the fuck? This cracker thinks I'm an Indian.

"Where you headed?"

"To the Stampede."

"Well this is your lucky day. That's where I'm going."

We rode along for another minute in silence and then he gave me a long appraising look and said, "You're not Indian, are you?"

"No."

"Well, then, what the hell are you?"

I studied him for a few seconds and then said, "Chicano."

He studied me for a few seconds and then said, "You speak English pretty good. What do they speak where you come from?"

"Vato-neese."

"Vado-knees," he repeated. Well, welcome to Canada-o.

CHAPTER 2

Up on the Rooftop

Meanwhile, twenty-two years earlier...

I, Richard Anthony Marin, was born July 13, 1946, at 1:00 p.m. in South Hoover Hospital, in South Central Los Angeles. My parents, Oscar Marin and Elsa Meza, were also born in more or less the same area and attended Jefferson High School, which was a racially mixed but predominantly African-American school that became even more so each succeeding year.

By the time I was born, the neighborhood was about 90 percent black with a sprinkling of Mexicans, a few Asians, and a couple of "What the hell are you doing here?" whites.

It wasn't a "sketchy" neighborhood; it was straight up "ghetto."

Right from the beginning I knew it was a violent place. By the time I was seven, I had seen two homicides committed right before my eyes, but I had friends and most of my family all around.

My large and tight-knit family with grandparents, uncles and aunts, fake uncles, fake aunts, and a swarm of cousins all lived in close proximity. They generally had the same racial mix in their neighborhoods except for one part of the family that moved to Pico Rivera and became Jehovah's Witnesses...guys...but whatever.

I started grammar school at Trinity Street School, just three blocks from our house. The first day of school my mother walked me hand in hand to the playground. The chain-link fence enclosed what looked like a million loud, yelling, screaming, and running kids. It looked like a vortex that would swallow me up if I came too close. I gripped my mother's hand tightly as we entered the gate. The first thing I saw as we stepped into the yard was a fight between two young girls. A black girl and a Mexican girl. The black girl had a grip on the Mexican girl's long, black hair and was swinging her around with her feet off the ground.

Worried, I looked up at my mother and said, "Don't leave me here!"

"It's all right, you'll be OK," she said. But the look in her eyes told me that she really just *hoped* she was telling the truth.

The whole scene changed as we entered the kindergarten area, which had its own little garden and grass for us to play on. It was like a cool oasis next to the steaming cauldron of the playground.

I was soon put at ease by Mrs. Brown, the kindergarten teacher, who had a smile and a glass of lemonade for each student. My mother gave me a kiss on the top of my head and said, "I'll see you at noon," then quietly slipped out.

Before I could panic, Mrs. Brown started introducing the children to each other. She introduced me to the cutest little Chinese girl in the world, Mary Lee, and from that moment forward I was OK.

We were shown where the crayons and paper and paint supplies were and told to try to draw pictures of each other. Mary and I quickly paired off, and I learned something that still holds true today. Most every female loves to have her picture made, whether it's painted or photographed or Instagrammed or even selfied. So the quickest way to get a girl's attention is to say, "I'd love to do your portrait." If only I were a better artist or even any artist at all. When I showed Mary my efforts, her face looked like she had just sucked on a lemon.

"That doesn't look like me."

I had to learn to deal with rejection early. It would help out later in showbiz.

I quickly settled into a routine and started making friends. My best friend would be a young boy named Jesse. We spent a lot of time at each other's houses getting into mischief. I was always a rascally, curious kid, and Jesse was my partner in crime. Jesse was, in a way, a school celebrity because his mama did Bobo Brazil's laundry.

Bobo Brazil (real name Houston Harris) was the first black World Wrestling Association heavyweight champion. He was a very large man, about six foot six inches tall and 270 pounds of solid muscle. All the kids in my school watched wrestling, and Bobo was every kid's hero.

About once or twice a month he would pull up in front of Jesse's house, in his long, white, Cadillac Eldorado convertible with zebra upholstery, right across the street from our school.

As soon as he got out of his car, the whole schoolyard would come rushing over to the fence to see him and shout out his name. They'd yell out for him to crush "Killer Kowalski" or "Dick the Bruiser" or whoever he was wrestling on Wednesday night.

I was always glued to the TV set on that night with my grandmother, who spoke no English, but you needed no particular language to enjoy wrestling. It was the only time I'd ever see my Gramma Lola so animated. She would jump up and down and scream at the screen in Spanish, "Watch out! He's behind you!" When her favorite would win she would hug me and dance around. The "spirit of wrestling" possessed her way more than anything that happened at church.

When Bobo came out of the house with his new bag full of clean laundry, he would scan the crowd and find Jesse and motion for him to come up front. Bobo would hand him a quarter through the fence. Of course, being his best friend, I got a quarter, too. It was my first brush with showbiz and I was mesmerized. Bobo Brazil was on TV, drove a big, white Cadillac, and made the kids go nuts. I was drawn like a moth to the flame.

The hook was really set when I appeared in my first Christmas musical. I was six years old. It was a presentation at night in the auditorium, and the whole class was to sing the Christmas classic "Up on the Rooftop." Everybody was fitted with a blue paper headband with a big gold star right in front. For some reason, I was singled out to play the kettledrum. Now, the kettledrum is a big-ass drum and I was a little-ass kid. Even while standing on a stool, the only thing you could see was the gold star on top of my head.

The class started to sing and I waited for my cue. I gripped my mallet tightly and tried to slow down my breathing…and then it came:

"Up on the rooftop" boom, boom, boom.

A tiny hand holding a mallet appeared out of nowhere and hit the drum with perfect timing…*boom, boom, boom.*

The whole audience burst out laughing. "Where did that hand come from and what's with the floating star?"

The first time I did it I didn't even hear the audience, I was so concentrated on hitting the drum. The second time the laughter was even louder and I could hear people talking and giggling. The third time the people were convulsing with laughter. The song ended and the audience erupted in applause. The whole class took a bow and then my teacher motioned for me to step out from behind the drum. As soon as the audience saw me, they started screaming and whistling and laughing and applauding.

That was it. From that moment on, I knew it was the high life for me.

I don't know why but, in those early days, it seemed that I was always being picked for special events. In 1952, there was a radio show called *House Party*, hosted by Art Linkletter. It was a huge show that went on to become an even bigger television show. Mr. Linkletter was a very prominent TV personality whose amiable nature made him one of America's favorites. I loved him and watched him all the time. He later had another big TV show called *People Are Funny*.

This radio show was broadcast live from a studio in Hollywood. In one of its regular features, Art would ask young kids all kinds of questions to try to elicit funny answers. Usually he tried to get the kids to spill the beans on family secrets, like their mother's pregnant and their dad doesn't know. That kind of stuff.

Four kids from my first-grade class were picked to be on the show, and I was one of them. On the appointed day a big, black limousine pulled up and the whole school watched as the four of us got in and waved good-bye. Inside, the limo was loaded with candy and sodas and cookies, which we all set upon devouring immediately. When we finally pulled up in front of the studio, four little sugar-filled first graders burst out of the limo like mad bumblebees. I had never been out of my neighborhood before, let alone to the middle of Hollywood. It was like being dropped into the Land of Oz. We were quickly herded into a room where a nice man with nice manners patiently explained what was going to happen on the show.

"When Mr. Linkletter asks you a question, don't be afraid, just tell him the truth and . . . have fun out there!"

This guy had all the makings of a future community theater director. He was talking to four first graders who had just guzzled down two cans of soda and eaten twenty pieces of candy apiece. Our attention span was set on BZZZZ . . . and we all had to pee. The door to our room popped open and another assistant stuck his smiling face inside and said, "OK, it's time to go."

"I have to pee."

"No time, you're on," he chirped.

He turned on his megawatt smile and led us to the stage. There were four tall director's chairs set up on the stage and then, out of nowhere, a bunch of stagehands rushed out, picked us up and set us on the chairs, and then disappeared. As a parting shot, Mr. Megawatt chirped, "Have fun with it!"

There was a large studio audience and lots of lights and then Mr. Linkletter came out…and everything was cool. He had such an ease and a charm that he could even relax squirming first graders…and we were squirming!

He got the audience laughing and then eventually us kids. When he came around to me he asked, "And what does your father do?"

"He's a policeman."

Linkletter feigned horror. "A policeman. That's a very dangerous job. And what do you want to be when you grow up?"

For my whole life I have never known why, but I said, "Policeman."

Even at that young age, I knew that the last thing I wanted to be in life was a policeman, but the lights were on and I cracked under pressure. Hey, I was six.

Then Mr. Linkletter asked, "What if you were a policeman, and a burglar came into your house at night?"

"I'd get my gun."

"Well, what if you didn't have a gun? Say you left it at work that night."

I cocked my head down and then looked up at him and sneered, "Maybe I have a knife?"

"I give up!"

Art got a big laugh from the audience and then the show was over. Mr. Linkletter said good-bye to all of us and left the stage. Four stagehands again appeared out of nowhere and lifted us out of our chairs. We all made a beeline for the bathroom. Most of us made it.

As the 1950s wore on, Los Angeles established itself as a hub for television production. All the national shows were shot either there or in New York, but local shows, especially kids' shows, were what I really loved. They talked to kids in the studio and showed cartoons, but you could write in and request to be in the audience. I did and I got on the *Webster Webfoot Show*, which featured a ventriloquist

(Mr. Jimmy) and a talking duck (Webster). I wrote in to all the shows whether they had an audience or not. They would always send you something, a membership card or a badge or pin.

Other shows I liked were *Sheriff John's Lunch Brigade, Engineer Bill* (who would play "Red Light, Green Light" to get kids to drink their milk: "On the green light you go, and on the red light you stop, because no engineer would ever run a red light."), *Thunder Bolt the Wonder Colt*, the show about a young horse that was hit by lightning and gained superpowers. Kind of like Spider-Man with hooves, acted out by puppets.

It's hard to believe now, but in those days, television was a new thing. I remember, although vaguely, that there was a time when there was no TV...and then there was! I told this fact to my young son Joey when he was about nine years old. I went to call him out of his room for dinner and I looked around at all the electronic gadgets and computer games and remote controlled TVs, and I said, "When I was your age, we didn't have TV."

He rolled his eyes because he had heard many times the tales of my tough upbringing.

"I know, you guys were too poor."

"No, it wasn't that; it's that television wasn't invented yet."

It took him a few moments to process this information. I could hear him thinking.

"What do you mean there was no TV? How could there be no TV? That was like saying there was a time when there was no air. Just how old are you?"

Then in wonderment, he added, "What was it like the first time you saw fire?"

"Wash your hands and come to dinner...and turn off that TV."

Growing up, I had my share of those moments that leave indelible marks and stay with you your whole life.

One of those occurred for me when I was in the second grade.

Our school was very near the Grand Central Market, an enormous building that sold almost everything that grew on earth. They had every vegetable, every fruit, every grain, every flower, literally anything that you could imagine.

Mrs. Harding, my teacher, announced that we would be going on a field trip to the market. We all hopped on a bus and within a few minutes we were there. We walked through the doors, and it was like stepping into the Garden of Eden. I'm surprised harp music didn't play. We all had a blast running around and seeing every exotic plant in the world.

When we got back to class, Mrs. Harding passed out the *good* paper and crayons and told us to draw the thing that impressed us the most. We had an assistant teacher in class that day who was, I guess, completing the requirements for her teaching certificate, and she helped pass out the supplies. I couldn't wait to get started.

The things that impressed me the most were these giant banana squashes that were a yellow-orange color and were taller than I was. I spread out my paper and got to work. I thought I was doing an amazing job illustrating these vegetables that were almost two feet over my head. I drew myself as a little stick-figure kid standing next to them with a big smile.

After about half an hour, the teachers came around to view our work. As they went around the class, I heard them making comments about each kid's work like "Oh, that's very nice" or "I like how you used all the colors." I couldn't wait for their comments about my amazing squashes.

Finally, the assistant came over to me and picked up my work. She let out a little laugh and shook her head.

"Well, you'll never be an artist."

She took my drawing with her and moved along. If I was older I would have thought of something witty to say, like, *Die and rot in hell, you evil, soul-crushing bitch!*

But I was only seven, and I just tried not to cry while the artist in me crawled off to shrivel up in some dark, unlit corner of my soul.

I never tried to draw again after that, but later in life I would become a world-renowned art collector. So, yeah: *Die, bitch!*

When I wasn't in school, life in the hood went on pretty much as usual. Every half hour or so a police car with its siren blaring would go speeding down the street and then drive away. Sirens used to freak me out and I would look for someplace to hide and cover my ears. It is no wonder that African-American men have a higher rate of early heart attack and hypertension than anybody else. The tension is constant. You don't ever really get used to it. It's not a matter of race; it's a matter of poverty. The same neighborhood today is still a very poor one and it is now 100 percent Latino and the exact same problems exist. I've been back and have seen it firsthand.

My mother countered this environment by joining the Parent-Teacher Association. She eventually became president of the Trinity Street School chapter. She was always a joiner and would become president of a few more organizations in the following years.

My father, Oscar, was a policeman. He joined the force because the Department of Water and Power, where he had been working, would not promote Mexicans past the rank of cable splicer. He took the advancement test three times and all three times was ranked number one...and still only a cable splicer. He saw the writing on the wall. It was nothing new; he had seen it all his life. He heard that the police department was hiring, and without my mother's knowledge, signed up for the job that he would hold for the next thirty years.

Since we only had the one car, a 1952 Plymouth, it was her duty to take my father to work and pick him up at the end of his shift each day. Taking him to work was always uneventful. We dropped him off and he walked into the station and that was that. Picking him up was where all the action was.

Policemen are always moved around from station to station in different parts of the city. We never knew when he was going to get off because he could get involved in some case and be hours late. So there we would be, sitting in our Plymouth waiting and waiting and waiting.

Each station had a different specialty. Georgia Street was a police station and also an emergency hospital. We watched the ambulances pull in with red lights flashing and sirens blasting, and the doors would burst open to reveal some blood-soaked person on a gurney who would be rushed inside, just like on television. One time two rival gangs arrived at the hospital and continued to duke it out in the parking lot as they carried their wounded inside.

The worst one was the Lincoln Heights Jail. We would be waiting in the parking lot and the paddy wagon would pull in right next to us. They had been out on the street picking up drunks and derelicts. One of the policemen would open the doors and out would fall some drunk who would go *splat* on the cement. Usually, they had pissed their pants and crapped their drawers, and the stench that wafted across the parking lot could knock a buzzard off a shit wagon.

One station I particularly remember was University Station. It was right next to the University of Southern California, hence the name. There was a bar across the street from the station called the "502 Room"—*502* was police code for drunk driving. More often than not, my dad would be there before us, sitting in a car with three other policemen, each with a six-pack of beer in his lap, downing them as fast as they could. It took that much for them to come down from the pressure of the job.

Policemen have an abnormally high rate of alcoholism, divorce, domestic violence, and suicide. You deal with the worst and most dangerous segment of society every day. You never know if you're going to come home at night. I knew right away that this was not the job I wanted to have, despite what I told Art Linkletter.

You know the funny thing about growing up in this kind of neighborhood is that you don't know anything else. You have nothing to compare it to. It all seems so normal. That was about to change very quickly.

In the dead of night

*B*am, *bam, bam!*

In 1954 I was only eight years old, but I knew exactly what those sounds were. They were gunshots and they were coming from right outside my bedroom window.

Bam, bam, bam!

Three more shots and I hit the floor and crawled into the front room where my mother and father slept.

"Mommy, they're shooting out there."

"I know, *mijo,* stay down."

I looked around the room and couldn't find my father.

"Where's Daddy?"

"He's out there, *mijo,* stay down."

I stayed down on the floor wrapped in my mother's protective arms for what seemed like forever. Finally, after a long silence, my mother went to the window and peeked through the shades. Swirling red and blue police lights flooded the room.

"What's happening?" I asked my mother, my body shivering with fright.

"There was a burglary."

A narrow, five-foot alley separated our duplex from a barbershop that had indeed been robbed.

Around 3:00 a.m., an alarm had gone off. It was faint, but loud

16

enough to awaken my father, by now a nearly ten-year veteran of the Los Angeles Police Department.

He got out of bed and pulled back the window shade and saw someone in the barbershop walking around with a small flashlight. He pulled on a pair of khakis and a white T-shirt, and got his gun. He told my mother to call the police, give them the address, and tell them that her husband was LAPD and he was going out to investigate. He told her to *be sure* to tell them that he was the one in khakis and a white T-shirt.

He entered the alley from the street side and walked halfway down to the window that had been jimmied open. He shined his flashlight on the man inside, identified himself as a policeman, and told the man to come out with his hands up. The man complied and put his hands on the side of the shop as my dad frisked him. He found three straight razors in the coat pocket and turned him back around.

"What are you going to do with me?"

"I'm going to hold you here until the police come. They're on their way."

The man looked around nervously and heard a siren wailing just down the street. It had been raining that night, and the man had brought an umbrella that leaned against the building. The siren was now just yards away.

"I'm not going back to prison."

He made a lunge at my father's gun and knocked it out of his hands. They wrestled on the wet ground, each trying to find the loose gun. Whoever got to that gun first was going to live. Luckily, my father found it first. The burglar broke free and grabbed the umbrella and proceeded to repeatedly whack my dad over the head with it. The cops were spilling out of the patrol car, guns drawn. My mom yelled out of the window.

"My husband's a policeman! He's the one in the white T-shirt!"

My dad, on his hands and knees, found his gun with the guy still whacking him with the umbrella. He rolled over on his back and fired. Though hit in the shoulder, the burglar turned and tried to run away. The cops opened up and my dad continued to fire. At the end of the alley the man collapsed, dead.

Another day in the hood.

The only difference was that my family was right in the middle of it.

As in all officer-involved shootings, there was an inquest in which all the facts were examined. Testimony was given by all the officers involved. Even the deceased man's parents, who lived in the area, testified that they tried to do the best they could in raising their son, but he had a significant criminal record and had served four years in prison for armed robbery. They insisted that he didn't deserve to die for this burglary. In the end, the inquest ruled that it was justifiable homicide in the commission of an armed robbery, case closed.

There were rumblings in the neighborhood newspapers because it was a Chicano policeman and a black victim. People would come by and point down the alley but after a while it became just another shooting in the hood, and everything went back to normal.

It never went back to normal for me. I had nightmares every night. Any little sound woke me up. The grocery store two doors away would get deliveries early in the morning, and the sound of trucks being unloaded woke me right up and had me looking out the window.

CHAPTER **4**

A change of scenery

One Saturday in the summer of 1955, my dad said that we were going on a trip to see a police buddy of his, Ernie Dicken. We all piled into the Plymouth and headed out to Granada Hills in the Northwest section of the San Fernando Valley. It was my first time in the country—or what I thought was the country.

We drove until the freeway ended in Van Nuys and then continued on surface streets until we'd been through all the towns and then there were just orange groves. I counted every backyard swimming pool I could see on the way to our destination.

Finally, we arrived at the Dickens house. It was a fairly new tract house on a suburban street surrounded by other semi-identical houses. Ernie, Virginia, and their son, Mike, were very nice; they welcomed us and ushered us into the kitchen where Virginia had prepared a lunch. My dad and Ernie fell into that easy camaraderie that most cops share, brothers in arms. Virginia and my mother got along great, and the Dickens would remain our lifelong friends.

After lunch my father and Ernie took a ride, and we were left at the house to get acquainted. Mike was a big, tall kid who would go on to be an all-league football player for Granada Hills High. He would be my protector for a lot of years.

Finally, my dad and Ernie came back, and it was time for us to go. On the way home, my dad was very silent.

Then, about halfway home, he suddenly announced,

"I bought us a house."

My mother's jaw dropped open.

"What do you mean?"

"I just put a down payment on a house one street over from the Dickens. We can move in next week."

My mother was eight months pregnant with my twin sisters. It was July. She started breathing heavier and started to sweat. I thought she was going to deliver right there and then.

A week later I was riding in the cab of a moving truck with my father on our way to our new home in Granada Hills. I was excited and scared. One day everybody in my neighborhood was black, and now everybody in my neighborhood was white. It was like going from Nigeria to Knott's Berry Farm. The drive still seemed endless, but my swimming pool count was up to seventy-two. Finally, we pulled up in front of our brand-spanking-new home.

We were the first family to ever live in it. It stood glistening in the middle of a dirt lot. I looked up and down the street, and every other house looked basically the same: new house, dirt lot. I would eventually spend many hours rototilling, seeding, fertilizing, and watering our new lawn into existence. We opened the front door, and it smelled just like a new house. Not that I had ever smelled one before, but if you could bottle *that smell* and let people inhale it, everybody would do whatever they had to do to get a new house. My dad turned on the taps in the kitchen and mud came out. Now, baby, *that's* new.

Our neighborhood was all tract houses bordered by orange groves. At night, the aroma of the orange blossoms was intoxicating. The first night in the house, I was awakened by a noise. I was afraid. It sounded like the house was being electrocuted. I went to the window and the sound grew louder. I opened the window and it got louder still. Then I realized what it was. The sound of a million crickets had replaced screaming sirens and gunshots. I'll make that trade every time.

In the afternoon, when my dad went to work, my mother and nine-year-old me would wander around the house. I would wander, she would waddle. When she got tired, we would sit in one room and just feel the ambience and look out the window of our brand-new house. It was like we were in a dream. It was a four-bedroom house with two bathrooms and a large backyard, where I would learn all the basic gardening skills while being overseen by "Oscar Legree," my father.

We soon met all the neighbors and tried to be as friendly as we could—which wasn't hard for my mom, as everybody loved her. My dad exchanged tips with all the other dads about how to put in the perfect lawn. The big raging debate was grass versus dichondra. All the families with kids went for grass, which could take a beating, and the childless couple opted for dichondra, which looked prettier.

Every day, it was a new decision: white plastic plates vs. sea foam green plastic plates. I was learning new words and phrases like *off-white* and *sandstone*. Then one day our new furniture arrived all in Colonial Maple, perfect for a young Chicano family in the Valley.

I never felt so American.

The highlight of the suite was a big cabinet with a hi-fi inside. It was a radio–record player combination that could play the latest invention: "long play" record albums, or LPs.

There was a limited selection of albums at first but I quickly, unbeknownst to my parents, signed us up for an album-of-the-month club. Every month we would receive Original Broadway Cast show soundtracks, Johnny Mathis's *Greatest Hits* and the latest Scatman Crothers album and other popular records of the time.

It was hot in the Valley; like hot, *hot*. Summer days would often be over a hundred degrees. My poor mother would sit in the coolest shade she could find and pant like a large German shepherd. Then, on August 2, she delivered my twin sisters, Monica and Margaret. I didn't know how to feel about the arrival of my sisters. After all, I was an only child for nine years and the center of my parents' attention. Now I would have to share the spotlight. When I went to the hospital with my dad to pick them up, they were so tiny and adorable, and I realized right away: *I can make them my slaves.*

The summer was over, my new twin sisters were safely ensconced in their matching cribs, and I was ready to start third grade at a new school. While my grandmother Carmen watched over the twins, my mother and I took the shortcut through the orange grove to get to Granada Hills Elementary School. We arrived at the playground, and all the kids were playing nice. They were just as loud as the kids from Trinity but nobody was fighting...and they were all white.

OK. Not all white. There were a few Mexican kids but no Asians and not one black kid. I thought, *This is weird, but whatever.*

My mom took me to my new classroom and I met my new teacher, Mrs. O'Brian. She was very nice, and we liked each other right away.

I was assigned a desk and I sat down, trying not to wrinkle my new clothes. I moved like a starched robot. I was trying to be on my best behavior and make a good impression. After a few preliminary instructions and directions as to what and where everything was, the recess bell rang, and you could feel the tension let out of the whole class. Mrs. O'Brian dismissed us, and everybody rushed out the door.

I looked around this new playground, and everything looked bigger and newer than my old playground. I searched for something familiar and spotted a tetherball pole. Every school had tetherball, so I walked over and sat down on the bench to be next to play. I watched the two kids playing and they played the same way we played tetherball at my old school.

Then, I saw two kids walking straight toward me. They were laughing and pointing in my direction. As soon as they got to the bench, the bigger of the two shoved me and said, "Hey blackie, get at the end."

They started laughing together while repeating, "Yeah, blackie."

I couldn't believe it. They were calling *me* blackie.

Now, I wasn't familiar with the correct procedure here in Granada Hills. I only knew what I knew from South Central. So I stood up and swung as hard as I could and hit this little fucker right in the mouth. He turned red as a thermometer and didn't stop crying for half an hour.

As I was usually the littlest kid, I learned to get in the first punch. I had been hit many times, both at the playground and at home, so it was no great shock. I guess this was the first time this kid's sense of entitlement was ever questioned.

A teacher came running over when she heard little Johnny screaming and marched us off to the principal's office. Now the thought of the thumping I was absolutely going to get from my father (and I did) paled next to the thought that at least one little a-hole was not going to ever bother me again. Nice first day.

This incident demonstrates one of the tougher aspects of my upbringing. My father had no tolerance for any fooling around or kid stuff. If I got called to the office, no matter the situation, I had done something wrong. And I got hit. Every time. Which was a prevalent form of punishment in those days. But my dad was a policeman and a former boxer.

We had a neighbor in Granada Hills. He once said to my dad, "Oscar, you are the most even-tempered man I've ever met. You're always mad." Sadly, that was true.

My dad dealt with a drinking problem in these early years of living in our new town. Those after-work beers developed into black-out-drunk periods. He'd come home after a shift, pretty drunk, and wrestle with me—playfully, in his mind—but he'd rough me up a bit because of his size and the shape he was in. Then he'd get up, try to make himself something to eat, and pass out facedown on the plate.

As time wore on, though, he got a grip on it and no longer drank to such excess. He didn't stop. He cut back. It wasn't until he was almost retired that he gave any thought to his health. He lived to be ninety-two...so go figure.

The rest of the semester went all right. There were a few more altercations with some kids but, all in all, it was OK. The one thing that I established was a profile that would stay with me through the rest of my academic life.

I was a little wiseass who got straight As.

Even if some teachers didn't like me (and there were a few), I still got an A in their class. It wasn't so much that I was a troublemaker, it was that I couldn't shut up. I was always talking, making jokes with the kids around me. Some teachers put up with it and thought I was cute; others were not amused. They would make me stay after class in detention or make me do extra work, but I would still get an A. Must have pissed them off.

In those days, the public school year was divided into two sections, A and B. You started off the year in section B, and after a semester you switched to section A with a new teacher.

After a few months, Mrs. O'Brian handed out our report cards and told us to be sure that they went straight to our parents and not to open them until we got home. Good luck on that one.

As soon as I was off the schoolyard, I opened the envelope and saw that I had straight As.

Cool, what can I get out of this?

The next semester brought a new classroom with a new teacher, Mr. Steakly. Not my favorite teacher ever. His teaching style was dead boring, so of course I started my little comedy class in the back of the room. I was quickly moved up to the front of the class, away from my friends, where he could keep an eye on me. That seemed to work for him, just not for me. I squirmed as much as I could, but I was right under his thumb.

There were a couple of kids in class that I didn't get along with, and they were always needling me. One day we got into a little altercation in the schoolyard that carried over into the classroom. Mr. Steakly blew his top and grabbed a softball and threw it on the floor so hard it hit the ceiling. He marched us off to the principal's office. I waited there for my father to arrive.

When he arrived at the office he listened to the teacher's complaints. It was the only time my father ever took my side against a teacher. Mr. Steakly was a real dick, a semiracist, who made it clear that things were going to hell since they started having Mexicans in the school. I saw my dad doing a slow burn as he listened to this idiot. After he finished, my dad looked him in the eye and very calmly said, "Thank you very much. If you need to get ahold of me, call this number."

He handed the teacher his police card. That seemed to chill Mr. Steakly out more than a little.

When we got into the car to go home, we drove along in silence until we pulled up in front of the house and he said, "We've got to get you into a new school."

My father didn't hit me this time, either. He saw what was happening. I was dealing with the same kind of racism he'd known his whole life. He stood up for me. He *knew* it wasn't my fault this time.

CHAPTER 5

Father Marin?

The great thing about Granada Hills during this period was that *anything* that happened in town was the *first time* it ever happened.

Hughes Market was the first big supermarket to come to Granada Hills. The opening was a three-day festival with carnival rides, free samples of everything edible, and appearances by celebrities whose claim to fame was supermarket openings.

I played in the first year of Little League in town. In 1963, Granada Hills would win the Little League World Championship in Williamsport, Pennsylvania.

For my family, the opening of St. John Baptist de la Salle Catholic School was the most important "first" in town. After my run-in with Mr. Steakly, they enrolled me for fourth grade immediately, even though it was an added expense that would mean an extra job for my dad.

Catholic school didn't play that "blackie" stuff or that "whitey" stuff; they played straight up corporal punishment. The first day you walked into the classroom, you saw a cross with Christ nailed to it. You got the picture right away. Once I got to de la Salle, it was clear sailing as far as school goes. I remember no real drama or any huge problems.

All my cousins were in Catholic school, so we were all speaking the same language and had the same references. We all also learned something very Catholic: how to sell door-to-door.

In Catholic school, you were always selling something whether it was Christmas seals, raffle tickets, subscriptions to Catholic periodicals, or whatever. It was all fund-raising for the school and it was mandatory. It was key in our family to be the one who got to our grandparents first!!

Actually, I came to love selling door-to-door. It was a real eye-opener to get to see into everybody's home. I saw firsthand the diversity that made up my neighborhood.

One time it would be a sweet little old lady who would smile before she closed the door in my face. Another time it would be a pissed-off husband in the middle of a fight with his wife.

The most unique encounter I had selling door-to-door was with a man who had had some kind of operation that left a hole in the middle of his throat. He spoke with a voice box. At first he scared the hell out of me, but he was the nicest of my neighbors and he bought a whole book of Christmas seals. Going door-to-door was also a great experience for me to have as a future actor. It really taught me a lot about self-confidence and hard work, and not to take rejection personally. I learned that you have to work to get what you want. Those lessons have stayed with me all my life.

There is another thing that is drilled into you all during Catholic grammar school: the concept of having a vocation.

At first, I thought they said *vacation* and I replied, "Cool, I'm all for it. The longer, the better."

I quickly found out that they were talking about being a priest or a nun.

There is a point in every Catholic grammar school kid's life where he or she considers joining the clergy. It is unavoidable, because it is pounded into you every day. I have to admit that I was not immune to the indoctrination. I was an altar boy and a choirboy, and I won the Religion Award when I graduated from eighth grade.

Eventually, I decided that I would pursue joining the priesthood. I was accepted to St. Vincent's Junior Seminary, a high school for future priests. I had passed all the tests, and my clothes were at the school awaiting my arrival.

It was becoming a family tradition. My older cousin Louie was already at St. Anthony's Seminary in Santa Barbara. My younger cousin Ray Gene Castro would go to the same school two years later, where he would become student body president. My cousin Rosalie was at St. Joseph's Convent studying to be a nun, which she would be for the following thirty years. My mother was elated. Her son would be a priest. Her place in heaven was secured.

And then after eighth-grade graduation, I started going to parties during the summer. I started to slow-dance close with girls. I even made out with a few.

Wait a minute. Time out. Let me rethink this for a minute.

Let's see . . . priesthood. No girls ever . . . ever.

I don't think so.

My mother was crushed. And it was my father's turn to be elated. After all, I was the extension of the family line. So it was off to Bishop Alemany High School in Mission Hills, still a Catholic school but without the no-girls part.

And all was right with the world.

CHAPTER 6

A Hard Day's Night

High school was like jumping in the deep end of the pool without knowing if you really knew how to swim.

There were kids from all over the Valley, from other Catholic schools that were way older and more established than mine. I was in de la Salle's first graduating class. We had played some of the other schools in sports (baseball, basketball, and football) and got soundly thrashed. Now it was time to see if we measured up academically. As it turned out, we had nothing to worry about and did just fine in comparison.

I loved all subjects except math. During some math classes, all I could think of was how to get my erections to go down. During geometry, I could spring one during a discussion of the Pythagorean Theorem. *I got your right angle right here!*

I played every sport. I found out very quickly that although I loved it, I was too small for football. I didn't look forward to getting creamed by big, fat guys. I played basketball, which I also loved, but I was too short to make varsity. I had a hoops nickname, though. Wilt Chamberlain was called "Wilt the Stilt." I was called "Wilt the Stump."

Then, in 1962, during my sophomore year, the Great Folk Scare happened.

Folk music of all varieties exploded across the country. It came at a time when rock and roll had stopped being rebellious and had slipped into a very syrupy stage. The hit parade was full of singers taking good care of their babies and telling Laura that they loved her.

Folk music represented something that was raw and real. It took no time for it to become commercial, too, but it set up a big divide in its young audience right from the beginning. There were the "real" folkies who played and sang only traditional folk songs, like Child Ballads and tunes that featured "silver daggers plunged into lily-white breasts" or were at least a hundred years old. These diehards seldom washed, ate all their meals from oversized handmade mugs, and disdained anyone not as completely devoted as they were to the purity, as they saw it, of real folk music.

At the same time, there was a hugely creative group led by Bob Dylan, Phil Ochs, Paul Simon, and others who were moving out of the traditional style and writing their own songs that reflected what was happening today. I didn't care, I liked them both. I don't know how authentic I was, being a Chicano singing about Gypsy Davy roaming the country-o. I just liked singing and being in show business.

I had been singing since I was five years old. An old friend of my mother's had a little recording machine that produced playable discs. An acetate coil would be carved out as the needle incised a groove in the record and sound would be imprinted into the disc. I was this little squeaky voiced five-year-old singing "Amorcito Corazón" in Spanish. The one quality that distinguished me then and now is that I could sing in tune.

I started taking guitar lessons when I was about twelve. I had bugged my dad nonstop until he relented and took me to a music store and bought me the cheapest guitar he could get away with. Actually, I paid for it by mowing lawns in the neighborhood, but he fronted the money. It was a Stella acoustic. It was more like a two-by-four with bailing wire but, hey, it was a start. I wanted a candy-apple-red electric guitar. Dad asked what the price was, and when the salesman told him he gave me a look that said, *Are you out of your fucking mind?* So I got the Stella and got busy learning "Michael Row the Boat Ashore." I learned just recently that Willie Nelson started with a Stella as well, so I was in good company.

Parents are always proud of you when you start playing a musical instrument. Well, other than the violin, which can make sounds that can take the enamel off your teeth. They also get less patient when you play and sing at the top of your lungs at two in the morning, but it's all part of the process.

I played every chance I got from living rooms to school assemblies, to open mike night at every coffeehouse I could find. We even formed a large group a la the New Christy Minstrels at our school. It was called the Mission Hills Singers after the location of our school.

The center of the folk scene in West Los Angeles was a club called the Ash Grove, which was a performance space and guitar shop. I saw every single major folk, blues, or bluegrass act that came to town: Lightnin' Hopkins, Mance Lipscomb, Son House, Reverend Gary Davis, Sonny Terry and Brownie McGhee, Mississippi John Hurt, John Lee Hooker, legendary flat-picker Doc Watson, Ian and Sylvia, the Stoneman Family, the New Lost City Ramblers, Pete Seeger, and many more, but the act that made the biggest impression on me was a totally unknown blind singer and guitarist named Jose Feliciano.

Jose ambled onstage with his dog, his wraparound Batman black sunglasses, and a guitar case. He opened his case, took out his nylon string guitar, and without one word launched into a lightning-fast flamenco run that segued into him singing Ray Charles's "I Got a Woman." When he finished, the entire jaded, seen-it-all folkie audience gave him a thunderous, stomping, screaming ovation. Every hotshot, "I'm so bad" guitar player in the house suddenly started thinking about selling insurance.

I got on the phone and called all my friends and spread the word.

The next night we were all there at the now fully packed Ash Grove to see this phenom. The next night he was even better...and funny. He did blues, he did rock, he sang in Spanish, and then he did the most astounding thing I have ever seen live on a stage.

In the middle of a song, he broke a string. Instead of stopping, he kept on playing scales, nursery tunes, anything that crossed his mind while at the same time pulling off the broken string, reaching into his guitar case, finding the right string, stringing it on to the guitar, tuning it and then continuing on with the song, right where he left off.

Did I mention he was blind?

I loved the Ash Grove. I went every week not only for the great music but because they would sell you beer no matter how old you were. I was sixteen but I looked twelve. Didn't matter, I had money. Ahh, the folk process.

And then the Beatles landed in America...and everything changed.

When the Beatles first came out, they were viewed by my folkie friends as just a teenybopper fad that would simply fade away like a press-on tattoo. What really turned them off was the same thing that turned the teenyboppers on: the "wild" haircuts. When viewed through the lens of today, John, Paul, George, and Ringo look like bank presidents, but at first they were put in the goofy novelty category.

There was, however, something infectious and energetic about their music. Sure, they were doing a lot of Chuck Berry covers, which I recognized right away because the first record I bought was a 78 rpm of "Sweet Little Sixteen."

But there was something else.

The Beatles stood out in one important way: Right from the very beginning they were writing their own tunes. They *sounded* familiar because they were inspired by their early rock-and-roll idols like Berry, Elvis Presley, Little Richard, and especially the Everly Brothers. They also covered their favorite artists early on, like Carl Perkins and

Smokey Robinson. But from their first album on, they wrote many (and later all) of the songs on their albums.

What was really amazing about this early period was their sheer output, which led some people to assume that they didn't write their own songs because nobody could write that many great, memorable tunes in that short a period. With every new release, I became more and more of a fan, much to the chagrin of my purist folkie friends, who viewed me as a sellout to juvenile rock and roll and a traitor to the virtues of crusty folk music.

Then in 1964 the Beatles released their first film, *A Hard Day's Night*, and all bets were off. I went to my local theater to see it the first day it opened and stayed for three showings. To this day, it is my favorite film ever. No other movie before or since has taken you to the white-hot center of a pop phenomenon with more authenticity, humor, *and* a soundtrack that will stay with you for the rest of your life. And it introduced the modern music video. I was enthralled and couldn't wait to spread the word.

I dragged all my folkie friends to the theater and they were converted in a flash, especially the girls. For weeks, we only talked in quotes from the movie. It was like a secret language. If you didn't understand it...well, you just didn't understand. All the guys immediately started to grow their hair as long and as fast as they could.

Looking back, what we were involved in was the start of the baby boom takeover that would last for the next fifty years. The Beatles were just the beginning. It seemed like the next week Bob Dylan, the folk god and oracle, went electric and promptly got booed at the Newport Folk Festival. The battle lines were being drawn and just as quickly erased as more and more defectors rushed over to the electric side. The times were a-changing from all directions at once. The country had no idea what was about to happen to its youth. And I was there, front and center and at the head of the line.

CHAPTER 7

What else have they been lying about?

Just to recap my life so far: I was a Cub Scout, a Boy Scout, an altar boy, a member of the choir, a straight-A student. I got the Religion Award when I graduated from eighth grade. I almost went to the seminary to become a priest...and my dad was a cop.

I was who I was raised to be.

When I went to college, I had my mind set on becoming a lawyer. I was going to uphold the law and fight for "truth, justice, and the American way."

Then one day in college, I smoked a joint with my roommates. As I felt the full effect of the marijuana smoke altering my consciousness, my first thought was:

And what else have they been lying about?

It was like pulling that first thread and then seeing the whole garment unravel.

Growing up, the only thing I knew about marijuana was what I read in the newspapers. It was usually a report about a "drug bust," accompanied by a black-and-white photo of two Mexicans in handcuffs and wifebeaters standing at the back of a car with what looked like a bale of hay in the trunk.

I asked my dad why they were arresting farmers for having alfalfa and he would say something along the lines of "Ah, they're a bunch

34

of hypes [drug addicts who used hypodermic needles]. Don't you ever smoke marijuana or that will be the end of your short little life! Now get me a beer."

Sometimes I'd see a reference in the story about how Gene Krupa, the swing band drummer, got arrested for marijuana possession. In most pictures, Krupa had wild hair and a wild look in his eyes, but he looked like he was having fun. My dad said he was a hophead. "Don't you ever do marijuana or I'll break your neck!"

Robert Mitchum was next in the news after he got nabbed in a drug raid. His picture was splayed across the cover of *Hollywood Confidential* sneering defiantly as he was marched to the paddy wagon. This was serious, because he was one of my dad's favorite movie stars. "He probably got in with the wrong crowd," said my dad as he shook his head.

If I was to believe what I saw in the newspaper, the "wrong crowd" was apparently two hot-looking blonde starlets. OK, whatever. Marijuana leads to heroin and then straight to prison for stealing money out of your mom's purse to support your drug habit...and I would get thumped by my dad.

Aside from these very occasional news stories, I never really thought about drugs. My early teenage years were consumed with sports, studies, and, again, trying to figure out how to make this erection go down. I followed the rules, drank my milk, ate my spinach, and dreamed the American wet dream.

My second semester at San Fernando Valley State College (now called California State University, Northridge), I moved into an apartment building with two of my fraternity brothers. I was working for Nordskog, a company with a factory in the San Fernando Valley that manufactured airplane galleys (kitchens) for all the major airlines. I worked about thirty-five hours a week as well as carrying a full load of sixteen units at school. I was the first worker that they hired on a part-time basis, because I was the first guy who went to college while working there.

I worked in the tool crib, which was the place that everybody came for tools or rivets or glue or anything else they needed to make airplane galleys. To this day, I cannot walk onto an airplane without checking out the galley and thinking, *Hey, I might have had a hand in making this.*

Once I got to work, all I had to do was clean the area and then wait for everyone to come up and order what they wanted. I filled up the waiting time by studying for my various classes. I think it was a testament to my powers of concentration that I could study with a hundred rivet guns going off at the same time.

Much of the above is the backstory to establish clearly that I was a hard-working, solid citizen, believer of the company line, and drinker of the Kool-Aid.

After working late one Friday night, I came home to find a party going on in my apartment. My roommates and several of our friends were there, as well as a few guys that I didn't know. There were no girls, which was not unusual. There was music playing and everybody was having a good time and I was really ready to have a good time.

From out of nowhere, my roommate Jerry pulled out what looked like a hand-rolled cigarette, lit it and handed it to me. He knew I didn't smoke, so what was this all about?

"It's a reefer."

"What?"

"A joint…grass…marijuana."

I don't know what possessed me, but I reached out and took it.

"Take a big hit and then keep it in till you can't keep it in anymore," instructed Jerry. All eyes in the room were on me now. I took a big hit and immediately coughed it out and kept on coughing. Everybody laughed.

"Try it again."

This time I kept it in for what seemed like forever and then finally let it out followed by a few more coughs. Jerry took the joint from my fingers.

"Hey man, don't bogart it."

"What?"

By now there were several other joints circulating the room. Everybody seemed to know what they were doing. A floating joint came my way again and I took another hit. I held it in as long as I could, but this time I didn't cough when I let it out.

Now I have heard more than a few people say that they can't get high no matter how much they smoke. I am not one of those people. The next time another joint came floating by *I was high as a motherfucker.*

The whole world seemed to go into slow motion. Sounds were louder and softer at the same time. The music that was playing, *Herbie Mann at the Village Gate,* which I had heard a hundred times before, sounded new. I heard each individual instrument like it was being played live in my living room. I could make out the voices in the audience and hear them having conversations and ordering drinks from the waitresses, glasses clinking and chairs being moved. They had always been there in the recording, but I had never heard them. I thought, *But how could I not have heard this stuff before?*

I was hyperaware of everything...and then I started to laugh... and I laughed and I laughed and I laughed at everything. One of my friends asked me how I was doing.

"I'm fucked up."

And *that was the funniest thing I had ever heard in my life.* I laughed until tears came out of my eyes. I looked around, and everybody else was fucked up, too. I felt this warm, overwhelming sense of well-being...and yes, love. I loved everybody in that room.

Now some people also say that they get paranoid when they smoke grass.

Wow, too bad.

Maybe they were just paranoid to begin with.

I have always found that marijuana is an enhancer of whatever state I am already in. I never smoke when I have anything to do, like homework or my taxes or walking a straight line. I usually only smoke when I have nothing to do. I find I can do nothing *better* if I'm high. Doing nothing is boring, but at least if you're stoned something might happen. You might find God or go to sleep...or something.

What marijuana does, among other things, is change your perspective. It slows things down and you get to see them in another light, from another angle. You are able to think about things in a new way.

In every culture since the beginning of time, man has sought to alter his consciousness through various intoxicants. If you don't seek to alter your consciousness every once in a while, you are prone to buy the company line and join in lockstep conformity and become a faceless, easily manipulated worker bee. The history of the world is rife with examples of geniuses who got high and thought about a different way to do things. Progress is sometimes made this way, not by accident but by a purposeful act.

The next morning was really the revelation. I didn't wake up hopelessly addicted to marijuana and craving heroin. I didn't even wake up with a hangover like I did when I drank. But I knew I had been to a place I had never been to before. And it was definitely not the scary, horror-filled, haunted house that the establishment wanted you to believe it was.

And *that* thought that kept reverberating in my mind:

And what else have they been lying about?

Herbie Mann had been trying to tell me. But I wasn't listening. The entire second side of his *Village Gate* live album was the Gershwin song "It Ain't Necessarily So."

I was listening now.

CHAPTER 8

A cross-fire hurricane

College was by far the largest pool I had ever been thrown into. There were students from all over the city, state, country, and even the world. There was every color and ethnicity all thrown together in pursuit of an education. So this mix was an interesting environment for me because my face has some kind of international malleability to it. Add your own preference or prejudice to it and I could be anything.

I also must say that I've used it to my advantage over the years, especially in the quest for, let's say, romantic adventure. In those college days, I convinced three separate girls at a frat party one night that I was Dutch Indonesian. Three bottles of Pagan Pink Ripple wine helped, too. They helped me because I had no idea what a Dutch Indonesian looked like, sounded like, or smelled like. I had eaten some Dutch Indonesian food once before at my next-door neighbor's when I was eleven. It was there that I first heard the term "Dutch Indonesian." At first I thought it was where the Dutch kept their "Nesians." You know—indoors, the same place the Chinese kept their good plates. Indoor China. Only later did I learn that Indonesia was someplace I would probably never visit, but at some time I guess the Dutch did... well, anyways, back to the party.

I belonged to a fraternity in college, Sigma Phi Beta, which was a local frat in that it existed only at the one campus, Valley State College (go Vallies). We later affiliated with a national fraternity, Phi

Sigma Kappa, but we were the same greasers we always were. The fraternity came together because it was composed of guys who were in two different car clubs at two different high schools. Kinda like in *Grease*. Anyway, all these guys went to college because they were smart but still wanted to hang around together. So they said, "What do we call a car club in college…a fraternity? OK, we're a fraternity. Let's get matching jackets."

So over the years Sigma Phi Beta attracted like-minded smart greasers. There are many reasons for joining a fraternity: social networking, academic support, a feeling of deep brotherhood, etc. I joined Sigma Phi Beta because they had the best parties—and the best parties attracted the hottest girls.

The game at our parties was to see how many girls you could hustle in the same night. I think the girls had the same agenda, so it worked out well. It was like a pre-DVD version of *Girls Gone Wild*, but without the cameras, only because they hadn't been invented yet.

The first girl I talked to asked the inevitable "What are you?" I don't know why Dutch Indonesian popped into my head. I guess I was just bored with all the other options and I was young, dumb, and…well, you know the rest. The only thing I elicited from her was a blank stare and then, "Is that in the Valley?"

"Hold that thought, I'll be right back."

The next girl also stared blankly (I think they were from the same sorority, Phi Beta Blankly) and then, "Cool, wanna make out?"

"Sure, that's why I'm here!"

The third girl stopped in her tracks and fixed me with an intense stare (nice variation) and then started speaking Dutch. I backed away quickly, stammering something about "I, I, I don't really speak Dutch, that was on my mother's side and she was born here and, and, and I gotta go."

Dutch Indonesian went out of the rotation for a long time after that.

It's June 1968 and there I was, covered in wet clay, striding barefoot across the quadrangle of Valley State College. I was heading for a temporary stage that was set up by the local draft resistance movement. I was spending all of my time in the pottery lab, because I had discovered I was an artist despite what that assistant teacher believed. My friend Steve had come to see me and tell me how there might be a riot in the middle of campus.

"These guys are going to turn in their draft cards and the football team is going to beat them up."

"Oh yeah, I forgot that was today. Let's go!"

Steve was bouncing up and down like a kid going to a hanging in a western movie. I flapped my way across campus, my bell-bottom pants slapping the pavement with every footfall. As I passed the Science Building, I caught my reflection in a window. My hair was definitely flipping up in back and my sideburns had reached the bottom of my jaw. I was no longer the altar boy, choir boy, straight-A student. *I was turning into one of them.* I smiled a crooked little smile as I flapped on.

I didn't doubt for a minute that a riot was a possibility and I was heading right for the center of it. At that time earth-shaking events could happen...and did, one right after the other.

Bobby Kennedy had spoken at our campus a month earlier during his presidential nomination campaign. A week later he was assassinated in the kitchen of the Biltmore Hotel right here in Los Angeles. We all watched it on the 11:00 news. Young Bobby lying there, his head in a pool of blood, while everyone around him screamed in panic.

Jack, one of my roommates, was a Kennedy volunteer and had been there at the hotel when it happened. He came back to the house ashen-faced and shaken.

This can't be happening. This is America.

We were all still reeling from the assassination of Martin Luther King in Memphis, Tennessee. The black ghettos of Los Angeles,

Chicago, Detroit, Philadelphia, and Washington, DC, had rioted and gone up in flames. The leaders of the young, the disenfranchised, and the minorities were being gunned down in cold blood. The nation was being torn asunder...and in the middle of all these events was this war...this evil war...thousands of miles away in the jungles of Vietnam. I was like everybody else in my generation when I asked, "Where the fuck is Vietnam?"

The war was escalating every day, and the government needed warm bodies that they could turn into cold corpses. That was the wedge that split my generation apart. The baby boomers were being drafted and sent halfway around the world to fight in an undeclared war. Nobody had bombed the Twin Towers. Nobody had sunk our ships in Pearl Harbor. We were not being invaded. We were not even coming to the aid of our allies. There was no reason for this war. Well, there were reasons, but the government was not sharing that information at the time.

My father had been in WWII and was now a veteran police officer with the LAPD. When I asked him about Vietnam, he said, "I don't believe in what they're doing over there, but if they called me I would go."

And there was the difference.

My generation was asking questions and we didn't like the answers—when we even got answers, that is. We were also the biggest generation (numbers-wise) in the history of America. When we said "Hell No We Won't Go," the battle lines were set.

My college became a hotbed of radical student dissent. The Students for a Democratic Society (SDS) had a very strong and active chapter on campus. A series of radical speakers made fiery speeches at our school. Floyd McKissick of the Congress of Racial Equality (CORE), Eldridge Cleaver of the Black Panthers, Reies Lopez Tijerina of the Chicano Land Movement, Cesar Chavez of the United Farm Workers, and Timothy Leary with his LSD consciousness movement. Timothy and I would become great friends years later and spend a lot of time hanging out together.

Timmy was essentially a psychedelic Irish pub rabble-rouser. He was also a well-respected clinical psychologist at Harvard University and the author of more than thirty books, and he had been in more than twenty prisons around the world. I don't know *anybody else* who has those credentials. He anticipated the coming computer revolution twenty years before it started to rear its digital head . . . and he loved to have fun. He was the most positive agent for change I have ever met. I still miss him very much.

But of all the speakers who came to campus, David Harris of the antiwar group the Resistance was by far the most influential for me.

Harris was soft-spoken, with bushy blond hair and wire-rimmed glasses. He wasn't full of fiery rhetoric; he was just full of common sense. I sat on the grass listening to his speech with a thousand other students, but after a while it seemed like he was talking just to me. He reasoned that this was an unjust, undeclared war, and the way to oppose it was not to participate. If you were under eighteen, don't register for the draft. If you were already registered, don't cooperate. Don't show up for a physical exam, and if drafted, refuse induction. In short, do not recognize their authority over you in this illegal war. It made so much sense to me. It was nonviolent but efficient. We would use the bureaucracy against itself.

One of our favorite methods was to comply with their change of address requirement. Every time you moved, you had to notify your local draft board. So we did. We would move to each other's houses at least three or four times a month. Usually the move was down the block or just next door, but it got the draft board running around in circles. We got really creative in how we notified them, too. The draft board was required to physically keep all correspondence in your personal file, so we sent them a change of address information burned on wooden roof shingles. (I knew that Christmas wood-burning kit would come in handy one day.) Then we switched to carving the change of address onto watermelons and then finally onto the bellies of dead fish...and they had to keep all the correspondence in your file. After about six months they changed the rule so that they just had to keep a picture of the correspondence in your file. Killjoys!

We also demonstrated at local draft boards, urging the inductees to resist the draft. We would hand them pamphlets as they walked into the induction center informing them of their rights and telling them not to cooperate.

One time two of my buddies got a notice to appear for a physical and spent the night before dropping acid and body painting themselves with antiwar slogans: "Drop acid, not bombs," or "LBJ kiss here" with arrows pointing to their butts. They went into the induction center fully dressed, and as soon as they got the chance they stripped off all their clothes except for their underwear and cowboy boots and went running up and down the halls screaming, "Resist the draft! Resist the draft!"

Needless to say, the authorities frowned on these forms of protest. Still, I would take part in many of these activities before too long. At the moment, though, I was being mesmerized by the logic that David Harris was spinning out. When he finished his talk, I pushed through the crowd to shake his hand and tell him that he made a lot of sense. And then walked away firm in the knowledge that I was not going to participate in this war. I didn't talk to anyone about it and I didn't solicit any other opinions. I just knew.

About a month after David Harris's talk, there was going to be a big antiwar demonstration at the newly constructed Century City Hotel in Los Angeles. President Lyndon Johnson was going to give a big speech to his supporters, and the antiwar faction mobilized in force. There must have been at least seven or eight thousand people already gathered at Rancho Park adjacent to the hotel when I got there. It was a carnival atmosphere, with face-painted hippies blowing giant soap bubbles to a background of bells, bongos, and guitars. Patchouli incense filled the air. People everywhere carried banners and signs denouncing the war. One group, from Topanga Canyon, made giant papier-mâché puppets of various government figures that they held aloft on long poles as they marched through the crowd.

Two antiwar provocateurs, "General Waste-more-land" and "General Hersheybar," dressed in comic military uniforms with Day-Glo plastic missiles on top of their general hats, roamed through the crowd handing out antiwar material. They were satirizing General William Westmoreland and General Lewis Blaine Hershey; at the time, the former commanded U.S. troops in Vietnam, and the latter was the director of the Selective Service System, also known as the draft. There was a succession of speakers, each fierce and adamant in their opposition to the war. But the one person that everybody came to see and hear was Muhammad Ali, the controversial heavyweight boxing champion of the world.

He had shocked the world with his improbable win over the seemingly unbeatable Sonny Liston and shortly thereafter announced that he had become a member of the Black Muslims and had changed his name from Cassius Clay. Now he was refusing to be drafted on conscientious objector grounds, saying "I ain't got no quarrel with them Vietcong. No Vietcong ever called me nigger."

To the nation at large he became either the biggest villain or the biggest hero. I believed the latter. As he climbed up on the back of a stake-bed truck, the thing that everybody noticed immediately was how big he was. He was almost six foot four and at the height of his youth and physical prowess. As he had said many times and in many ways before: "I'm the prettiest champion that ever was." No shit, Sherlock!

Even when modestly dressed in a plain black suit with a bow tie, he was the most physically impressive human being I had ever seen. He addressed the crowd in a short speech that combined humor and commitment and completely charmed everybody. When he finished, the whole crowd surged forward, calling out his name and holding up bits of paper for him to sign.

I pushed my way to the front and thrust up my draft card for him to sign, which he did with a clearly legible "M Ali." I got it back and looked at it like it was a holy relic. It didn't matter that I had broken another federal law by defacing my draft card. *I had Muhammad Ali's autograph on my draft card.*

He climbed down off the truck and slowly made his way through the crowd surrounded by fellow Black Muslims, but still shaking hands and saying "I'm with you, if you're with me." I stuck out my hand and he shook it. He had the biggest hands I'd ever felt in my life. It was like sticking my hand in a giant mixing bowl. The only thing I thought was *God, I would hate to get hit by these fists.*

I wouldn't see him again in person for more than thirty years, when he showed up in his hometown of Louisville, Kentucky, for the premiere of the movie *Tin Cup*, in which I costarred with Kevin Costner, Don Johnson, and Rene Russo. Though he was struggling with Parkinson's disease, he had a big smile on his face as he congratulated me on my performance. In spite of his infirmities, there was still the undeniably sly charisma of the one and only Muhammad Ali. He will always be one of my all-time sacred heroes.

As we demonstrators made our way out of the park to start the march, the first thing we were confronted with was a line of at least fifty black-and-white police cars and hundreds of helmeted cops with billy clubs in their hands. The first marchers stepped out into the street, and the second they did, the police started breaking the windshields of a few cars parked across the street. They dragged the occupants out of the cars and started beating them with their clubs. With blood streaming down their faces, the people were dragged down the street by the police to a waiting paddy wagon. The police were deliberately trying to start a riot. The leaders of the demonstration, however, were very seasoned by this time and through their bullhorns they shouted out for everyone to immediately sit down, which we all did. Panic did not ensue.

After about ten minutes they instructed us to get up on our feet and start the march. Again the police started beating people up and again the demonstrators sat down, this time for twenty minutes. By now, every news outlet in the nation had their cameras there and were broadcasting the cops' every move. The police backed off and the march continued.

By the time we got to the hotel, our numbers had swelled to about ten or fifteen thousand chanting protestors. It felt almost medieval, like we were barbarians about to charge across the plain against the Roman army. We looked like barbarians, too, with long hair and painted faces, carrying banners and blowing horns. It was scary and thrilling at the same time. We were a bunch of kids who thought we were bulletproof.

The police waited until we got in front of the hotel. It was starting to get dark when they made their big move.

The middle of the demonstration line had reached the front of the hotel and faced hundreds of police in riot gear. They stopped and started chanting:

Hey, hey, LBJ, how many kids did you kill today?

The police wanted them to keep moving but they were staying put. Their chants grew louder. Suddenly, the police dove into the line and tried to form a wedge in the line by swinging their billy clubs and firing tear gas. Their goal was to disperse the crowd and they eventually did, although it took them all night. This demonstration was big news in the city for weeks and seemed to further polarize the older and the baby boomer generations. Demonstrations like Century City were happening all over the country.

As I said, as events intensified I increasingly sought refuge in the pottery lab at school. All my life I felt deep down inside that I was an artist of some kind but I didn't have a medium. To be an artist you had to draw or paint or sculpt or something, right? Well, that teacher's aide in elementary school had taken care of my artistic urges for a long time. Her cutting, thoughtless remark was like a knife right to the center of my little brown heart.

When I eventually took an Art History class in college and had to draw something as one of the requirements, I paid one of my fraternity brothers five bucks to draw a pair of glasses for me.

In my last semester in school, I was finally taking the few required classes that I had put off for four years. I found myself with a big open space in my schedule that I could fill with any elective I wanted. As I was registering for the various classes, I saw this really cute girl that I had a class with the previous semester in line right next to me. So I struck up a casual conversation.

"Hey, what classes are you taking?"

"I just signed up for a pottery class."

"Pottery, no kidding. That sounds kind of cool."

"Yeah, they have a couple more spots open. Why don't you take it with me?"

And that was all it took. I followed her scent right into Pottery 101 with Professor Howard Tollefson. I'm always amazed at how a casual encounter can change your entire life.

Professor Tollefson walked into the pottery lab the first day of class and wrote his name on the blackboard. Then he walked over to the clay bin, opened it up, and grabbed a big wad of clay. He threw it on a big plaster wedging table and kneaded it for about ten seconds.

"First you wedge the clay to get all the air bubbles out and then you put it on the center of the throwing wheel, like this. And then you turn on the wheel and then center it, like this. After you center the clay, you make a cylinder like this. Any questions? Good. Do that."

And then he walked out of the room.

The whole class stood there with a big "Huh?" on their faces. I looked over at the girl I signed up with. She was still cute. So I thought, *What the fuck? I'll give it a shot.*

From the moment I centered my first piece of clay, I was hooked. It was like a tuning fork went off in my loins and reverberated throughout my whole body. It woke up my dormant Mexican handcrafting genes. The spirit of generations of long gone Mexican potters pushed me to do what I was born to do.

Within a week, I had quit all my other classes and now spent all my time in the pottery lab. Professor Tollefson noticed that he had a live one in the corner and started giving me more personal instruction. He started letting me stay late and then finally gave me a key to the lab so I could come and go as I pleased. Everything else became subordinate to pottery, because now I was an "artist."

Even the cute girl in class had to compete for attention. It must have been a first for both of us. There were a million clamorous events happening out there in the world, but inside the lab there was peace and tranquility.

During this time, I also started practicing Transcendental Meditation as taught by Maharishi Mahesh Yogi. I continue to meditate to this day. It was right before the Beatles joined the movement, so it was still bubbling under. Between the meditation and pottery, I was the most calm, clear, and centered I had ever been in my life. I was smiling in the eye of the hurricane. It was then that my friend Steve came bouncing in the lab to tell me of the Draft Card Turn-In Day.

As we approached the quadrangle, we could see a crowd building. On one side were the SDS guys carrying antiwar signs, but they were taped to what looked like baseball bats or clubs. These guys were definitely not flower children. On the other side were the jocks in their letterman jackets. Each side was snarling at the other. Any little spark and we could have a melee.

There was a long-haired, bearded peacenik onstage running

things. One by one, young guys were coming onstage and handing this guy their draft cards. He would take it and hold it overhead and announce, "Joe Smith refuses to recognize the government's authority over him."

The radicals would cheer and the football team would snarl.

Steve said, "Let's stay here in case some shit goes down." But when he turned back I was not there. I had continued walking right up to the stage. I got in line behind two other guys and when my turn came I walked up and handed him my Muhammad Ali–autographed draft card. He announced my name and there were cheers and snarls.

When I came offstage, Steve was there waiting for me. He looked at me like I had volunteered to go to the moon on the back of a propane tank.

"Dude, what the fuck are you doing?"

"What's the worst thing that could happen? They give me a new draft card?"

I would find out very soon what the worst thing was.

Since it was a national event, it got the government's attention. A week later, General Hershey issued a notice that anybody who turned in their draft cards, burned their draft cards, demonstrated at draft centers, or in general did anything he didn't like would immediately be reclassified I-A, drafted, and sent to the front lines in Vietnam.

By this time, I had done all of the above, so I was on his hit list. As a matter of fact, my draft card had been included on an antiwar collage that accompanied David Harris and his new wife, Joan Baez, the world's most famous folksinger, on a speaking tour of college campuses. The collage eventually ended up on the cover of *Time* magazine, and if you looked hard enough you could make out my name on a card in the corner.

Talk about throwing gasoline on the fire. Never mind that what Hershey was doing was *totally illegal*. He was the high and mighty General Hershey, and everybody else could eat shit.

Eventually, four years later, my case, along with over six hundred others, went to the U.S. Court of Appeals in a class-action suit and the court promptly nullified General Hershey's order and declared it *totally fucking illegal*. I think that was the legal term.

Meanwhile back in reality, one month later I received a new draft card in the mail. Sure enough, I had been reclassified I-A (fit for military service) even though I was a full-time student and entitled to a II-S Student deferment. Another month went by, and the government started sentencing the leaders of the movement. The first three sentenced got eight years each in Leavenworth Federal Penitentiary in Kansas.

A big chill ran through the movement. Sure it was illegal and it would be overturned, but in the meantime guys had to wait out the process in the federal can. Leavenworth was no country-club, day-at-the-beach "camp cupcake" where white-collar government criminals like the Watergate felons went. It was hard time in general population.

During an Easter-break camping trip in San Felipe, Mexico, with Professor Tollefson and a few other students, I discussed the situation with him over a late-night joint around the campfire. He knew my situation and was totally sympathetic.

"Man, I didn't do anything wrong. I did something right."

"Yeah, I know, I know."

We both took another long hit off the joint. Howard stared into the fire and then said, "You know, I have this ex-student from Washington State who is living in Calgary, Canada, and is just starting a pottery business. Maybe he could use an assistant."

I mulled this over as I watched figures dance in the flames. "Maybe...maybe."

The school year was ending and I was still I-A. I hadn't been drafted yet, but I knew it was coming. I meditated on the problem for days, and then one morning I woke up with the answer. Proper deliberation, combined with instinct, has always led me to the right choice at key points in my life.

I gathered as much cash as I could ($80) and bought a bus ticket for Calgary. I was leaving everybody I knew and loved and was heading for a country where I knew no one. I didn't know if I could ever come back. I just knew that I was not participating in this war.

I stopped by my mother's house to say good-bye. My parents' divorce was finalized that day. They'd been having trouble for years. I gave my mother a big hug. With tears in her eyes she said, "Everybody's leaving me today."

It hurt to see my mother in that way. But I knew she'd be OK, because she had my three sisters: the twins Monica and Margie and the younger one, Elena Marie (three years younger than the twins). (We call her Orbie because she had a toy called a Li'l Orbie that could crawl up a wall. My sister could climb the walls, too! People call her Orbie today and have no idea what her real name is.) My mother and my sisters grew incredibly close over the years, and they treated her with great love and care. They had an incredibly close bond. My sisters still visit my mother's grave to this day and talk to her.

Fighting back my own tears, I stuck out my thumb and hitchhiked to the bus station. I got on the Dog and took that bus out of my old life and into my new one.

CHAPTER **9**

A big day of castrating

The last place I stopped in the United States, in June 1968, before crossing the border was Great Falls, Montana. The bus pulled in late at night and stopped in front of the only hotel open at that time of night. I just wanted to get a room, get some sleep, and get up early in the morning. I was on my way to my room and passed by the bar in the hotel where three or four cowboys were having a late drink. One of these geniuses noticed that I had longish hair and yelled out, "Hey, get out the sheep shears, one got loose."

They all had a hearty cowboy laugh. I wanted to just go up into my room, but the wiseass in me went right up to them and said, "Hey this is my first time in Montana...do you guys really fuck sheep?"

Three of the guys burst out laughing...one did not. The one who did not said, "You better not be getting on the bus to Canada in the morning. We'll be here waiting for you."

"That's so nice of you, but don't bother."

He glared. I split.

In the morning, I crept down the creaky, wooden stairs and peeked around the corner. I shouldn't have worried. The cowboys were passed out on top of each other sorta *Brokeback Mountain*-ish.

Maybe they do fuck sheep here...I don't know.

To pick up where I left off in the intro, when Jerry Kaufman and his family came back we set about building his pottery studio in an old chicken coop. We gutted the interior and hauled out what seemed like 23 million metric tons of chicken shit. Good preparation for my future career in show business. We built shelves and tables and constructed a brick-lined space for a kiln. We worked night and day and it was a labor of love.

Priddis, the area where the family lived, wasn't really an official place. It was just farmland for as far as you could see. There were no public buildings at all. It was a thrill to see deer, moose, bears, coyotes, raccoons, ducks, geese, and pheasants everywhere you looked. Quite spectacular for an inner-city boy whose only previous contact with wildlife was rats.

At night, after the day's work and dinner was over, we would sit around by lamplight and fill each other in about each other's lives. Sometimes their friends Helen and Hank would come over for a beer. Hank was the foreman of the nearby Burns Pig Farm. One time while he was sharpening his knife he said, "Come on Helen, let's go, I got a big day of castrating tomorrow." I had never heard that phrase before…or since.

One of the most striking things about where I landed was that it was exactly where Tommy Chong grew up. Calgary, and its outskirts, during his young years, was a combination of hick town and unincorporated land in flux. It was here that I first heard the accent that I would recognize later when Tommy whipped it out in the studio. That Sergeant Stadanko voice. His straight guy. I used to love listening to that guy because I knew him so well. Tommy would go into him when he really wanted to crack me up.

When we finished building the shop, Jerry couldn't afford to hire me, and I needed to find work. He mentioned that there was a famous local potter that lived eleven miles away in Bragg Creek. Jerry said maybe he needed an assistant. That was all I had to hear.

I got up early the next morning, put on my boots, and headed off to Bragg Creek through the back roads. I walked a whole lot, hitchhiked a little, walked a whole lot more, and then got a little ride at the end. The guy who picked me up knew exactly where I was going, because he had made a delivery there.

"I'll drop you off at the bridge," the driver said. "I can't go over because of the weight."

It was only a couple of miles more until I hopped out and flashed him the peace sign.

In parting he told me, "Just go across the bridge and then up the hill. The first road you come to on your left, that's it."

"Thanks for the ride, buddy."

I did as I was told...and crossed the river and went deeper into my new life. I walked forever up this hill until I came to a stunning wood-and-glass house that looked out over a huge valley. The bottom floor was the studio. Ed Drahanchuk and his beautiful artist wife, Ethyl Egg, were working on a tile mural that they had laid out on the floor. They just looked up and stared at me. I didn't know if this was going to be another "Chief" situation, so I started talking as fast as I could.

"Hi, you must be Ed. My name is Richard Marin. I'm a potter from Los Angeles. I was just working with Jerry Kaufman over in Priddis and I heard that you might be looking for an assistant..."

And on and on and on and on until he said, "You're hired," if only to get me to stop talking.

"When can you start?"

"Right now. What would you like me to do?"

"Well, see those bricks over there? Start cleaning them off. Get all the crud off." And so would start the purest, most-at-one-with-nature time of my entire life.

Bragg Creek was a little summer cabin community about twenty-five miles northwest of Calgary in the foothills of the Rocky Mountains. People came out from the city during the summer to enjoy the outdoors and play in the Elbow River. During the winter, nobody lived there. I can't exactly say *nobody*, because there were about seven or eight of us that could endure the winter out there. The year I got there Alberta had its coldest winter in eighty years. For a few hours one winter night, the temperature plunged to seventy-five degrees below zero, breaking all the thermometers. One week it was fifty below five days out of the seven. I got to where I could work all day outside when it was twenty below.

Ed was a successful and established potter when I met him. He won the Bi-Centennial Exhibition Award for Crafts the year we met. He had designed and built this beautiful, functional home and studio in the mountains for himself, his wife, and their daughter, Katrina. They were living the ideal potter's life only they made it work as a business enterprise. Ed would do special commissions like giant planters for the Vancouver Airport or big clay murals for bank buildings. As a matter of fact, he made the first clay mural in Calgary's history. He also had a line of production pottery, cups, plates, bowls, vases, and so on, which he made on a daily basis.

Ed was tall, thin, and wiry, and of Ukrainian heritage. He looked like a younger, handsomer Leon Trotsky. Ethyl was the beautiful homecoming queen of the art college that they both attended. She laughed about it, because she didn't even know they had a homecoming, much less a queen, but she graciously accepted the honor. Katrina could have passed as Heidi from the storybooks.

Drahanchuk was the best thrower I have ever seen. He could center 150 pounds of clay, about what he weighed, on the wheel at one time. He immediately put me to work learning to throw his production line. That meant that I would have to get up early each morning while it was still dark and walk about two miles through the woods to his house in order to practice throwing before he got up. As soon as I learned, I could get paid for throwing his line, but they had to look exactly as he threw them, not an easy task.

After practicing for about an hour or so, I would clean up the shop and get everything ready so that Ed could start working as soon as he woke up. Some people have this idea that a potter sits around throwing pots all day. The throwing is the smallest part of the production. It's almost like recess. The rest of the process is hard work. Mixing two thousand pounds of clay from big bags of powder, running it through a pug mill, cutting it off and wrapping it in plastic, storing it in a damp "green room," mixing glazes, trimming newly thrown pots, and on and on. There was always something to do in the process. Sometimes, when we were firing a kiln load, we would work seventy-two hours straight.

The biggest problem I had when I first started working for Drahanchuk was finding a place to live. I first rented a little cabin next to the general store. How little? I could stand in the middle of the floor and touch everything in the room. Mrs. Elston, who owned the store, showed me how to make kindling for the little stove and gave me a fifteen-gallon drum so that I could walk across the street to the river and get water for all my daily needs.

That process got to be a real chore real soon. I came up with the bright idea that I would put the drum in a little wagon she had and roll it across to a little temporary bridge they had erected across the river for the summer when the water narrowed. My idea was that I would lean over the bridge and put the drum in the water where the flowing water would fill it up much faster than I could do it by hand. I leaned over the side with the drum and as soon as the drum touched the water I was pulled off the bridge and into the freezing, fast-flowing river, and I was gone fully clothed, boots and all, downstream.

It wasn't just that the water was fast. Even though it was summer, the river was *freezing*. I struggled to catch my breath as I went zooming down the river, the cold water squeezing my heart like an iron fist. Finally, the river widened out downstream and the current slowed down a little so that I could swim to shore. I crawled out of the water on my hands and knees and stayed in that position, hyper-ventilating until I could catch my breath.

Well, that was a brilliant move! I thought to myself as I watched the drum speed out of sight down the river. It was one of the many, many things I learned the hard way about living in the frozen North.

Recently I was watching the movie *The Revenant*, which was shot in the same general location I lived in when working for Drahanchuk. Leonardo DiCaprio really deserved his Oscar as much for surviving as for acting.

Every day after work, I would go knock on cabin doors, introduce myself, and explain that I worked for Drahanchuk, whom I assumed everybody knew, and inquire if their cabin was for rent for the winter. It seemed that not many people were aware that they had a renowned artist living in their midst. They assumed that I was an Indian, so I got a lot of doors shut in my face. After a while, I just got used to it and didn't pay much attention to their ignorance.

One time after a shut-door rejection, I was walking away and I noticed a neatly stacked woodpile next to the house. I stopped to see what size they had cut the wood, because I knew I would have to be cutting wood all winter. Suddenly the cabin door reopened and the owner stuck his head out and yelled out, "And don't touch the wood-pile!" and slammed the door.

I couldn't wait to touch this motherfucker's woodpile... and I got the chance to, as I eventually rented a cabin right across the street... while he was gone all winter.

One afternoon on my daily cabin rental rounds, I noticed a cabin with some people in it. As I got closer I saw that it was a black man and his young daughters hanging out in the main room. The man was sitting in the middle of the room on a small chair getting his hair braided by one of the girls. I introduced myself and gave my usual spiel. The man smiled and introduced himself as Georgie Dunn. In the course of the conversation, I came to find out that he was lightweight boxing champion of Canada. Later on, Georgie would go on to work as equipment manager for the Calgary Stampeders professional football team for sixteen years. He couldn't have been nicer, and when I asked him about the cabin he said without hesitation, "Sure, no problem, but it gets cold out here and this cabin isn't winterized."

I assured him that it would be no problem because…in reality, I had no idea what I was talking about. He gave me the key to the cabin and an address where I could send the money and wished me good luck.

The cabin had electricity, but that was about it. It had a big pot-bellied stove in the middle of the room, which I would have to learn to bank with coal and wood in order to keep a fire going throughout the night so I wouldn't wake up in the morning *all froze up.* Sometimes I would get that stove so blazing that I would have to open all the doors and windows even at twenty below zero. That stove would suck air louder than one of George's boxing opponents, too. I had to chop wood every day and go to the river for water every five days or so. I had a hot plate for cooking, and a radio, so I was good to go.

One morning, a few days after I had settled in, I awoke to find that a foot and a half of snow had fallen overnight. I had never seen a snowstorm before, so I wandered outside, awestruck. It only took a few minutes until I heard the first loud crack. The snow had fallen very early in the season, so the trees still had all their leaves on them. That much snow created so much weight that the trees were snapping in half all over the place. *Snap, snap, crack!* Trees were falling all around. The upshot was that trees had fallen all over Drahanchuk's long driveway, and we spent the next three days sawing the fallen trees and hauling them off the road.

Every day it was something new.

Besides being a world-class potter, Ed was an avid hunter. He took me with him many afternoons after work to look for deer.

During my first excursions into the wild as a hunter, I couldn't help but laugh at the situation. Although I was raised by a policeman, I had never fired a gun in my whole life. I had come up to Canada to be a potter, never guessing that the potter who would give me my chance would also be so into hunting. I had nothing against this stalking and shooting; I just had never been in a position to do it. They didn't have a lot of wild deer or other game in South Central LA. But here I was in the wilds of Alberta looking for the elusive, giant moose or whatever!

When I informed Drahanchuk of my inexperience with firearms, he broke out in a sly smile and said, "Grab that shotgun and let's go." He walked me out to a grove of giant pines, pointed to a large tree, and said, "OK, hit that tree." I aimed my shotgun, closed my eyes, and fired. I missed the tree by a good ten yards. Ed almost doubled over from laughing. "OK, try it again, but this time keep your eyes open." I tried it again and this time it was much better; I missed the tree by only five yards. Ed shook his head and said "Well, you need practice."

So I practiced every day with my newly acquired single-shot shotgun. On the way walking to work every morning I took my shotgun and looked for partridge, which were plentiful in the area. It took more than a few tries, but eventually I bagged a few and proudly laid them on the kitchen table for Ethyl to prepare for lunch. Ed couldn't believe that I had actually shot them myself, but eating is believing. During all the time I worked for the Drahanchuks, I ate beef maybe once or twice. The rest of the time it was venison, moose, elk, antelope, pheasant, partridge, duck, quail, goose, and trout.

I had fished all my life with my father and grandfather, but now I could really live off the land if I had to. Every day as I chopped wood and hauled water from the river I became more and more independent and confident that I could be dropped off anywhere and survive. This way of life did not faze me. Still, I was a long way from velour jackets and Beatle boots.

One afternoon, I went out with Ed and his two buddies to hunt a moose that had been seen in the area. Whatever. The agreement was that Ed and I would go one way and the other guys would go the other and if either of us landed a moose, we would fire three shots in a row and the other guys would come and help. We left the truck on the road and disappeared into the forest.

We looked and looked and looked and lo and behold, late in the afternoon we came upon a giant moose standing in a frozen muskeg, which is a shallow swamp. Drahanchuk told me to go to the other side and see if I could scare him out and make the moose run toward him. I got to the other side and made a few stomping noises. I didn't want to scare him too much because I didn't want him running toward me. After a few more tries, it was evident that the moose was not going to move. He just stood there chewing on some frozen bugs or something.

Finally, Ed motioned for me to come back to him, which I was glad to do. It was starting to get dark, and Ed said, "I'm going to have to drop him right where he is."

"Why don't we just come back tomorrow?"

Ed looked at me like I was nuts. He lifted his rifle, took aim, and fired. He hit the moose right through the heart, and the moose fell over right where he was standing. Eddie let out a yell and gave me a big hug.

"We better signal the other guys."

He shot into the air three times and then said, "Let's go see."

We tromped our way through the muskeg, breaking ice with every step, until we got to the moose. He was huge. He must have weighed at least fifteen hundred pounds. We both grabbed one leg and tried to pull him. Not a chance that we could move him an inch.

"We can't wait for the other guys. Let's go back to the truck and get the saw and harness."

"What?"

"We're going to have to cut him up in quarters and haul him out piece by piece."

This was my chance to look at Ed like *he* was nuts.

"Come on, we have to hurry. There's bears around."

Eventually we got back to the truck. Now it was really dark and no two other buddies. Ed opened up the truck and pulled out a small chain saw and what looked like a harness.

"After we cut him up, we'll hook him up to this harness and pull out the pieces one by one like a team of horses. Ready?"

We got back to the moose and Ed expertly gutted him and quartered him with the chain saw. I thought I was in a slasher movie. Eddie was smiling and laughing all the way. Piece by piece and frozen step by frozen step we pulled out four giant chunks of frozen, bloody moose. Aah, the good life.

The next hunting adventure occurred right at home. It was a sunny, early autumn afternoon. Ed had been on the wheel throwing big vases all day. I was at the table wedging clay, trying to keep him supplied. Ed called a break and said he was going outside to stretch. Within thirty seconds he came running back into the shop yelling.

"Ethyl, Ethyl, where's my gun? Where's my gun?"

He pulled open a lower cabinet and pulled out his hunting rifle and a box of cartridges. He crammed them into the gun so fast that they were popping out. Finally, he got the gun loaded and went back outside. I'm standing at the table thinking, *What the hell?*

Ethyl called out, "Ed, what's the matter?"

"There's a bear out there."

I dropped my ball of clay and went to the window just in time to see Drahanchuk drop to one knee, raise his rifle, and fire two shots. A big golden-brown bear came rolling down the hill and collapsed right in front of the door. He was still twitching and steam was coming off of him when Ed said, "OK, grab a hind leg and we'll pull him down into that gulley."

Still in a state of shock, I said, "And then what?"

He looked at me, puzzled.

"Why then, I'll teach you how to skin him. Come on, grab a leg."

I barely knew how to roll a joint at this point, and here I was yanking on some twitchy bear with steam coming off him.

Ed strung the bear up between two trees, and cut by cut he showed me how to skin a bear. I haven't had to do it since...but I can if I'm asked.

Of all the adventures I had with the Drahanchuks, and there were many, many more, the one that affected me the most physically, mentally, and spiritually was seeing a spectacular display of the Northern Lights.

Once again Drahanchuk wanted to go hunting. This time we were going pheasant hunting. The good fields were farther south, so I had to get up and be ready at 4:00 a.m. for him to pick me up. I was out front waiting when he pulled up. As soon as he stepped out of his truck, the whole sky changed. It was like we had stepped into a dome with a hole at the top. Out of that hole a dozen long rays of light reached all the way to the ground, surrounding us. The colors would shift from red to blue to green to yellow to purple. It was as if we were stuck inside of a kaleidoscope with the most vivid colors you've ever seen.

The air was very still and quiet, but charged with electricity and with a slight electric smell. I thought for sure the sky was going to open up and we were going to be abducted by aliens. We stood there dumbfounded, not uttering a sound. There had been previous reports of UFOs in the area, so it was not without foundation that we viewed this phenomenon as otherworldly.

When you hear of the Northern Lights, it's usually described as some sheet lightning off in the distance. You can admire it and say *ooh* and *ahhh*. But this experience was transformative. If we were living in Biblical times, it could almost be described as the Burning Bush without the voice. Just as suddenly as it appeared, it disappeared. Without a word we got in the truck and drove away, stunned and humbled.

No matter how much I was into pottery and the potter's lifestyle, music had a way of finding me. The Steak Pit was Bragg Creek's only restaurant, but it remained open all winter. It was owned and operated by Gordy Schultz, a musician who was a contemporary of Chong's in the early music scene in Calgary. Chong, with his rock-and-roll and blues band, took some of the park gigs away from Gordy and his more "trad-jazz" sound. Gordy was a cool guy who could cook and play bass and saxophone. On the weekends, he brought in a dine-and-dance trio that consisted of his brother Kenny on bass; Kenny's wife, Joyce, on keyboards; and Rob Mallileau on drums. I would sit in with them and sing every Johnny Mathis song I knew. They liked the way I sang and invited me to join them at an upcoming gig in Banff.

Banff National Park, in the Canadian Rockies in Alberta, is one of the most beautiful and majestic spots on earth. It's what you picture in your mind when you think of the Canadian Rockies. They had a gig at the Cascade Hotel, right on Main Street.

I took a bus from Calgary and arrived around midnight in Banff. The first thing I saw when I got off the bus was a huge moose walking down the center of Main Street. Nobody seemed to even notice. I found my way to the hotel and bunked up with Rob. The next day we rehearsed a little and that night we went on and I got everybody dancing by singing "Watermelon Man."

The weekend was a great hit, and the trio invited me to play with them at their next gig…in Hawaii. It obviously was a no-go for me, traveling to the United States, but I had been rebitten by the performing bug. I went back to Bragg Creek, where Drahanchuk told me that there would be much less work in the winter, so he had to lay me off for a little while.

I thought, *Perfect. I can do something musically.* I got turned on to an agent in town, and she said she could put something together for me singing and playing in clubs and bars "Up North." I thought, *How much farther north can you go?* She said it would take a little time, so I had to find something to do for a month.

I had a solution. While playing at the Cascade in Banff, I met a waitress named Rosanne, who was from Huntington Beach, a suburb of Los Angeles. She was glad to see a homeboy, and we got along famously. Nothing romantic, just friends. She was renting a cute little house there and said if I was ever in town, I was welcome to stay with her. A couple of days later I showed up at her door, and Rosanne took me in.

I wandered around Banff for about a week, taking in the sights. One night, Rosanne came home from work and asked me if I wanted a job. I think she figured that I'd better get a job or I would be at her house forever. She said they were looking for a grill cook at Sunshine Village, a ski resort just out of town. I applied for the job, and I made up a cooking résumé on the bus ride up there. They just wanted a fresh body, and they hired me right on the spot.

Being a grill cook at Sunshine was a job from heaven. I had to make very few things, like hamburgers, steak sandwiches, and fondue, and maybe heat up some escargot. I didn't have to work breakfast or dinner, only lunch and evenings at the bar. The rest of the staff could not go to the bar during the evenings, as it was strictly for the guests. I was there alone listening to the entertainment, talking to the young female guests, and making the occasional steak sandwich. At the end of the shift, I would raid the kitchen for leftovers from dinner, fill my chef's hat with fried chicken, and take it back to my buds at the staff dormitory. There was often a poker game going on, which I was welcome to join seeing as I had all the fried chicken. Somehow, I was usually very lucky at those games and walked away with quite a bit of extra money.

Working at Sunshine also allowed me to learn to ski. As I said,

I had never seen snow before, so skiing was like science fiction to me. My roommate, Len MacMillan, got me a pair of skis and boots and took me up to the top of the mountain. He showed me the snowplow position, told me how to turn left and right…then pushed me out onto the ski run. Len showed me how to stop, but that was easier said than done. Whenever I picked up too much speed or was out of control, I just fell over.

Every morning I would be the first one up and out on the hill. I was picking up more speed but no technique. After about two weeks, I was starting to get a little cocky, but I still could not stop quickly when I wanted to. One time I came zooming down the hill and simply could not stop. I got down to the bottom, ran out of snow, and continued across the street and into the side of a bus that was just delivering new guests.

Fairly soon my nickname was "the Brown Blur." I was having a ball and felt more and more Canadian every day. Late one Sunday afternoon, just before closing time, I came zooming down the hill and hit a trench at the bottom and got launched into the air. I landed very hard and did three somersaults before landing flat on my face. I thought I had broken my neck. I moved my head and saw that I had not. I checked my mouth and all my teeth were present. My nose was not broken, nor were any of my ribs. I remember thinking to myself, *Wow, I can't believe I came out of that unscathed.*

I looked back uphill, where my ski tips were planted in the snow, to see my right leg was broken in half. It looked like a number seven. My leg had been broken right at the boot top, a compound fracture. Len had seen me take the fall and came skiing up.

"Are you OK?"

"No, I broke my leg!"

Len looked at my leg and immediately threw up.

"Ah man, don't do that, just go get the ski patrol."

My friend Gordy, head of the ski patrol, came skiing up and just about retched, too. I'm sure I went into shock, but it was the kind of shock that brought calm. I instructed Gordy how to move my leg as he transferred me onto a sled and prepared to ski me down the rest of the mountain. I had never broken a bone before, but this was a doozy.

I was in the hospital for a month. There were some complications, and they had to operate twice, but in the end I was discharged with a full-length cast and crutches which I had for the next six months. Thank God for Rosanne, who let me stay at her house when I got discharged.

While hobbling around her house, I discovered one of the few record albums she had was *Love Child* by Diana Ross and the Supremes. One of the songs on the album was "Does Your Mama Know About Me?" It was a very touching and beautiful song about an interracial love affair. I played it over and over. One day I turned the cover over to check the credits and the lyrics were by T. Chong. I thought, *What kind of name is Chong for a brother?* Not too far in the future I would find out.

As the ski season ended, Len said that he was going back to Vancouver, his hometown, and that I should come with him. We could continue being roommates and have fun in one of the most beautiful cities in the world. Sounded good to me, so I crutched my way onto my first airplane and got ready for the next adventure.

CHAPTER **10**

Meeting Tommy Chong

Vancouver is one of the most beautiful cities in North America, and at that time it was the "San Francisco of Canada," with all the counterculture implications—only Canadian, so it was more polite... as in "Can we please have a revolution?" On my first day, Len took me to Chinatown.

It was the most exotic city I had ever been in. It had a beautiful ocean view from Stanley Park, colorful hippies from all over the world, and dried bats on a stake in Chinatown. Canada, unlike the United States, always had political, diplomatic, and trade relations with Red China. After San Francisco, Vancouver has the second largest Chinatown in North America. It is a port city and "China White" heroin comes straight off the boats and into town. It was and still is a big problem for Vancouver. Mixed with the "anything goes" hippie ethic of the time, it was quite a carnival I found in this most idyllic of Canadian cities.

We were standing on the corner of Main and Pender, which was, and still is, the most squalid point in the city. It was the conjunction of Chinatown, Skid Row, and Junkyville.

As we walked by a nightclub named the Shanghai Junk, I couldn't help but notice their promotional photos in a little waterlogged glass showcase. "The Junk," as I was to come to know it, was Vancouver's first topless bar. Light-years from what we know as a topless bar today, these ladies wore large pasties with tassels and sequined underwear.

The photographs in the case showed the ladies interacting with some fully clothed hippie/greaser guys dressed in police uniforms with army helmets on.

My first reaction was *What the fuck is this?*

Oddly enough, I had seen something similar when I was in high school. There was this place on Ventura Boulevard in the Valley called the Zomba Cafe, and it was a burlesque house that featured strippers and comedians. But I just thought these photos were odd and funny and walked on.

About a month later, I ran into a high school buddy of mine from Los Angeles who was in Vancouver because of *his* difficulties with the draft. Hank Zevallos was an odd character. He was senior class president. He also ran track and was an aspiring writer who wrote for the school newspaper.

Hank told me that he and another guy, a Ukrainian named Ihor Todoruck, had started a music scene magazine called *Poppin*. They had ambitions to be bigger than *Rolling Stone*, but right now they were selling their publication on the streets of Vancouver. Hank, who was the editor, remembered that I used to do some writing for the school newspaper and suggested that I could write some pieces for *Poppin*. Whatever.

"I could put your name on our masthead," Hank continued. "You could get free albums and get into shows free and get free drinks and food."

Now I was listening.

In short order, I went to a bar and was introduced to Ihor, the magazine's publisher. After a long conversation and a few short drinks, in which I briefed him on my background, Ihor said I could work with Hank and write for them.

I was one of those kids who could always figure out how to get into some place for free. Whether it was a high school football game or a dance in the gym or later into a nightclub or a rock-and-roll concert, I could concoct some story that some gatekeeper would buy. It was usually some variation of "I'm with the band."

When I was on my way to Canada for the first time, I stopped for a week to visit some friends in Lake Tahoe, California.

The Crystal Ship was a club that featured emerging rock bands. I convinced my friend Kenny to hang out with me by the back door and wait for the bands to arrive. As soon as their van arrived, we ran up to them and started helping them unload their equipment. The band thought we were with the club and the club thought we were with the band. At any rate, we got in and disappeared into the crowd. It was the least I could do to help this new group called the Santana Blues Band. They had this great lead guitar player; I think his name was Carlos.

Anyway, I was always good at being part of the scene, so when I got offered this job with *Poppin* magazine, I fit right in. There was never any money involved, but what they did offer was free entrée to any show in town. That, plus having my name on the masthead, meant that I got all the free albums I could handle. Eventually they asked me to do interviews with the big acts that came to town.

My first assignment was to interview Little Richard, who was playing at the Cave, the biggest club in town. Little Richard was one of the founders and most influential figures in early rock and roll. He was in the first group inducted into the Rock and Roll Hall of Fame along with Elvis Presley, Bill Haley, and Chuck Berry, among others. He was the most flamboyant performer I have ever seen and one of the best singers in rock and roll. He described himself as "omnisexual." No doubt.

The interview was a rollicking, hilarious performance that started in his dressing room and ended in his hotel room early in the morning, where he discovered to his delight that these two hippie interviewers

(Hank and I) smoked grass. What a revelation! He disappeared into the next room and came back with a shoe box containing a handful of scraggily Mexican weed that was mostly stems and seeds.

Hank and I took one look at his stash and said, "You know, we have this chunk of hashish that might be better."

Without further ado we proceeded to get high with Little Richard.

Richard told more stories but at some point he realized that we actually were journalists and that nothing else was going to happen. He yawned and said that he had to get some sleep and wished us a merry good-bye. I would run into Little Richard a few more times in the years to come in Los Angeles.

The next time I saw Richard Penniman (his real name) was at a concert at the Olympic Auditorium in downtown LA. I was there to see my friend John Hammond Jr., the blues singer and guitar player. Headlining the bill was Little Richard.

There was a lot of unrest in the crowd. People were being busted and dragged out. Onstage it was just John Hammond Jr. and a guitar. It was like playing to a riot. Hard to get a groove.

After John's set, we were hanging out in his dressing room. He was trying to decompress, after having done acoustic combat. All of a sudden, he remembered that he hadn't got paid. He said that the promoter had his check: "I just have to find him." He mentioned the name of the guy, someone I knew. We had done a show for him earlier. I also knew exactly where he was.

"Yeah, I saw him when you came offstage. He's onstage now with Little Richard."

I told John to chill and that I would get his check.

"Ahhh, man, that would be great. Thanks."

The dressing rooms were high above the stage at the Grand Olympic Auditorium, and as I came out of the dressing room I could see our friend clearly, on the stage below. As I got down to the stage, he saw me and signaled for me to come onstage.

Richard was in the part of his act when he has the crowd whipped into a frenzy and is dancing on top of the piano, hot and sweaty, with his shirt off and his wig bouncing at an odd angle.

On both sides of the front of the stage, there were these enormous stacks of very large speakers. They looked wobbly.

I shouted to the promoter that I was here to get John's check. He nodded and reached into his back pocket and pulled out the check. He looked at it, nodded again, and handed it to me. I put the check in my back pocket and looked up to see Little Richard's wild gyrations. All of a sudden I felt a cracking sensation at my feet. And then another. I didn't even think; I just turned and ran until I was off the stage...which collapsed right behind me.

The tall stacks of speakers tumbled over one another and crashed onto the stage, smashing into people, equipment, instruments. The stage cratered right in the middle. There were arms and legs and organs and guitars sticking out from everywhere. Luckily, Richard had just gotten off the piano and didn't get hit by anything. He still had to be carried from the middle of the rubble. Other band members and stage crew weren't as lucky. There were several concussions, three broken legs, and a broken back.

Humpteen years later I was doing a TV singing competition show called *Celebrity Duets*. Each celebrity was teamed up with a different famous singer every week. Where else but on a reality show would I get to sing duets with Randy Travis, Aaron Neville, Clint Black, Al Jarreau, and Peter Frampton?

One afternoon during a rehearsal break, we were all gathered around a piano with our celebrity judge, Little Richard. We were all listening to him reminisce and I asked him, "Do you remember playing the Olympic Auditorium when the stage collapsed?"

Slowly he turned around and looked at me.

"How you know about that?"

"I was standing on the stage when it started to crack." Then I told him the story of how I got there and at the end he looked at me and let out a high pitched falsetto. "Woooo! The Lord is mighty! Wooooo!"

My next assignment for *Poppin* was to interview Richard Pryor, who was just starting to heat up. He had two comedy records out that were causing a lot of noise not only in the hood, but in Hollywood as well.

Pryor started out as a traditional stand-up comedian. He played the standard clubs and had an act that resembled Bill Cosby's. Then Cosby saw him doing it one night at a club in New York and told him to stop using his material. It is the oldest argument in the history of comedy. (And it came up many years later with Tommy and me and Jimmy Komack. Keep reading!)

"You're using my material."

"Oh yeah, well I'm black/brown/white/Asian/female/gay, too."

My wife, Natasha, is from Russia, and when we first started dating I took her, in ten days, to see George Lopez, Paul Rodriguez, Carlos Mencia, and Culture Clash. I asked her what she thought. She said it was the same show and pointed out all the similar jokes. She speaks perfect Spanish, so nothing had escaped her. There is a lot of similarity in what we find funny, and Richard was just starting out and finding his voice. He wasn't ripping off Cosby. The similarities between them fell away pretty quickly anyway.

Richard had been infected by the same sociological, revolutionary, and spiritual changes that were spreading across the country and had infected Tommy and me. His point of view was straight from the ghetto, and it was hilarious and incendiary. For my money, Richard Pryor was the funniest, most insightful, and challenging stand-up who ever lived. I saw him many times over the years. This interview occurred after the first time I ever saw him live.

He was playing at Izzy's nightclub in Vancouver. His act was raw and offended some in the all-white audience of Vancouver. I laughed my ass off, but there was an edge that he kept inserting into the audience, and you could feel the tension with every off-color remark that he made.

I met him in his dressing room after the show. I told him that I was from LA and had lived in South Central. He smiled and nodded, and we set a time to do the interview the next day at his hotel.

I came the next day at the appointed time and knocked on the door. Somebody from inside called out.

"Who is it?"

"I'm here for the interview."

I heard rustling in the room that sounded like people getting dressed and finally, after a long wait, the door was opened by a young, blonde German woman. She motioned me inside and there, in the middle of a king-sized bed, with his legs under the covers, sat a naked Richard Pryor.

"Yo, South Central, come on in."

OK, whatever. The girl sat in a chair off to the side and Pryor motioned for me to sit in the chair next to the bed.

"How you doing? Can I get you anything?"

"No, I'm cool."

I set up my tape recorder on the nightstand next to the bed and proceeded to start the interview like we were in a television studio. I asked him a lot of questions that I hoped sounded intelligent and at one point I asked him, "Do you ever worry about getting shot by somebody who takes offense at what you're saying?"

He laughed and shook his head at the same time.

"You know, you're the second person in a week that's asked me that question. No, man, I don't think of that at all."

He continued to laugh and look at me like I was crazy. During the course of the interview, there was one exchange we had that has always stayed with me.

"Who is Richard Pryor?"

"It's not important who Richard Pryor is; it's what Richard Pryor sees."

In that brief moment, I learned, from one of the best ever, that it's about the material, not the performer.

I thanked Richard for the interview, and I knew somehow I would see him again in the future. It would not be in Vancouver, however, because he was fired that night from Izzy's for saying "motherfucker" one too many times.

In a few years I would see him again at the Bitter End West nightclub in Hollywood. By this time, he was the hottest comedian in America, and a who's who of Hollywood were crammed into the small nightclub every night for a week: Harry Belafonte, Sidney Poitier, Diana Ross, Bill Russell, and just about every other music, film, and sports star was there to laugh their asses off. Luckily, Tommy and I knew the people at the club, and they would let us in to stand along the back wall. We saw every single show that week. It was a wild week, and anything could and did happen.

On Friday night during the first show, some woman in the second row kept interrupting him and giving him a hard time. He tried to ignore her, but she kept it up. I couldn't hear what she was saying, but it was obviously irritating Pryor. He asked her to be quiet to no avail. Finally, he had had enough and said, "Oh, I know what you want!" and proceeded to whip out his dick and wave it in her face. The whole club erupted. They couldn't believe it and went wild yelling and screaming. The heckling woman finally got up and walked out. When she was gone, Richard said to the crowd with his dick in his hand, "Sorry for ruining the myth."

To paraphrase one of his later album titles: That nigger was crazy. Richard Pryor went on to achieve the highest highs in his stand-up and movie careers. And experience the lowest lows when he almost burned himself to death while drinking and smoking crack. Through it all, Richard Pryor was a once-in-a-lifetime comic voice, and I'm glad I was around for all of his brilliant career.

Back to our story!

Before I left the bar, Ihor gave me a mischievous smile and said, "There's this guy I think you should meet."

Ihor said he knew this guy named Tommy Chong who was running an improvisational theater company in a topless bar in Chinatown. I quickly realized that he was talking about the Shanghai Junk, the bar I had passed when I was walking around with Len that first day.

Eventually, I'd realize that Tommy was the musician that everybody in Calgary knew because he had cowritten the song "Does Your Mama Know About Me?" that Diana Ross and the Supremes had recorded. It was first a hit for Tommy's band, Bobby Taylor and the Vancouvers, on Motown Records. He was a legend in Calgary. The song went on to be recorded by other performers, too, like Stephanie Mills, Jermaine Jackson, and the Harlettes, Bette Midler's backup singers.

Ihor set up a meeting and we were to meet at a farmhouse out in the countryside. On the appointed day, I drove out there and knocked on the door, which was quickly opened by a very pretty, young, blonde, hippie-type chick. It was Shelby Fiddis, Tommy's girlfriend, a person I would come to know very well for the next forty years (and counting). Crawling around the floor was an angelic little one-year-old girl with cookie smeared all over her face. I would know Precious Chong for her entire life…so far.

Tommy came out from a back bedroom, and at the instant we first laid eyes on each other, we both had the same thought: *What the hell are you?*

Tommy was wearing brown leather pants held up by a wide leather belt fastened to a handmade hippie belt buckle. He was also sporting a blue nylon wifebeater T-shirt that revealed a crude, homemade eagle

tattoo on his left arm where one wing was bigger than the other...
and not on purpose. He had long, wild black hair parted in the middle. To top it off, he had a scraggly and sparse Fu Manchu moustache
and goatee...and he was brown, which I took to be a good sign.

The overall effect was of a hippie–biker–Mongolian–weight lifter.
And he had gold-framed eyeglasses and a big gap in his front teeth.
You know, your typical topless, improvisational-theater look.

I was sporting the exact opposite look.

Working at Sunshine Village Ski Resort required a short haircut
and no facial hair. I looked like a narc, which everyone in the troupe
would suspect at first.

I started filling Tommy in on my background, starting with my
draft-resister status and ending with my experience as a member of
Instant Theater, an improvisational-theater group in LA. A total
fucking lie, but a very good improv.

I had seen Instant Theater many times and immediately knew I
could do improv. The Theater had been started by Rachel Rosenthal,
who went on to become the grand dame of performance art, and her
husband King Moody, who went on to become the original Ronald
McDonald in all the McDonald's commercials.

Tommy knew that I was a writer for *Poppin* magazine, so he hired
me as a writer for the group. But first I had to come down and check
out the show to see if we were a fit. I asked him how much the job
paid, and he said sixty Canadian dollars a week.

Right away, I knew we were a fit.

CHAPTER 11

We want tits!

I went down the next night to see the show that Tommy and his group were putting on at the Shanghai Junk. I was more than slightly distracted, because my on-again/off-again girlfriend, Sara, had come to Vancouver from Los Angeles that day to pick up where we'd left off. I really didn't want to go that night, but I had promised Chong that I would. So, with Sara in tow, I ventured down to Chinatown.

I loved the hippie days; anything was possible. Sara didn't even blink when I said we were going to Skid Row to see naked improv theater. There was a thin line between the hippies and the homeless, and we moved in and out of each other's worlds effortlessly.

The show was just starting as we were guided to our table by Shelby, Tommy's girlfriend, who worked as a waitress. Over the years, various stories have said that Shelby was one of the strippers. She was not. However, she did wear the skimpiest costume possible because, well... tips are tips, and she did OK.

The show started off with three naked but chiffon-covered strippers dancing slowly to some Indian-sounding guitar raga music played by Tommy and sung by troupe member David Graham. It went on forever, but I really didn't pay much attention, because my focus was on Sara. I did look around, though, to see who would come to see this show. The audience was composed of bikers, loggers, run-of-the-mill drunks, pimps, and quite a few hookers. I would soon find out that, for the hookers, this place was their office. They took care of the office and the office took care of them. What was apparent right away was that the rest of the crowd was as befuddled by the show as I was. I heard more than one biker say, "What the fuck is this shit?"

After the music ended everybody disappeared from the stage, which didn't go over too well with the loggers. "Hey, we wanna see some tits!" was, I think, the exact phrase they used.

Next up was a mime. I kid you not. A fucking mime in whiteface and a beret with a striped shirt...in a strip bar.

Ian (the mime) began his silent routine searching for truth and beauty by employing classic mime routines like running against the wind and picking every petal off a flower.

Accompanying Ian on classical guitar was Gabriel Delorme, the greatest guitarist I have ever heard...bar none. He was the guy who wrote the music for "Earache My Eye," one of our biggest hits. Every guitar player on earth knows that riff: *Da da da, da da da, da, da da!*

The crowd was growing visibly angry. More important, they had stopped drinking, which was death for the club. Ian quickly exited before he was assaulted. Another blackout and a few in the crowd started chanting, "We want tits!"

Quickly the stage lit up and David Graham walked out looking like Buffalo Bill Cody. He stood center stage and started to sing:

> *I dream of Brownie in the light blue jeans*
> *She's just as neat as licorice jelly beans*
> *I dream of Brownie and it makes me melly-er*
> *Cause Brownie is my favorite wire-haired Terrier.*

The audience stared at David, stunned. The bikers started to growl. All of a sudden one of the doors on the back wall of the stage flew open and there stood a pissed-off Tommy Chong, shirtless with his hair a mess like he had just been awakened. He had a rolled-up newspaper in one hand. Slowly, he approached David, silently looked him over and then he started beating him with the newspaper while slowly, but loudly, saying, *"What-kind-of-fucking-song-is-that?"*

Blackout.

I almost fell off my chair laughing. Even some of the bikers laughed and they are not known as an overly jovial lot. It was pure guerilla theater played to an actively hostile crowd, and it got them.

After the show, I went backstage to meet the cast. Tommy had told them that I was this great improv actor from LA. As I said, they thought I was a narc. Tommy was glad that I laughed, and I told him I would see him Monday morning at the club. I was hired as a writer, and I was confident that I could help the show.

Even the most glamorous, sexy, and seductive nightclub looks entirely different in the cold light of day. When the lights are on and the people are gone, you see every stain, every tear, and every uphol-stery gash that is invisible in the night, when colored lights and naked women cloud your vision. Sitting in the Junk with the chairs upside down on the tables and faint daylight streaming in from an overhead skylight was a definite reality check. Even the girls, who the night before were the definition of desire, sat there without makeup, pimply and bored. They still thought I was a narc, and they were not going to say anything in front of me.

I started talking to Tommy and the rest of the cast, congratulat-ing them on their bravery. I threw out a few suggestions, which they seemed to like, and then I performed a mime bit about an astronaut who goes from preflight preparation to takeoff and then, finding himself all alone in space with nobody watching, decides it's the per-fect time to jack off. Ian was entranced. I had written a solo piece for him. I was welcomed into the group.

Every night was a new adventure. You never knew what was going to happen. Some nights the crowd was in a good mood and even laughed at some bits. Other nights they were drunk and hostile and tried to climb onstage and beat us up.

Thank God for Stan Chong.

Tommy's brother was our bartender-bouncer. Stan was nobody you would want to mess with in life. He was the kind of man referred to in the saying "Beware of the man with the sloping shoulders."

For example, one week Stan kept complaining that his knuckle was sore. Finally, Tommy got tired of listening to him and told him to go to the doctor to get checked up. Reluctantly, Stan trudged off to the doctor, who found the source of his trouble. It seems that Stan had a tooth embedded in his knuckle and it had gotten infected. Thank God Canada had socialized medicine.

How the troupe got started in the first place was a great story. While touring with Bobby Taylor and the Vancouvers, Chong got to see Second City, a famous improvisational-theater group in Chicago. In San Francisco, he saw the Committee. He found them as he walked along the street below a sign that said FUCK COMMUNISM. He was fascinated by this new form of theater, and it made a mark on him.

Long story short: The band broke up in 1968 and Tommy eventually found himself back in Vancouver.

Tommy had always been a club owner. He started nightclubs so his various bands would have some place to play. His most successful club was the Elegant Parlor, which was a mostly black after-hours club. You could drive through Vancouver all day and not see one black person, then go to the Parlor and see three hundred.

When he got back home, he found that the last club he had, which he had left in the care of his parents and Stan, had been turned into, of course, Vancouver's first topless club.

He'd been gone a little while so when he tried to enter the club, the doorman almost didn't let him in because he had such long hair. Once inside, Tommy saw what was going on and started working the lights to try to give it more zip. He watched the strippers who performed without much enthusiasm. There was a live band and the girls came out, shook 'em for three songs, and then went off. Even the audience treated them as background.

What he did notice, however, was that when the dancers showed up for work in their tight, hip-hugger, bell-bottom jeans and their little short crop tops, they were much sexier than when they were naked onstage. One thought led to another until he came to the conclusion that he would start an improvisational-theater company...but with naked girls.

It was a stroke of genius. The girls came out fully clothed and then somehow or another in the course of a very rudimentary skit, they would take off their clothes. It was almost like a porno movie at first. You could hear a pin drop in the house. Every voyeuristic tendency in the male and female audience came to full attention. He had stumbled upon the next evolution: "Hippie Burlesque."

Since I didn't have a definite role to play in the show at first, I watched from offstage. Fairly quickly, I learned everybody's role and could fill in anywhere in the show. Except for certain strippers. If I saw something that could work better or if I came up with a new line, I could get it in right away. This period was great for me, because I could watch the show critically as an audience member more than as a performer. It helped me develop an intuitive sense of what works onstage. And what doesn't. Performer, critic, fixer.

We did four hours of improv a night, six nights a week. We were piling up more onstage experience than anybody we knew. It was an apprenticeship, but it also reaped very strong material.

I remember one night everybody was in a panic because Ian, the mime, hadn't shown up yet.

What about the "Astronaut"? Ian's not here!

I volunteered that, since I wrote the bit, I could probably fill in.

Oh, yeah! OK.

I got the costume on and went out and did the bit to a rousing response. In the middle of the performance, Ian walked into the club and saw what was going on. He was never late again. In the years to come, "The Astronaut" would be a bright spot in the Cheech and Chong show for a long time.

Every night something hilarious or dangerous would happen. Every show we would throw in some counterculture reference from the street's-eye view we saw all around us. This approach is at the heart of Cheech and Chong's shows and records.

For example, there was a really nice cop in San Francisco who smoked pot and was generally sympathetic to the kids and the hippies. We read about him in the paper, and Tommy immediately wrote a song based on the cop's nickname, "Sergeant Sunshine." It went right into the show. Tommy and I had that song in and out of our show for years.

For Tommy and me, this was the incubation period for what would become Cheech and Chong. Many of the bits that we performed at the Junk formed the basis of future Cheech and Chong routines. We learned how to work together, what made each other tick. We learned how to inspire each other. And we each learned how the other thought. We learned how to work and read the audience. The Beatles had Hamburg. We had Vancouver.

When word started getting out about what we were doing, we started getting a lot of attention, and other actors would drop by to check it out. Even other strippers would come by to jam. The main dancers, Wendy and Maureen, were told by Tommy that they were no longer strippers, they were now actresses...who took off their clothes. So they would get paid less. I think their reaction was, "Uh...OK."

The troupe, now named the City Works, was quite a collection of characters. Besides me, Tommy, Ian, and David, there was Gabriel and, most important, "Strawberry," our light man.

Strawberry, whose real name I never knew, was so named because

Cheech Marin

of his long, flaming-red hair. He was just a kid. Tommy discovered him in the alley behind the club sitting on a box, eating a ham sandwich. When Tommy asked him what he was doing he said, "Nothing, just eating a sandwich."

"Do you have any place to live?"

"I've been staying in this alley lately."

Tommy told him that he could sleep in the club. After a few days, Tommy told him, "As long as you're here, you can learn to run the lights during the show."

"OK."

Strawberry would become our light man. And sometimes he'd get the light cues and sometimes he wouldn't. One time he told me, "Sorry I missed that cue, man, but I scored some dynamite acid this afternoon. It really started coming on when you were doing your bit. Wow, you were really good. But I just tripped out."

Sometimes he was a very incisive critic, like "Man, that bit really sucked...Sorry I missed the cue."

How can you get mad at a guy like that?

Tommy used Strawberry as the basis of his "Man" character in all the records and movies.

As you can tell, pot and psychedelics were all around us. They were part of our act from the very beginning. We didn't have to introduce drugs as a topic or a reference. They were just *there*. We tapped into stoner culture very naturally. And our later success showed we weren't alone. We were just the first act to reflect it so openly. We didn't become hippies. We *were* hippies.

After I'd been with the troupe about three months, the *Vancouver Sun*, the main newspaper in town, sent their theater critic down to check us out. He was told that there was this edgy, avant-garde, experimental, improvisational, naked theater company working in Chinatown. I bet he envisioned something like Living Theater from New York, which was all of the above. What he found was low-brow, hippie burlesque. He was not amused...but he was intrigued by some of it.

The dichotomy he sensed, broad comedy with insightful characterizations and situations, would be our hallmark for the rest of our career. In other words, sometimes you have to be smart to understand why something so dumb can be so funny.

Many years later, our good friend Timothy Leary told us that we were modern exponents of classic comedy forms. He even showed us the definition in an encyclopedia. We were a combination of both high and low comedy.

At any rate, it took that critic three pages to dismiss us.

The next day the club was packed, because people had read about us in the paper. It didn't matter that he'd put us down—nobody remembered that part. It only mattered that we were in the paper... with a picture!

Tommy took a cue from that and put an ad in the paper that week that consisted of a large picture of the cast and a few out-of-context quotes from the review. We were packed from then on.

We now had an educated, college-aged crowd. The bikers, loggers, pimps, and hookers were relegated to a few tables in the back. The new crowd was very attentive. It was remarkable how good we became when people actually listened.

The only fly in the ointment was that the new crowd didn't drink. They would nurse a glass of white wine the whole show and then stiff the waitresses. A couple or three drunks could keep the place open. The hooker trade generated plenty of drink revenue. Now we had neither.

One Saturday night after the show, Tommy and I were sitting at a table going over the act when his brother, Stan, walked up with a large stack of bills in his hands and dropped them with a big thud right in front of us. He didn't even say anything. He didn't have to. After nine months, we were ready to give birth to something. We knew that playtime was over.

We were done with the main room at the Shanghai Junk. We took over the upstairs back room and made it into an after-hours nightclub, where our now reduced-in-size troupe and Django, Gabriel's band, would play.

One day, Tommy found out that Three Dog Night would be playing a big arena in town. Tommy's brother-in-law, Floyd Snead, was their drummer. Tommy prevailed on Floyd to bring the band over to see our act. We met the guys and became friends. One of the guys in the band, Danny Hutton, would play a pivotal role in our career within the next year.

CHAPTER 12

Do you have a nickname?

I knew that the end was near when David Graham announced that he was quitting to manage Django. There was this persistent buzz that Vancouver was the new San Francisco and that all the cool new bands were coming from Canada. Chilliwack, a local band, had just signed a deal with A&M Records. David figured that whatever Chilliwack got, Django should get at least twice as much because they were that much better.

Django included bass player Kenny Passarelli from Denver, who would go on to cowrite "Rocky Mountain Way" with Joe Walsh when they were members of Barnstorm, and then go on to play with Elton John, Hall and Oates, Dan Fogelberg, and Stephen Stills among others. So, they probably *were* twice as good as Chilliwack, but they would have had to stay together longer than three months to be the next big thing...which they did not.

Then, Ian announced that he was going to the woods to get his head together. I had been to the woods. Moose carcasses, skinning bears. I prayed for him.

The club went back to the old format. I saw the "show" a couple of times and it just broke my heart, so I didn't go back. Then one night, Tommy called out of the blue.

"I got what we can do. We form a duo, me and you. You're a singer. I'm a guitar player. We get a band together and do music and bits from the show. We could play like lounges and clubs and who knows, maybe even Vegas."

I thought, *Well, I'll see if I can cram it into my busy career of being broke and jobless.*

So Tommy started putting the band together. He brought up Tony Riley, a drummer from Los Angeles, and the rest were local musicians. We started rehearsing a couple of tunes at the club in the daytime. Some R&B standards and some of Tommy's guitar raga stuff.

Very quickly we heard of this "battle of the bands" at the Garden Auditorium. Perfect place to try out our new act. We got a time slot for Tommy Chong and the City Works. I had heard Tommy say more than a few times that the next act or group he was in would have his name in the title. He didn't want to be anonymous like he was in Bobby Taylor and the Vancouvers.

I totally understood. I wanted exactly the same thing.

We decided to start out with a couple of comedy bits and then play some music. We started out with "Old Man in the Park," where Tommy plays a crotchety old geezer and I play a biker. We have a conversation, which is pictured on the back of our first record album. We started performing the bit while everybody was still milling around. Very quickly a bunch of people rushed to the front of the stage. I thought they were going to jump onstage, which is what we were used to, but they just wanted to hear what was going on. These kids, for the most part, would never have gone down to the Junk. So while they never heard of us . . . *we were them.* When we finished the bit, we got a big cheer. We knew what a rock-and-roll audience was like. We both had been musicians and performers all our lives. I had been in a number of bands all through high school and college. Tommy, the same. We had more to give them, and we did.

We went into another bit, and most of the arena had quieted down and were following us. They wanted another bit and then another.

We never got around to the music. The band stood there the whole time. We got a rousing rock-and-roll reception and bounced offstage.

As we came off the stage, one of the band members asked, "Well, when's our next gig?"

Tommy and I both looked at each other and knew the answer. There would be no next gig for the band. We were now a bona fide comedy duo.

As we drove home in Pop Chong's car, we were floating on a cloud of euphoria. In Vancouver, where it always rains, it is necessary to have windshield wipers that work. Ours did, but the windshield wiper motor had been broken for a while. The wiper was hooked up to a straightened-out wire clothes hanger that the driver used to move the blades back and forth...by hand. We didn't care, though, as we drove along bursting with joy. We went back and forth going over the show and how the audience responded. We were thrilled that they not only listened and laughed but that they didn't throw shit at us.

Soon we were driving along in a happy silence. While working the windshield wiper, Tommy seemed lost in a reverie.

"We need a new name."

We both realized that "Tommy Chong and the City Works" would not work if there were just the two of us. So we tried out all the combinations.

Marin and Chong.

Chong and Marin.

No. Both sounded too much like an ambulance-chasing, "*Se habla Espanol*...and Chinese" law firm.

Tommy and Richard.

Richard and Tommy.

No. Sounded like two white guys.

Then finally, Chong asked, "Do you have a nickname?"

"Well, my family calls me Cheech, which is short for *chicharrón.*"

"What's a *chicharrón*?"

"It's a pork rind, you know, a deep-fried pig skin. They're all curled up and small. When my uncle Bano saw me for the first time in my crib he said, 'He looks like a little *chicharrón*.' It very quickly got shortened to 'Cheech,' and that was always my nickname in the family. Everybody in my family had nicknames, usually two or three."

Chong said softly, "Cheech, Cheech."

And then "Cheech and Chong." And that was it.

We didn't even try "Chong and Cheech." We were both musicians, and our ears told us that name had the right sound. Cheech and Chong...and that's the way it's always been. We drove into the rain, over a bridge that was condemned and had a big sign that warned PROCEED AT YOUR OWN RISK.

Tommy, while still working the wiper by hand as we disappeared into the fog, softly chanted, "Cheech and Chong, Cheech and Chong...Man we're gonna be big."

CHAPTER 13

One small problem

Though we didn't know it at the time, and hadn't planned it, our first gig as Cheech and Chong was at that battle of the bands at the Garden Auditorium. We played one more gig in Vancouver at Ronnie Scott's Blues and Folk Club on Davie Street. It was May 1970.

Scott's was the epicenter of the blues and folk scene in Vancouver. We were opening for blues great T-Bone Walker. Once again, people in this scene had never seen us, but we went over great.

T-Bone was very late getting on, and when he did show up he was totally drunk and had to be helped onto the stage. He sat down in his chair, and a roadie laid a guitar in his lap. The band, which had already started to play, waited for him to join in.

Finally, he started playing his guitar and singing in a very drunk voice, slurring all his words. The strings on his guitar had been loosened for the plane ride, so they were all out of tune. But it didn't bother T-Bone, because he just kept singing and playing. I don't think he even knew where he was. A roadie crept onstage and tried to tune as he played, which only seemed to annoy him. The band finished the tune and the audience leapt to their feet to give him a standing ovation.

Tommy and I almost fell over laughing in the back of the room. Later on, Chong would use that performance as the basis of his blind blues singer Blind Melon Chitlin, which is still in our act today.

After the show, Chong and I had a conversation about what we would do next. If we really wanted to make it, we would have to go to either Los Angeles or New York. New York was cold and we knew nobody there, Los Angeles was warm and I grew up there. There was only one problem: I was wanted by the FBI because of my draft-resistance activities.

You must remember that there was total bureaucratic and administrative chaos in the United States at this time. The Vietnam War was raging and a huge portion of the country, especially college-age kids, were doing everything they could to fuck with the government. I figured they were never going to notice li'l old me. This was well before the computer age. They were still making carbon copies of shit.

So I went to the airport armed with a phony ID. It was the driver's license of my friend Bill Knorr... *with his picture on it.*

Still, I was a little bit nervous... so, I looked for a bar at the airport. I saw something Irish sounding with a shamrock on it so I went in and ordered a double vodka on the rocks.

My cover story, if I needed one, was that I was a writer for *Poppin* magazine, which I was, and I was going down to the U.S. to do some interviews with the Grateful Dead, Santana, and the Jefferson Airplane. I ordered another shot. I downed it as soon as it came and then got up and walked to Gate 34.

Rounding a corner into a long hallway of gates, I saw Led Zeppelin coming out of a door at the other end. Robert Plant and Jimmy Page led a gang of roadies. There was nobody else in the hallway. They acted like they were being attacked by a hundred groupies. They were laughing at the top of their lungs as they pretended to kick them away and fight their way through the nonexistent crowd. I thought I was in the movie *Blow-Up*.

I steeled myself for my interaction with the U.S. border officer. As I showed him my phony ID, I leaned in closely so that he could get a whiff of the vodka on my breath. I wanted to make sure he believed that I was a journalist. I started telling him my story of going to get interviews. He stopped me in the middle of the story, handed me back my ID with Bill Knorr's picture on it, and said, "Welcome to the U.S."

I stepped across the line and, after three years, I was back home.

CHAPTER 14

What happened to the leopard you had last night?

The most immediate problem when I landed in Los Angeles in 1971 was figuring out where to go. I couldn't go to my mom's house, because the FBI used to drop by every so often to check and see if I was there. Tommy had come in the day before and met me at the airport. He said we could stay with his soon-to-be-ex-wife, Maxine, and his two daughters, Robbie and Rae Dawn. Sounded ideal.

We showed up at Maxine's apartment fairly late. It rained pretty hard that night in LA, and our only transportation was Chong's Honda 90. It was more a motor scooter than motorcycle. It would have been great in Hanoi. Maxine opened the door to two drowned-rat brown guys. She immediately understood our situation, and to my eternal gratitude, she said...come in.

Maxine Snead Chong was a saint then and has remained one to this day. She is one of my favorite people in the world. Tommy, who had known her since she was fourteen, said she had the best body he had ever seen. I have no reason to doubt him. Robbie, her daughter, would become an in-demand Paris ramp model for many famous designers such as Issey Miyake, Matsuda, and Karl Lagerfeld. The apple doesn't fall far from the tree.

Maxine showed me the couch where I was to sleep, and she and Tommy adjourned to the bedroom.

I was awakened early in the morning by cartoons blasting out of the television, which was located right next to my head. Half unconscious, I pried one eye open to see two stone-faced little girls with bowls of Cheerios staring at me. I started to say something and thought better of it and turned over and tried to go back to sleep.

In a little while, Maxine, dressed for work, came out of the bedroom and shouted at the girls in a loud voice, "Don't wake up your daddy! He's sleeping," and then slammed a hard-to-close front door. I turned over once again to see Rae Dawn giving me the stink eye. I moaned and turned back over. This scene would be repeated every morning I was there. We would use it as the opening sequence for *Up in Smoke*, our first movie.

Once the girls were off to school, Chong and I would roust ourselves up and get ready to do what we had to do: find a gig.

We actually had two things to do: find a gig and somehow get our hands on $1.50. For that amount of money, we could make ourselves some sort of Chinese meal and stave off starvation. As we walked around the neighborhood, we pulled a little red wagon and looked for pop bottles that we could return for the five-cents deposit.

With Tommy's experience and connections in the black music scene, we were quickly able to get some spots in the thriving black nightclub circuit in Los Angeles.

The traditional floor-show format was still in effect: A professional MC would open up and address the audience, and introduce the opening act, usually a comedian, and then the main attraction. We fit right in.

We related to the black audience and they related to us, especially in regard to marijuana and music. Once they got past the novelty of nonblack performers in an all-black club and listened to the material, they were on our side all the way. To this day, we still have a large and appreciative black audience. It was also a sign of the times that there was more comingling between groups, at least in the large cities.

At any rate we played a lot of black clubs in LA: Maverick's Flat, the Parisian Room, the Total Experience, and the York Club, which was the first place we ever played with armed guards in the parking lot. The two biggest black clubs we played were the Climax II club and P. J.'s in the middle of Hollywood.

The Climax II was a wild place and indicative of the emerging anything-goes-psychedelic-hippie aesthetic, crossed with a black after-hours club, which was right up our alley. The building, located on the corner of La Cienega and Third, where the Beverly Center is now, looked like something right out of *The Jetsons*. It was painted in a surrealist mural style by the L.A. Fine Arts Squad and was originally called the Millionaires Club.

When it opened as the Climax Club, it was the hottest club in town. You had to pay a membership fee of $2,000 and then monthly dues of $250. For these fees, everything was free once you got in. There were six or seven bars in the three-story building and two or three lavish buffets on every floor. There were also many themed rooms that catered to every fantasy and a large Moroccan Room that you could smoke in . . . and many did.

As I mentioned, it was an after-hours club, and so didn't open its doors until after midnight. You saw every wild character that Hollywood had to offer, wearing as little as possible, wandering around dancing, singing, and interacting. At 4:00 a.m., there was often still a line outside two blocks long.

Eventually, the owner absconded with all the money and left all the after-hours people wandering around the parking lot looking for a Quaalude at five in the morning.

But you can't keep a good idea down.

After a few months, the club reopened under new management and with a *totally* new name: the Climax II club. It featured the same basic attractions, but this time it had live entertainment. Every night, live onstage you could see Ralph Mathis, Johnny Mathis's look-alike brother, who sang all of Johnny's songs, new emerging comedy duo Cheech and Chong, and, for the first time anywhere onstage, a brand new group called Earth, Wind and Fire. Maurice White and his brother Verdine had just put this group together and were still trying to fig-ure out the right combination. Some nights there were fifteen people onstage, including a mini gospel choir, all dressed in flowing red robes.

It was a great gig. We were making up new stuff every day and couldn't wait to try it out that night. We used to riff on the audience as they walked by. One time I saw a black guy dressed in white leather bell-bottoms, a white leather cape, and a big, floppy, white leather pimp hat. This guy was *leading around by a leash* a platinum-blonde white girl dressed in black leather hip-hugger bell-bottoms and a black leather bra.

I shouted out, "Hey man, what happened to the leopard you had on the leash last night?"

The guy glared. But the girl smiled and shouted back, "I ate her... and he filmed it."

You couldn't help but be inspired.

The best club was P.J.'s, right in the heart of Hollywood on Santa Monica Boulevard. For years, it was the center of the go-go scene, and its house band, the Standells, had many good-sized hits ("Dirty Water," "Try It"), especially for what was essentially a local band. Trini Lopez recorded a live album at P.J.'s.

After it had run its run, it floundered, and then out of the blue it was sold to some guy who owned like thirty pizza places and wanted to meet girls... specifically black girls.

So P.J.'s reopened as the uptown black club in Hollywood.

We were hired, sight unseen, due to a pitch from Sally Marr, Lenny Bruce's mother. We were now the house comedians at P.J.'s. We opened for Carmen McRae, who christened the place with a demonstration of what jazz singing was all about. That was a great night.

We were the opening act for, among others, the Isley Brothers, who had just released "Who's That Lady?" the instantly recognizable song from the L'eggs commercial with the innovative fuzz-tone guitar lead. They were right there on the cutting edge of the fusion between R&B and psychedelic. The Isleys had an incredible live show featuring a long list of huge hit records. They were the first ones to record "Twist and Shout." Ronny Isley even did comic impressions of other singers. His impression of Ray Charles brought down the house.

One night Marvin Gaye got onstage and did the title song from his new album, called *What's Going On*. Another magical night.

Every week it was a who's who of R&B stars like the Whispers, the Impressions, Little Anthony and the Imperials, Edwin Starr, the Chi-Lites, the Delfonics. We were the opening act for all of them.

By necessity and by inclination, our act became very black oriented because of the audience we were playing to. But at the same time, we were playing to very white audiences at the Troubadour in Hollywood and the Ice House in Pasadena. The big difference was that the black clubs paid and the white clubs paid very little . . . or not at all.

The Troubadour was the most important club as far as being discovered in the folk and folk-rock music scene. It showcased such acts as Linda Ronstadt, Randy Newman, Joni Mitchell, JD Souther, the Eagles, the Nitty Gritty Dirt Band, Jackson Browne, and just about everybody else in that emerging Los Angeles country rock and singer-songwriter scene. They all got record deals based upon being seen at the "Troub."

But the bar was the real star. Every hot-to-trot young musician, actor, actress, and young Hollywood talent, hung out there. Over the years, you could see Janis Joplin, Jim Morrison, Mick Jagger, Eric Clapton, Linda Ronstadt, or a young Don Johnson, and many others, all scheming on each other. (More on Don Johnson later!)

At the Troubadour, they had this thing called Hoot Night, which was essentially an open-mike night in which amateur acts could get up and perform. The deal was that the first six acts that were at the box office when it opened at 6:00 p.m. could go on that night in reverse order. The first in line could go on sixth—which was a great spot, because by that time the audience was all in, had ordered drinks, and were ready to listen.

We were *always* first in line, because we would get there at 9:00 a.m. and sit on the sidewalk until 6:00 p.m. We did this about seven or eight times, and we very quickly gathered a following.

We'd be alone in front of the club until 2:00 or 3:00 p.m. After all, we had nothing else to do. We sat there and killed time until the other guys started showing up. We heard the dreams of many young singers and songwriters who weren't really going anywhere, and we knew it. But they didn't know it yet. And it was fun to hear their delusional, folksinger stories.

Tommy and I would also talk about our act and try out routines and scenarios on each other. Or we would look at the passing parade of characters and start from there. Our comedy was based on observing this hippie revolution that was going on all around us. And as I said before, very few people were presenting it as a form of entertainment. Which astounded us, because we found it so rich. It was there for anyone to use. But I'm glad we were the ones to capitalize on it.

And once we were established, any act that came close to doing any hippie/stoner stuff was told, "You're just ripping off Cheech and Chong."

Other comedians would tell us later, "You guys stole home plate. We can't follow you guys. You got there first."

An example of this was in the cult classic movie *The Groove Tube*. They ripped off a bit from our album and stage show in which I pick up a hitchhiking Tommy. We ignored it and moved on. Accept no substitutes!

During the rest of the week, we would scramble for gigs and then on the weekends play P.J.'s.

We would play anything that we could get, from the lunch yard at USC to the just-opened Scientology center, which was one of our stranger gigs. I knew it would be different when I went into the men's room and the graffiti on the walls read, *"I was thrown into the maelstrom of the universe blind and unaware."* I was used to "Here I sit in stinky vapors." We went into our doper routines, and the audience stared at us intently. I thought they might have been a painting.

We became a sight around Hollywood traveling from gig to gig on Tommy's Honda 90 wearing all our costumes at the same time. We would have on three or four coats, two or three hats, and a few pairs of shoes strung around our necks. We'd get to the gig, walk onstage, and basically undress, piling all our costumes in a heap, then pick whatever we needed for the next bit. We would do two, three, or even four gigs in one day.

We were growing as a duo by leaps and bounds because we had nothing else to go to onstage. No naked girls. It all came from us. We were also growing because we had nothing else going on offstage. We were either doing the act or thinking about the act. The one thing that we never questioned was our natural affinity. We were like the Everly Brothers; our voices just fit together. No matter what the bit or song or whatever, we both found a way to harmonize together. We understood each other's backgrounds and instinctively, as musicians, knew what notes to play. That was why we could go into a studio or onto a movie set with little or no script and improvise with confidence.

CHAPTER 15

Bank error in your favor

July 1971. On the home front, things were coming unraveled. Maxine finally acknowledged that Chong had a girlfriend—his future wife, Shelby—and a baby (Precious) stashed on the other side of town in Venice. They had come down from Vancouver, and Tommy was going back and forth between the two families. At some point, Maxine had enough and showed Tommy the door. Which meant me, too. It was my first real glimpse into Tommy's chaotic family life, which would change little in the coming years. When you have children with three different women, complications will arise.

Having no other place to go, I went to my mother's house, but I was nervous all the time because of the FBI. Chong didn't make it any easier when he would announce from the stage that I was wanted by the law. He thought it was so funny. Typical Chong move. I was getting used to the fact that he had a mean streak.

Being a Chicano, I always had to have three jobs. I began to write, or pretend to write, for *Poppin* magazine from Canada. I went around to all the record company offices and introduced myself and showed them the magazine with my name on the masthead. They put me on their writer list, which meant that I got free record albums and invites to all the parties and openings. Though we were broke, Tommy and I went to more concerts than the average promoter.

Now and then, the record companies would want me to actually write something. Michael Ochs, brother of folksinger Phil Ochs, was head of publicity at CBS Records, and he asked me who I would like to write about. I mentioned Karen Dalton.

Karen Dalton was a blues-folk singer from Oklahoma who was part of the early Greenwich Village folk scene in New York along with Fred Neil, Dave Van Ronk, and others. She had a very unusual voice, which she accompanied on guitar or banjo. She was a white-folk-blues Billie Holiday. You either loved her or thought, *What the fuck is that?* I heard her first record when I was in Vancouver and was entranced. People thought I was nuts.

When I told Michael Ochs my choice, he stared at me quizzically for a long time and then said, "Well she's on our label, so whatever." He gave me an address in the middle of Hollywood, and I was on my way.

The house was diagonally across the street from the Whisky a Go Go on Sunset Boulevard in the dead center of Hollywood. Lots of heat and cop action in this area. Incinerator number one. Drug users and cops interacting. I knocked on the door of a (now long-gone) little house. After a while, the door creaked open a bit, and there stood Karen Dalton with a cigarette dangling from her lips and a drink in her hand.

"Hi, I'm here to interview you."

She looked me over.

"Oh man, was that today?"

With a great, hoarse, Okie laugh, she opened the door and bid me enter. There were some other people there and they just kind of wandered around. The first thing I noticed was that she had a front tooth missing and was pretty pale. It took me about ten more seconds to realize that most people in the house were junkies. It was a cool house, though, wooden, kind of handcrafted. I asked her a couple of music questions, and she pretended to think about an answer. The background people kept wandering around.

"How many people live here?"

"Six right now, but we have one room open."

"Oh really? I'm looking for a room."

She took a pull from her drink and gave me a more focused look.

"Well, we kind of have to be cool about who we rent to, if you know what I mean."

She laughed to herself and gave me a nod.

"But do you have fifty bucks?"

I was in.

The great thing about living in the same house with Karen Dalton was that every once in a while you got to hear her sing live in the chair across from you. She had a totally unique voice that could break your heart. I've never heard another one like it. The rest of it was *Trainspotting*, but I had a place to stay far from the tentacles of J. Edgar Hoover.

Around this time, our agent, Ron Smith, turned us on to a little club down the street from the Whisky on Sunset that was trying to do a comedy room before there were such things in Hollywood. Or anywhere else for that matter.

Konopow's Komedy Room, run by Gary Konopow, was a club-restaurant that featured only comedians. It was a tiny place. He got a bunch of us to work for a dinner a night…anything off the menu. So seven starving funny guys gorged themselves on steak and lobster for a week until Gary's 'ludes wore off, and then it was changed to a hamburger a night. It didn't matter. We were there to perform. We started to grow. Every night we could refine the bits we were doing. We could think of a new line that we could try out right away and keep or discard. We learned how to perform successfully in front of audiences that hadn't seen us before. We had to trust the material more than our personalities.

I was still living with Karen Dalton and the walking dead, but the house was being sold and we all had to get out. (Karen never became very well known, but she remains an icon to many musicians, if not the general public. Bob Dylan and Kim Gordon of Sonic Youth are fans.)

Night after night at work, I started to talk a lot with a very cute and sexy red-headed waitress/actress named Barbara Douglas, who just so happened to be Ron Smith's cousin. One thing led to another and we decided to get a place together. It was the first live-in arrangement I ever had with a girl, and it was nonstop drama. It had to do with how old we were. I learned what "fucking and feuding" was all about. It's what happens in your early twenties. Volatile times.

Although we had the gig at Konopow's, paying jobs were hard to come by. As the days slipped by, it started to get a little tense with Barbara, because she was the only one bringing in money.

To make matters worse, Tommy now needed a place to live, as Shelby and Precious went back to Vancouver due to lack of support. As she put it to Tommy, "If you can't buy me a pair of shoes, I'm leaving."

So Tommy moved in with us, and it was his turn to sleep on the couch. It was all good until once in the middle of the night I awoke to hear Chong screaming, "Help, Cheech! Cheech, help!" I sat straight up in bed and smelled smoke. I sprang out of bed and ran into a smoke-filled living room.

Tommy was on his hands and knees trying to stamp out the flames in three or four spots on the carpet. I grabbed whatever I could and joined the fight. We finally got the flames out and sat there dazed and confused and naked in the dense, thick smoke.

Meanwhile, Barbara had called the fire department and a big red truck pulled up in front of the duplex. Three or four firemen rushed into the house, assessed the damage, and set up a big fan that drew the smoke out of the room and into the street. The firemen looked at two naked, brown hippies and a white girl, and just shook their heads. It was West Hollywood; they had seen worse. After the smoke cleared, we figured out what happened.

The couch that Tommy had been sleeping on had some foam pillows on it. Right next to the couch was a floor heater. During the night, one of the pillows had fallen off and landed on the heater. The pillow heated up quickly; and as the foam melted and fell on the heater below, it exploded like a volcano and spewed molten foam all over the living room. We were lucky. It could have been much worse.

Not surprisingly, it did nothing to decrease the tension at home.

To make matters worse, Shelby announced that she was coming back with Precious after only a few weeks in Canada. I guess she had gotten some money from welfare or something. Tommy went down to pick them up at the airport on his Honda 90. The three of them drove back…in the rain…and arrived late at night soaking wet. As soon as they arrived, Shelby realized that she didn't have her suitcase. They started to argue until Chong cut it short, dropped his head, got on the scooter, and drove back to the airport…in the rain. I guess God was testing us or some shit.

The next morning Barbara got up early and found them a house right down the street. Now we were back to two, but with the same problem…not enough dough. Finally, she threw down an ultimatum; get a job or get out. I was faced with the reality of the dreaded "day job."

And then a miracle happened.

Tommy, who was as broke as I was, decided to go to his bank to check on his account.

He knew he had no money, so why did he go? Years later, he told me he went to the bank just to get out of the house and have something to do.

He asked the teller to check his account and tell him how much he had. She walked away and then came back and said: "You have two thousand dollars in your account, Mr. Chong."

Dumbfounded, Tommy said, "Uh, uh, I'd like to withdraw five hundred dollars." Improv to the rescue.

"No problem Mr. Chong, just fill out this withdrawal slip."

Tommy filled out the slip, handed it to the teller, and she disappeared. She came back with the signature of the bank president and counted out five one-hundred-dollar bills.

"Have a nice day."

Chong hurried out of the bank, stunned. He came back home and told Shelby the story.

"What happened to the rest of the money?"

"They still have it."

"Well, go back and get the rest."

Dutifully, Chong returned to the bank and asked for the remaining fifteen hundred dollars.

"Is there anything wrong, Mr. Chong?"

"No, no, I just have a lot of bills to pay."

Tommy filled out another slip and she gave him fifteen hundred dollars. Freaked out, he showed up at my place.

"I don't know what's going on, but the bank just gave me two thousand dollars."

"What?"

In those days we could've lived for seven years on two grand.

"Here, hide this."

He shoved a roll of bills in my hand then turned around and split. I looked around for where to hide the cash. Ahh, the sock drawer! They'll never think of looking there. Problem solved.

The next morning there was a knock on Chong's door. It was the bank president and his guy.

"Mr. Chong?"

"Yes?"

"I'm the bank president and this is my guy. You have something that belongs to us."

"Whatever could that be?"

"Two thousand dollars. You took two thousand dollars out of our bank and we want it back...now."

"Well, I withdrew two thousand dollars... but out of my account. I think I have the withdrawal slips... Oh here they are. Signed by the bank president. Is that your signature?"

His face turned beet red. The bank president was sitting in the only piece of furniture in the house, a blow-up beanbag chair that was slowly leaking air. He started speaking louder to Tommy.

"Well, we need that money back, Mr. Chong."

"Oh, I'm sorry man, but I spent it. I had a lot of bills."

The bank president struggled to get out of the chair with little success.

Finally, with Tommy's assistance, he got to his feet.

"What made you think that you had *any* money in your account?"

"Well, I'm a songwriter for Motown, and I thought that they deposited a check in my account."

"You owed us two dollars!"

"Well, how about that?"

"We'll be back, Mr. Chong."

The next day an earthquake struck, and we never heard from them again.

To keep the good news flowing, at around the same time that Tommy got the money from the bank, I saw an article in the *Los Angeles Times*. It detailed a U.S. Court of Appeals decision on a class-action suit involving more than six hundred defendants. I was one of them. It was officially known as *Bucher v. Selective Service System* but was basically the Draft Resisters versus the United States Government. The Court ruled that the reclassification of the defendants because of their political activities was a blatant breach of the First Amendment. The case was thrown out as everybody thought it would be. No more "Draft Dodger" status. No more being sent to the front lines in Vietnam.

Case closed, right?

Two weeks later I received a notice to report to my draft board to undergo an Army physical. They were trying to redraft me now that I didn't have any classification.

I knew immediately what to do. I sent forty-five dollars to Canada to have a copy of the medical report from my ski accident and copies of my X-rays sent down to me. I then spent my last fifty dollars to obtain a letter from a friendly ex–Air Force medical examiner saying that in his opinion, I was unfit for military service. I had never met him, but I liked him already. I crossed my fingers and went down to the draft board.

I followed the red line and followed the blue line until I arrived at the room where you're standing around in nothing but your "chonies." It was a big square room with doors on every wall. Across the room, a door opened and a doctor walked out for a smoke break. He lit up, took a big drag, exhaled, and looked around the room. His gaze came around to me. It seemed like he was staring at me. He motioned at me to come over to him. I crossed the room and stood in front of him. All the while he was staring at my leg.

"Are those X-rays of your leg?"

I nodded yes. He reached out to take them and then held them up to the light. He motioned for me to come into his office.

"You have about a six-degree angle of distortion in your leg where this break occurred. I'm afraid I have some bad news for you."

Now *I* was staring at *him*.

"I'm sorry," he said with a smirk on his face. "You are now officially classified as IV-F. Unfit for military service."

I waited until I got out of his office before jumping in the air and clicking my heels. The skiing accident that I had gotten into in Banff eventually got me out of the draft, and I was able to go forward with Cheech and Chong without fear.

Lucky break, I guess.

CHAPTER 16

Who's Lou Adler?

So you would think that with a little bank we could kind of cruise for a minute. Not that I got a penny from the bank mistake, but I felt that if anything drastic happened Tommy would help me out. Thankfully, nothing drastic occurred.

We just kept on plugging, and then about a week after the bank gift Tommy somehow found a shuttered nightclub right around the corner from us. It was owned by a man named Al Gilbert, who had friends in Chicago. Chong convinced him, club owner to club owner, to let us open the club. He had been using it for storage, and it was stacked to the ceiling with tables and chairs and a thick coating of dust.

The deal was that we would clean it out and use it to establish a nightly residence. It would also be a place for up-and-comers to get their first break. We called it the First Stage. We put a hand-painted sign on the roof; the lettering on the sign got smaller as it ran out of space. We found a band to play for the opening and even got a cameraman to film it. So we had everything but an audience.

Chong got a brainstorm and spent the last of the bank's two thousand dollars to take out ads in *Variety* and the *Hollywood Reporter*. The ads read, "Making a movie, need extras." The next morning there was a line around the block. It looked like a "Black Friday Sale." We took the people in five at a time and explained to them that we were making a movie about an up-and-coming comedy duo, played by us, and we needed them to play the part of the audience. Anyone who had any experience saw that it was bullshit, but an amazing number of people didn't have anything else to do and signed up to play the audience.

Opening night, we were packed. We even sold them food and drinks and everybody smiled and laughed. Why not? They were on camera.

Everybody comes to Hollywood with one purpose in mind: to make it in showbiz. We had jump-started the process and had an instant audience. As word got out over several weeks, we attracted more and more people. A band named Madura joined us for a stretch, and things were lovely…that is until Al Gilbert saw the crowd we were attracting and decided to take over. I guess in his mind people were coming because of his wonderful club that was a storage shed a few weeks earlier. He ousted us and we were back out on the street. Our attitude was, "OK, what's next?"

We learned, though, that we could attract our own crowds with word of mouth. We had a vague sense that something was going on with us.

We went back to P.J.'s, but that, too, would be short-lived.

When the pizza guy bought the club from the gangsters, he didn't change any of the staff. So the employees were still all *their* people. What they did was play it cool until a week came when the club made a lot of money. And then they robbed him.

Their plan was to follow the secretary taking the money to the bank. Two men would jump out of a car, kidnap her, tie her up, take the money, and abandon her in the hills. What *a coincidence* that these thieves knew exactly when she would be out on the street with the money!

They even did this a couple more times before "Mr. Pizza" began scratching his head. He was going to outsmart them now! He bought a safe that was cemented and bolted to the floor of the basement. The gangsters just waited for the next big week and spent all day and night Sunday breaking up the cement with pickaxes and stole the whole safe.

Tommy and I always knew when they were going to rob the guy by how the club did each week. So we would ask for an advance and they would give us a sour look because they figured that that was twenty-five dollars they weren't going to get in the upcoming robbery.

Needless to say, after that last robbery the club went out of business. Over the years, various clubs occupied that space. The best known was Starwood, a prime rock venue that launched, among other bands, Van Halen.

We also went back to do the Troubadour on Monday nights, but this time it was different. Our old friend Danny Hutton from Three Dog Night had been telling all his music industry friends about us, and he set up a slot for us and invited his buddies: Ted Templeman of Warner Bros. Records, Randy Newman, Brian Wilson of the Beach Boys, Van Dyke Parks, and a few others. (Recently, Steve Martin told me that he was in the crowd that night.) By this time, we had a small and vocal following, and we were hot that night. We came offstage to a lively reception. It was very warm that July night, and we walked out of the club to cool off in the street.

People were coming up to us and congratulating us on the show. Then I saw Melissa Montgomery stepping toward us. Melissa was Danny's latest girlfriend. She was also Dinah Shore and Robert Montgomery's daughter. Dinah and Bob were two of the biggest stars in Hollywood at the time. She smiled and gave me a big hug and said how much she loved our act. She leaned in and whispered into my ear, "Lou Adler just saw your show and he wants you to call him." And then she disappeared back into the club.

I told Tommy what Melissa said, and he replied, "Who's Lou Adler?"

Chong may not have known, but because I was a record reviewer I knew exactly who Lou was. He was the biggest record producer in the business. He had produced records for Sam Cooke, Johnny Rivers, Barry "Eve of Destruction" McGuire, Jan and Dean, the Grass Roots, Scott Mackenzie, and Spirit. He founded Dunhill Records, where he produced The Mamas and The Papas and other bands. Lou also produced the Monterey Pop Festival, which introduced Jimi Hendrix to the United States.

At this time, he was dealing with the success of another record he produced: *Tapestry* by Carole King, which would become one of the biggest-selling albums of all time. So I called him.

His secretary, Cheryl, told me that we should come to A&M Records, located at the old Charlie Chaplin Studios, the next day at 1:00 p.m.

At the appointed time, we showed up without a clue as to what was going to happen. Cheryl escorted us into his small office, where Lou sat behind his desk with his sunglasses on. He smiled, stood up, shook our hands, and took off his sunglasses. He told us he had seen our act at the Troubadour and really liked us. He really related to us, he said, because he was from East LA—Boyle Heights, to be exact.

Cool. Homeboy, I thought.

I looked around his office and noticed that his walls were covered in gold records.

"So what do you guys want to do?"

Chong and I had not discussed anything before we came to the meeting.

"Make a record, I guess."

"What kind?" asked Lou.

I looked around at the walls again and then said, "Gold, I guess. That seems to be what you make."

"Are you guys signed to anybody?"

We both shook our heads.

"Good," said Lou. "Do you have a manager?"

Again we shook our heads.

"Even better. Let me call my lawyer."

Lou called downstairs to Abe Somers, his company lawyer, and said he was sending us down to talk to him. Abe ushered us into his office and, with a big smile, said that Lou wanted to offer us a recording contract. He gave us a short speech about what a home-run hitter Lou was and how we would be the first comedy act he had ever signed. If anybody knew what to do with us, it would be Lou Adler.

My heart began to thump. We were going to be rich. These were the days in which new bands were signing for a hundred thousand dollars or more. Abe said that Lou was prepared to offer us *one thousand dollars* to sign. Tommy started to reach for the pen. I stopped him and said:

"Mr. Somers, there's two of us...so we'll need... *two thousand dollars.*"

Abe smiled a sly smile and said that he'd have to ask Lou. He picked up the phone and relayed the request to Lou. He almost laughed when he said, "Well, you drive a hard bargain, but Lou said OK."

We were now officially recording artists...without a clue.

CHAPTER 17

Dave's not here

The next day, we went into A&M studio #1, the biggest one on the lot, without any idea on how to proceed.

Lou suggested we act out one of our bits just like we did it onstage. We pulled up two chairs while the engineers set up the mikes and, when a whole control room full of technicians was ready, we went into "The Low Rider and the Red Freak."

Right away, I knew that this was not working. There was no audience to get feedback from, the few people in the control booth behind the glass wall were busy looking at dials.

After the first take, I looked at Adler in the control room, and he had a look on his face that said, *Well, there goes two thousand dollars.* We tried a few more bits, and they had the same effect... nada.

Lou called a halt to the session and huddled with us in the control room. He suggested that we do some writing to try to figure out how to convert our stage act to record. He said that we could use the projection room on the lot to work out whatever we had in mind. Our essential problem was that we were largely a visual act, and records couldn't capture any of that.

The next morning brought a hot, sunny July day in Los Angeles. Boiling, to be more precise. Tommy and I went into that projection room on the main square of the lot. It was where Charlie Chaplin screened all the dailies from his movies. It was hard to get over the feeling that his ghost was still in the room. Air-conditioning helped.

We started working on a bit that we had done a few times before. It was a scene about a guy that doesn't really want a job coming in to apply for one.

We had a little cassette recorder with us, which was part of our "signing bonus."

We decided to start with this bit because it was all talking and might be easier to adapt to a record. Chong suggested that I go outside and knock on the door to start the bit. "As long as you're out there," he said, "put on a coat and hat to get into character." That was one of the ways I always used to get into character, from the external to the internal.

I step out of the room and into the square that's open to all the surrounding offices. Then I get into character and knock on the door. Nobody answers. I knock again; still no answer. I knock a third time and, after a long delay, finally I hear Chong say, "Who is it?"

What do you mean "Who is it?" You're not supposed to say, "Who is it?" You're supposed to say, "Come in."

I knock again.

"Who is it?"

My improv training kicks in and I say, "It's me...Dave."

Back comes the reply:

"Dave?"

"Yeah, man. Dave. Open the door. I think the cops saw me come in here."

"Dave?"

"Yeah, man. Dave. Now open up!"

"Dave?"

"Yesssss! Dave! Now open up."

Long delay, and then: "Dave's not here."

I can hear Tommy trying not to laugh as he tortures me, which is his favorite thing to do. People walking by in the square stare at this long-haired, overdressed hippie banging on a door in the blistering heat. They don't know whether to alert security or what.

Chong keeps on going: "Dave's not here."

I'm banging on the door hard now and really getting pissed. Finally, Tommy opens the door, laughing his head off.

"What the fuck you doing, man? It's hot out here!"

Chong's laughing even harder. "You gotta hear this, man."

He pulls me inside and we sit down on the floor as he rewinds the tape and then hits Play. I listen for a few seconds, and against my will I start to smile. Five more seconds and I'm laughing. The longer it goes on, the harder we laugh. As soon as it ends, we rewind it and start laughing all over again.

Tommy explains that he was trying to see if the needle on the tape recorder was moving and if he was really recording, and that's why he kept repeating, "Who is it?"

We took the tape up to Lou's office. He had the same reaction and laughed hard until his eyes started to water. This simple-ass riff, "Dave," would launch our recording careers and introduce the world to Cheech and Chong. We couldn't really explain it, but we had stumbled upon the technique that we would employ our whole careers: improvisation in the recording studio and later in front of the cameras.

Here at last was the payoff of all those shows from the Junk, to the First Stage, to the Troubadour and P.J.'s. Tommy and I were seasoned improvisers and could follow each other anywhere. We were like jazz musicians, and that was when Cheech and Chong were at their best. When we were improvising.

Later that afternoon, we went into a mix-down room which consisted of a console that controlled the individual tracks we were using.

We just set up two microphones on the other side of the console and away we went. It was just the three of us: Chong, myself, and

Norm Kinney, our engineer for all the albums. Besides being a good engineer, Norm was a great set of ears and could always be counted on for an honest reaction.

The first thing we had to do was re-create the "Dave" bit we had done that morning. We got a pretty close version. Then we decided that we needed a door knock to match the one on the tape. We recorded all kinds of different knocks until we found the right one.

I was a big fan of Ken Nordine, who around 1960 had a series of records called Word Jazz. Nordine was in advertising out of Chicago. He had the most mellifluous baritone voice and was a mainstay of advertising voice-over work. If you knew his voice, you would hear it ten times a day on TV. He did a famous Levi's campaign that was taken from one of his pieces called "Flibberty Jib" about a stranger who walked into a town. It was animated and won every award in the industry. His records featured background atmosphere that really put you into the feel of the situation. I wanted to put that feeling into our recordings and Tommy did, too. He had heard the Word Jazz albums back in the day and understood what I was talking about.

The great thing about this era was the rapid advances in recording technique. We started out with four-track capability, and before we even finished our first album there was eight-track, twelve-track, and then twenty-four track. With all those available open tracks, we had a field day filling them up with other voices and sound effects.

We stood out from any of our comedy contemporaries—George Carlin, Lily Tomlin, Steve Martin, and Richard Pryor—who did albums that were recordings of their live stand-up acts. We did our albums in the studio. We were like radio theater for a new generation that appreciated stereo effects and layered sound. They used headphones. Sometimes we spent as much time on the background effects as the foreground.

Every day as we worked on that first album, we evolved this method and approach. We could do it because we were just two guys in a mix-down room. We didn't have the expense of a large studio or even a remote recording truck. As we finished some new bits, we would take them to Lou upstairs; after that first session, he was never in the studio with us again. He would produce some additional musical elements in the future when it was necessary, but by and large he left us to our own devices.

As Tommy and I worked together, we had the usual creative differences. We were two very different personalities and we would sometimes dig in our heels. Chong's method was to try to steamroll me, and I would curl up and be stubborn. The only thing that would break the impasse was when we would come up with something totally different that would crack both of us up. If it was funny, we *both* knew it. We were always very true to that method.

Our process was to go into the studio with a premise and a character or two and turn on the microphones. Four hours a night doing topless improv had prepared us for any situation that could come up. Something would catch a spark and we would go with it. Then we would go back and smooth out the performance if it needed it. A lot of times the bits didn't need any tweaking. Then we would add effects. With this method, you could capture spontaneous moments that you could never get if you sat down and wrote it out on paper.

One of our favorite techniques was to take an old joke that we knew or one that we just heard and render it with this new recording method. Instead of telling it, we would act it out and put in sound effects and atmosphere. "The Pope: Live at the Vatican" was an example of this. We referenced rock-and-roll albums and religion in the same bit.

Day after day and night after night, we would work in our little mix-down room crafting our first album. At first, we tried to develop a version of our show that emphasized the voices and sounds we used. A lot of times it wouldn't work. Some of the funniest elements were just too visual. But what we did discover was that we didn't necessarily have to have the characters in the same scenario as onstage. The characters themselves were funny, and we could put them in many other situations.

On the first album, we did this with "Blind Melon Chitlin," a character based on observing T-Bone Walker that Tommy still does to this day. We put him in the recording studio with a hotshot producer played by me. In our live act at the time, Blind Melon was simply drunk and trying to perform. (Also regarding Blind Melon, the vocal part of the character was influenced by Floyd Snead's uncle who answered the phone with "Ahh, yuh.")

What we also discovered was that we had to make stuff that *sounded* funny. It was like making a funny face, but for your ears. Whether it was a knife being thrown into a blackboard (some knives are funnier than others) or a needle scratch, or a nun's high-pitched scream of "Shut Up!" It had to tickle your funny bone by the way it sounded.

Finally, we finished the record in September of 1971. It was released immediately on Adler's label, Ode Records. And Lou's real job had just begun. For all his talents, his greatest strength was promotion. Not just any promotion, but promotion specifically tailored to the act. Being from East LA, he immediately got our distinct voice, and he created advertising that matched it. Whether it was album design or radio commercials or little Cheech and Chong roach clips, all the advertising reflected who we were. And we were you as you were me and we were all together.

During this time, I was talking to Lou about who we were and what we did. He was looking for marketing and design ideas for that first record. I was describing us to him and I said we did "Hard Rock Comedy." I used hard rock to distinguish us from the early days and Chuck Berry, because now rock was Led Zeppelin. Lou liked the phrase and used it on a sticker you could peel off on the front of the album.

The first thing he did was slip a copy of our album to B. Mitchell Reed, the biggest FM disc jockey in LA. "BMR" was the king of KMET, 94.7 on your FM dial. "The Mighty Met." He began previewing our album on the air, cut by cut. He would announce:

"Ten more minutes to the new Cheech and Chong album."

People flooded the station with requests for more "Ching and Chang."

I loved those days of FM radio. FM was taking over the airwaves, catering to a new generation of baby boomers who were sick of Top 40 AM radio. This was the album generation, and they wanted to hear albums even if they didn't fit into the regular radio format. It was happening all over. It was time to take our show to the rest of the country.

Mom and Dad, Oscar and Elsa (1944) *(Courtesy of the Marin Family)*

My first job with "Cirque du Mexican" (1946) *(Courtesy of the Marin Family)*

Me and my cousins Lollie and Louie enjoying a typical American breakfast of Cheerios and cola (1950). *(Courtesy of the Marin Family)*

Li'l Cheech…Chicanos always have to have three jobs. I started early. *(Courtesy of the Marin Family)*

My Dad and I were both members of the South Central mounted police. *(Photos courtesy of the Marin Family)*

My twin sisters, Monica and Margie, in their audition photo for Diane Arbus *(Courtesy of the Marin Family)*

Little sister Orbie Elena Marie *(Courtesy of the Marin Family)*

My sister Christy
before being sacrificed
to the god Chac Mol
*(Courtesy of the
Marin Family)*

"At the Granada Hills little league... and the next day, everybody was white."
(Courtesy of Cheech Marin)

Men with fish. (L–R: Nono [my grandfather] with a grouper in Baja California, Mexico; Oscar [my dad] with trout in Lake Crawley, California… *(Photos courtesy of the Marin Family)*

...me with a sturgeon in the Flambeau River, Wisconsin; and me with my son Joey with a sockeye salmon in Alaska) *(Photos courtesy of the Marin Family)*

Woody, my daughter
Jasmine, son Max, and
Jessie at Disneyland
*(Courtesy of the
Marin Family)*

My daughter Carmen
and son Joey
*(Courtesy of the
Marin Family)*

Me and two of my
grandkids, Katelyn and
Batman *(Courtesy of the
Marin Family)*

Signing our first record contract with Lou Adler (1970) *(Courtesy of Lou Adler)*

"What are you?" (1971) *(Courtesy of Bruce Kessler/ RockinHouston.com)*

Tommy explaining how the universe works *(Courtesy of Neal Preston)*

I have no brakes and I
cannot stop!
*(Courtesy of
Neal Preston)*

Mug shots from
Tampa, Florida (1973)

Alice Bowie live
on stage (1974)
*(Courtesy of
Lou Adler)*

Me, Tommy Chong, and Lou Adler, the director of *Up in Smoke* (1978) *(Courtesy of Lou Adler)*

Harry and Margaret, my favorite stage bit (1976)
(Richard E. Aaron/Getty Images)

Tommy Chong, Paris Chong, Cesar Chavez, Lupe Ontiveros, and me at East LA College (1979) *(Courtesy of George Rodriguez on behalf of the Estate of Rudy Rodriguez)*

Tommy and me working at our peak here in *Cheech and Chong's Next Movie* (1980) *(Michael Ochs Archives/Getty Images)*

Cheech and Chong at the 1984 Oscars *(Ron Galella/Getty Images)*

I've always loved
this photo (1981).
(NICE DREAMS © 1981
Columbia Pictures Industries,
Inc. All Rights Reserved.
Courtesy of Columbia
Pictures.)

I finally got to work with Betty White, "the Mother of God." *(CBS Photo Archive/ Getty Images)*

Chilling with Dale Bozzio (from the band Missing Persons), Peter Max, and my good friend Dr. Timothy Leary (1986) *(Ron Galella/WireImage/Getty Images)*

Me, Robert Rodriguez, and Antonio Banderas on the set of *Desperado*, the first of my eight movies with Rodriguez (1995) *(DESPERADO © 1995 Columbia Pictures Industries, Inc. All Rights Reserved. Courtesy of Columbia Pictures.)*

I never had more fun than with Don Johnson (1996). *(CBS Photo Archive/Getty Images)*

My wedding (2009). (L–R: Best man Stan Coleman, me, Mayor Antonio Villaraigosa, Natasha Rubin, and maids of honor Katya Lavrovskaya and Maria Demina) *(Courtesy of Ron Tanji)*

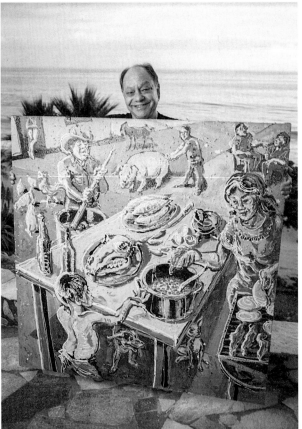

With my favorite Wayne Alaniz Healy painting (2012) *(Photo by Ethan Kaminsky, www.kaminskyproductions .com)*

CHAPTER 18

Hitting the road

After we did as much local and industry promotion as we could for the release of our album, it was time to go nationwide. But first, we launched our album at the Troubadour for a week... and got paid.

We opened for Cannonball Adderley, an iconic jazz sax player, and his group, which included Airto Moreira, a phenomenal Brazilian percussionist with whom we would have a lot of interaction in the coming years. Because of the overwhelming support of KMET, we drew as many fans as Cannonball.

Next stop, New York City.

All my life I've had a fascination with New York. As a kid I watched any movie that was set in Manhattan. It was the height of sophistication. I expected to see Fred Astaire and Ginger Rogers dancing down the middle of Broadway when I arrived.

The first thing I saw when we drove into the city was a bum that looked like Emmett Kelly, the clown, walking down the middle of the street in rush hour traffic like he was walking a tightrope with an umbrella in his hand. People paid no attention to him, like it was a common occurrence... which I guess it was.

Tommy and I dropped our bags in our room at the City Squire Hotel in Midtown and didn't come back for two days. We walked all the way to Greenwich Village.

It was 1971, and a great change was sweeping across America.

What was interesting was that the sixties were really played out in the seventies. It was Us against Them, and marijuana was still illegal and hush-hush, but still the most blatant fact of youth culture. That was part of the appeal of Cheech and Chong. We were blatantly out in the open and talking about it. People thought that the cops would always be on us, but the exact opposite was true. The cops always loved us. They could see the humor in the characters we portrayed, because they saw the real ones every day.

We made it down to the Bitter End, the club we would be playing. It was the most famous club in the Village in the folk days. Everybody's live album was recorded there, and if you didn't have a picture taken in front of their famous brick wall, you weren't anybody yet.

We arrived at the club around noon to drop off our stuff, and as I opened the door, my first reaction was *Who peed in the Bitter End?* It was a tiny club with nails all over the stage…but it was still a classic venue for us to play. The owner, Paul Colby, who didn't even look up when we approached him about playing the Bitter End West in LA, would soon become our buddy.

OK, here goes nothing. We played our first set opening up for the Flying Burrito Brothers. Mike Clarke, the drummer, who was also the drummer for The Byrds, and I would become friendly and go looking for action in the Big Apple. It was the first time we played anywhere other than the West Coast. The first set had gone relatively well. Nowhere near the reception as the black clubs in LA, but not bad. The Chicano element was missing. They didn't have "Low Riders" in Manhattan. We couldn't count on that boisterous recognition factor that usually propelled our act.

We had two A&M Records company guys in New York who were our constant companions. Jerry Love, the Jewish pimp daddy. He had a big, white Cadillac convertible, and he took us to every cool restaurant that was happening in the city, and we took him to Chinatown. The other guy was "Heavy Lenny" Bronstein, who was really the college rep, but he did a lot of the radio work, and he was very hip and loved comedy. After the first show he came up to us and said, "Why didn't you guys do 'Dave'? That's the big hit here."

We didn't know you could have a "hit here" so quickly. The record had only been out a week. We looked at each other, befuddled. Heavy Lenny told us, "All the radio guys, the guys who get the albums first, talk amongst themselves. If there's anything they like, they tell each other about it."

"I don't know. We don't have a way to do it," I said.

He stared at us for a minute and then said, "Do it in the dark. Open up with it, but in the dark, and then go into your routine."

Chicano humor didn't work so well in New York, but paranoia did. No wonder "Dave" was a big hit there. We tried it the next set and it went over great. We were always attuned to the slightest tweak that would help a recorded bit go over in the live act.

We had taken the first step in building the "Comedy Omni Burger." The show that had just the right kind of ingredients in just the right proportions. Not too many dick jokes...but not too few. A show that would work in Boston and then the next night in New Jersey and then the next night in Atlanta and then...San Antonio, Tejas homeboy!

The day before we finished at the Bitter End, we got a call from Lou, who told us that the record was going crazy in San Antonio and he'd booked us a gig there. It was at the last minute, so the only flight we could get put us in "San Anto" an hour before the gig. We had to go straight from the plane to the job. We hardly slept at all, as we had stayed up all night trying to squeeze the last few drops out of New York City.

We collapsed into our airplane seats and woke up five hours later, two sweaty, wet, hair balls with cement in their eyes in San Antonio, Texas. We drove for a little while, and as we slowly woke up, I realized we were in a field and it looked like a county fair but Mexican style.

There were folkloric dancers, *charros*, mariachis, and a couple of rock bands. We figured out that it was some radio station gig. OK, cool.

We stumble out of the car and they show us to a low, small stage right next to where they were grilling carne asada. The announcer introduces us, and we walk on, say hi, and start making jokes about where we were. I look out on the audience, and it's all Latino. "The Low Rider and the Red Freak." Let's go.

We settle into the routine and people are laughing and smiling and shaking each other... and coming from all over the lot. We were just up high enough to see them flowing like streams into a lake; a pretty sight. They crowded around close to the stage. They wanted to hear every word. They loved everything we did with an intensity that screamed... finally! After the show I remember thinking, *We should just live here—we could be gods.*

For some perspective, that San Antonio show was within six months of Tommy and I still collecting returnable bottles to scrounge up enough money for a daily meal. While we were on a seeming rocket to fame, we had put in the time and paid our dues. Which made the success all the sweeter.

We arrived back in LA, and as soon as we hit home, there was a package waiting at each of our houses. It was an itinerary that started in three days and ran for two months and would later be lengthened to three months.

The next four years were a blur. We worked an average of 250 to 300 dates a year and got to see the country up close and personal. We played with everybody from B. B. King to Alice Cooper, the Allman Brothers, Muddy Waters, Bill Withers, and even Harry Chapin. What a time to be out on the road! I was in my early twenties and I *was single and ready to mingle.* My guy friends have always shaken their heads and marveled when they ask me about those days. *Did you guys get all the pussy in the world?* That's the one thing they all want to know.

Well, I can only speak for myself when I say, *Yes, I did!*

I mean, the world is a big place, but I tried my best. I met some wonderful, beautiful, funny, and sweet young ladies in my travels. Some for just one night and others every time I was in their town.

People also ask, *Didn't you ever get sick of meaningless sex with new girls every day?*

The answer is yes, but then I would lay down and the feeling would pass and I was right back at it.

You have to realize that I was a late bloomer. I didn't lose my virginity until I was almost twenty-one. So for me it was all making up for lost time. Throw in the travel, the money, the fact that we were a new breed of comedy rock stars, and the free love ethic of the day, and it was about as much fun as a young man could have.

Youth is fleeting and I certainly couldn't do it again. But I did it when I could. I was young, dumb, and full of you-know-what at a pretty great time in American history. So sue me.

19

If you could please not do that dog bit

We were almost two months into our latest tour when we got the inevitable call from Adler.

"Do you guys have passports with you?"

As a matter of fact, we did, because we were playing Toronto and Montreal on this leg.

"Good, because you're going to London and then on tour in England for three weeks."

"Blimey!" said I.

I had never been to Europe before, so the thought of playing in England thrilled me beyond description. The stakes were upped even more when Lou told us that we had a very special fan in London.

It seemed Peter Sellers had heard our record and wanted to meet us as soon as we got to London.

"Holy fucking shit! Peter Sellers?" I yelled into the pay phone in some airport somewhere, immediately alerting all the security guards to keep an eye on this long-haired hippie with the big moustache.

Things were moving really fast now. Successful record, great shows on the road.

And now Peter Sellers wants to meet us?

You have to realize that Peter Sellers was probably the greatest comic actor of his or any generation. When we met him he was at the very height of his fame and popularity. He had starred in and created multiple roles in *Lolita* and *Dr. Strangelove*, both directed by Stanley Kubrick. He had made *The Party*, which to this day is one of my favorite comedies. *I Love You, Alice B. Toklas* was the movie that made Chong move from Detroit to Los Angeles. Tommy said that when he saw Sellers having a good time in warm, sunny Venice Beach, California, he said to himself, "What the fuck am I doing here in Detroit?" He immediately shoveled a path through the snow, got in his car, and drove to LA.

Peter Sellers was also Inspector Clouseau, the bumbling French detective in the mega-successful Pink Panther movies. They were huge international hits, both commercially and critically.

All these movies were *after* he had created a huge body of work on radio, onstage, and in English cinema that made him a comic sensation.

One of the big reasons he related to us was that he had created *The Goon Show* for BBC Radio along with Spike Milligan, Harry Secombe, and Michael Bentine. It was a scripted comedy-variety show that mostly satirized modern British life and used surreal humor, puns, and lots of sound effects. There were regular characters as well as one-offs. It ran for about ten years and made Sellers an English icon. The Goons were the forerunner to *Monty Python's Flying Circus*, *Beyond the Fringe*, Peter Cook and Dudley Moore...and Cheech and Chong.

A few years after we ran into him, Sellers created what for me was his greatest role, that of Chance, the gardener, in *Being There*. He was nominated for a Best Actor Academy Award for that performance and the movie also featured a cartoon of our hit single "Basketball Jones." Hal Ashby directed the movie, and he was a friend of Adler's. The script called for Chance to watch something on the TV in a limo. Hal put in Cheech and Chong, of course.

How did Peter Sellers even hear our record? It hadn't been released in England yet.

Incestuous Hollywood was the answer.

Peter Sellers had been married to Britt Ekland, the beautiful, blonde Swedish actress who had been a Bond Girl and was the "It Girl" of the moment. Brit was now cohabitating with Lou Adler but was still friendly with Sellers.

Terribly civilized, these Brits!

Usually, I want my ex-girlfriends to immediately volunteer for a ten-year expedition to Antarctica.

Britt and Peter had a daughter together (Victoria), so things were relatively calm. They even shared a flat together in London, and whoever was in town could use it, including Britt…with Lou.

Lou and Britt had been staying in the flat right after the first test pressings of our first album had been cut, and Lou had brought a copy to London with him.

Here's where the story gets a little muddy; either Lou left the record in the flat and Sellers discovered it, or Lou asked him to listen to it. At any rate, Sellers heard the record and flipped. He wrote Adler a letter to say that this was the most original comedy he had heard since *The Goon Show*, and he had to meet these guys right away.

So there we were on a plane to London, still in a semicoma from having toured more than three straight months without a day off, totally unaware of what was going to happen as soon as we landed. We were luxuriating in old-school First Class Intercontinental Air Travel. We were served cocktails and three different kinds of wine before they rolled up a cart and made a Caesar salad from scratch right in front of us.

Next came a rolling cart with a silver dome that contained your choice of prime rib or rack of lamb that they carved just for you at whatever thickness you wanted. "Don't worry, sir, there's plenty more in the galley."

Then it was cherries jubilee followed by another cart filled with every after-dinner drink known to man. I think of this flight every time I'm hit in the side of the head by the bag of peanuts that they fling at you in "first class" now.

All too soon, I was awakened from my sugar- and liquor-induced dream state by a British accent, like that chick from the Orbit gum commercial, and she announced that we were about to land in London.

I walked off the plane in a fog and then down a long hallway with no idea what time or even what day it was. As far as I knew, we were in the Central Stranded Twilight Zone. We must have looked like a walking hair explosion. There was Chong and I with our girlfriends, Barbara and Shelby, and Lou Adler and Britt Ekland, all in full "rich hippie" regalia, sleepwalking through some corridor in Heathrow Airport.

We turned a corner, and a wall of flashbulbs hit us like a nuclear explosion. There must have been thirty cameramen there firing off shots as fast as they could while calling out our names in a cacophony of British accents.

"What the fuck?" I mumbled to myself. I felt like King Kong on exhibit, when all of a sudden from out of the middle of the flashbulbs stepped Peter Sellers. He walked right up to me, extended his hand and said, "Hello, I'm Peter. So nice to meet you."

I stood there dumbfounded with my mouth open like a Venus fly-trap. Peter whipped right around to face the cameras, put his arm around my shoulder, and turned on his megawatt smile. The flash-bulbs exploded again, this time twice as ferocious. We took every combination of Sellers, me, Tommy, Lou, Britt, and girlfriends that was mathematically possible, and then we were whisked into three waiting limos. We didn't even go through customs. We just waved at them as we waltzed by their office, and they handed us back our passports. Before we were driven away, Sellers came up to our limo, stuck his head in, and said, "I'll see you tonight. Britt knows where. Cheerio!"

Tommy and I just looked at each other. "Did that just happen?"

That evening, as promised, Britt Ekland escorted us to a flat in some very posh section of London that was home to many international diplomats, because Peter was going out with the Swedish ambassador's daughter. We knocked on the door, which was immediately flung open and there was Peter with that "Peter Sellers smile" on his face, both warm and demented. There was not a stick of furniture in the place.

"We've just moved in here. Well, we haven't really moved in yet, but I wanted a private place we could come before dinner."

With that, Peter Sellers whipped out the biggest piece of hashish I'd ever seen. It looked like one of those giant chocolate Hershey bars that must have weighed at least a pound. He lit the corner of it, took a big hit, and passed it to me. Dumbfounded, I took it and did the same and passed it on.

"I do indeed love getting high," he said with that wonderful Sellers smile. Peter said that the thing he most enjoyed was getting members of the British aristocracy stoned, and he said he was on a mission to get them all turned on.

After everybody was sufficiently loaded, we got in our cars and were driven to the restaurant San Lorenzo in Beauchamp Place. I remember the name of the restaurant because it was the only good meal we got in London our entire stay. English food at that time was "raahther dreadful." It was all bangers and mash (mashed potatoes with sausages stuck in them) or "Wimpys" (their version of a fast food hamburger). Food in London has improved greatly since then.

We had the next day off and promptly at noon Peter showed up at our hotel. He announced that he and his friend wanted to drive us around London and then take us to lunch.

Sleepy-eyed, we crawled into his customized Mini Cooper, and he zoomed into the street like a Formula One driver. Tommy and I were still half asleep in the backseat when Peter and his friend launched into something I'll never forget.

Peter Sellers, the world's greatest comic actor, and his friend started doing all the characters from our album. Back and forth they went, assuming the voices of all our characters and acting out all the bits, laughing hysterically between lines and then right into another bit until they had done the entire album. And then they started doing them all over again.

At some point, I think they even forgot we were in the car. Chong and I sat there "gobsmacked," as the Brits say. I think they did our characters better than we did.

When we arrived at the next fabulous eating establishment, there was a pack of paparazzi waiting at the entrance. Very soon I got the picture that not only was Peter introducing us to England in a way that nobody else in the world could, but he wanted the public to know that he identified with us, that he was on our side. Peter showed up at every one of our gigs and made sure we had tons of pictures taken with him that were all over the newspapers the next day. No amount of money could possibly buy the kind of publicity that Peter Sellers gave us out of the goodness of his heart.

At the end of the week, there was a handwritten message from the front desk delivered to my door. I opened the envelope and the message said that a Mr. Sellers had called and he wanted me to call him right away because he wanted us to come out to his country house for lunch. OK, no problem. I called the number in the message and a man with a heavy Asian accent answered the phone.

"Hi, is Peter there? It's Cheech calling."

"Just one minute, I get Mista Sellwers."

I could hear footsteps walking away on a marble floor and then footsteps walking back to the phone.

"Mista Sellwers say he call you right back."

"OK, whatever."

A minute later the phone rang.

"Hello Cheech, it's Peter. Can you guys come out for lunch today around one?"

"We would be delighted."

"Lovely, I wrote the address on the message, so I'll see you at one. Cheerio."

We hired a car and we all drove out to the country. After about an hour, we came to the address, which was a very tall hedge surrounding a wooden door with a speaker box next to it. I pressed the buzzer.

"Hello." Again it was the Asian man.

"Hi, it's Cheech and Chong."

"Oh yes. Mista Sellwers say come in."

The buzzer buzzed and the door opened. We walked in, and halfway down the walk Peter came out to meet us. He greeted us effusively and said that he hoped we were hungry, because lunch was on the table. We came in and proceeded to have lunch and a very enjoyable afternoon, but not before hitting that giant-sized bar of hash again.

Peter regaled us with stories from the *Goon Show* days and asked us all about our process in the recording studio, and we just had a great old time.

At no time did I see another person in the house.

No Asian man, no maid, no gardener, nobody. I finally realized that Peter *was* the Asian man, and it was a pattern that he would maintain throughout all the time we knew him. He *never* answered the phone in his own voice ... ever.

Peter came to the two gigs we had the next week, one of which was Ronnie Scott's Jazz Club, a very famous venue. The bill read Blossom Dearie, the Modern Jazz Quartet and *Introducing Cheech and Chong*. We did our regular show, which ended with a bit called "The Dogs," where we became dogs and crawled around on all fours and did what dogs do: eat, shit, lick our balls, and hump each other.

Ronnie Scott, the owner, came up to us after the show wearing a bespoke Savile Row suit and said, "Lovely show, lads ... here's fifty quid, if you could please not do that dog bit tomorrow. Cheers."

After about two weeks, our time in London was over and we had to return home. We had one last dinner with Peter and one last hit of that giant hash bar, which never seemed to get any smaller.

We would meet up with Peter a handful of times in the ensuing years whenever we were in the same city. He would always leave a message that Leslie Horwinkle (one of our characters) called and we should call him right back. We always went through the same routine: We would call, the Asian guy would answer, we'd leave a message, and then Peter would call right back. I never asked him about it. I figured, *Well, that's just Sellers.*

In the end, it just seemed normal, because no matter how much time we spent with him and no matter how much hash we smoked with him, he was essentially unknowable. When he wasn't in a character, it was like he was in neutral and just floated along with that warm, demented smile. I was privileged to have spent time with Peter Sellers, because there will never be another like him.

CHAPTER 20

In and out of dry dock

As I said, the early to mid-1970s went by in a blur for me. We were successful and we were busy. It was a lot of work but it was work we loved. And it was fun.

At the beginning, it was one club date after another. We would usually play for a week in each spot. Each time we went to a new city was one more week that the album was out and people started to know the names Cheech and Chong. Clubs were starting to sell out the whole week in advance. The greatest thing, though, was that we were working and evolving every day, two, maybe sometimes three, shows a day. You can't help but grow. Every night it was like picking up the conversation where we had left off. We remembered something we meant to say the night before. Usually we saved it as a surprise for each other. Our favorite thing was to throw in something new that would make the other guy laugh. It was a constant evolution. We were the new underground FM radio stars, and people came prepared to like us. We didn't have to break new ice every time. The album was doing that for us.

When you are working every day, you are changing the act in small, imperceptible ways. We had regular bits but we would change them slightly in each performance. In the tiniest of ways. Improvisation remained at the core of our act.

Quite often, a guy from the record company or Adler's office would see us for the first time in a while. And he'd say, "Wow, you guys have really changed the act." We would have no idea what he was talking about. But we also knew he was right. Little increments every night. I see it as whittling. Basic stagecraft. It's a big part of my live performance approach.

Tommy and I were also together all the time. We would be walking down the street and out of the blue Tommy would say "Come out slower in that bit." Or "What if he says this?" And I'd know exactly what he was talking about with no more information than that. Or if we were talking about a bit and playing with it, Tommy, or I, would suddenly say "Say it that way *tonight*!" Or "What if he does *this*?" And it would be right to both of us.

Tommy and I were so attuned to each other that we could write for each other. I could see his characters and he could see mine.

We also had a vast trove of common knowledge and experiences. Again, from all the time together. We knew what made each other tick and what made each other laugh. Sometimes, this bond would allow for big laughs *for ourselves* onstage.

One time we were at the bar at the hotel after a gig. The bartender was a snotty, dismissive woman who had no respect for us. All her answers to us were curt and rude. She could barely tolerate us. We were talking about her and laughing at the situation. Tommy called out to her, "Excuse me, miss? Can I ask you something?"

She snapped back "*What?*"

Tommy said, "Where do you keep that stick when you don't have it stuck up your ass?"

Everybody with us fell on the floor laughing. She just gave us another death stare.

Later on during a show, if Tommy or I found a place to say, "Excuse me, miss?" we would. The other guy would crack up, but the bit would just roll on. That kind of shorthand kept it fresh and exciting for us. And kept it fun for the audience, because our joy was contagious and made the show better.

Another example of this bond we have is the bit "Hey, Margaret." It's an old couple going to a porn movie. The husband is trying to get the wife interested and the bit is essentially Tommy describing what he sees on the screen. It's one of my favorite bits even though I don't have a line. I played Margaret and my job was reacting to Tommy. He'd change it all the time, and sometimes I'd be unable to react I was laughing so hard. We'd hear the audience pleading for Tommy to pause so they could breathe. Eventually, Tommy would be disgusted by something on the screen and try to get Margaret to leave. But by then she's enjoying it and wants to stay.

I loved doing it because I could channel my mother. And I had to listen to him to react properly. Definitely my favorite bit of ours to perform.

We finally got home in the middle of November 1971. All I wanted to do was sit in my living room, on my couch, and just look out the window until the room stopped spinning. It took about three days.

Finally, we paid a visit to Adler at his office at A&M. He filled us in on how well the album was doing, which none of us could believe. It wasn't like he wasn't used to big numbers. He was still working on the unprecedented success of *Tapestry* by Carole King.

In those days, it was a big deal to sell five hundred thousand units, which would get you a gold record. Platinum records for the sale of a million units were so rare as to be almost nonexistent. *Tapestry* would eventually pass the *15 million* mark and just keep going. It would become *the* singer-songwriter touchstone of the 1970s. We were officially into the album age. It was like the recording industry had hit the Lotto. Before a year had passed, we had earned a gold record… and *we were a comedy act*. Before it was all over we would be the biggest-selling comedy act in recording history at that time.

Out of the blue, Lou asked if we had anything for AM radio. FM was cool, but it wasn't the big commercial locomotive that Top 40 radio was.

"You guys got anything for Christmas?"

"Of course. We're Chicano and a half."

We have to have three jobs at the same time.

We went into the studio with just this snippet of an idea: a musician who doesn't know who Santa Claus is. Go. We started to improvise. It took only two or three passes and we had it. We had been working together every day. We were so attuned to each other's rhythm that it was like telepathy. We called Lou into the studio. He cracked up and got a gleam in his eye.

A couple of days later he called us back to listen to some music. A great studio musician, Clarence McDonald, had written a jazzy backing track that was so good you hardly even knew that it was there. The first time we all heard it together, we knew it was a hit.

It went on the radio two weeks before Christmas and exploded. It shot to number one in LA and then many other cities. It really showed the power of the radio as the fastest of the popular media. You recorded it and it could be on the air the next day. Much more indicative of where the culture was heading. In the movies, you might wait two years after writing a screenplay.

From its very first playing, "Santa Claus and His Old Lady" became a funky Christmas classic. To this day, people still say to me that Christmas isn't officially Christmas until they've heard it.

I remember the first time I heard it on the radio. I was at a party with some of my friends and cousins. It had been out a couple of days and I'd been hearing that everybody had been keeping their radio on all day so that they wouldn't miss it. Finally, it came on. I'll never forget that feeling of wonder and amazement as we all gathered around and laughed at every line. When it was over, there was such a feeling of happiness bursting from everybody. Happiness that one of us, who shared the same sensibilities, had broken through.

After Christmas was over, it was back out on the road. We were so busy that when Lou called to tell us that our album was nominated for a Grammy for best Comedy Record of the Year, it didn't even register.

"Well, that sounds great, Lou. Listen, I've got to go or we'll miss our plane." I told Tommy as we were boarding and he was in the same space.

"Yeah, cool."

It wasn't until later in the flight that he turned to me and said, "A Grammy, huh? All right."

About a year later we were *still* out on the road and got a call from Adler.

"You guys have to come back to LA because you're opening for the Rolling Stones at the Forum."

"Uh, OK."

You don't get that call every day.

We were on a bill that read:

SANTANA, CHEECH AND CHONG AND THE ROLLING STONES

LIVE AT THE FORUM IN LOS ANGELES

FOR THE BENEFIT OF NICARAGUAN EARTHQUAKE RELIEF

Nicaragua had suffered a massive earthquake in December 1972 that killed more than ten thousand people and left three hundred thousand homeless. Mick Jagger's wife, Bianca, was Nicaraguan. She was one of the great international beauties of the day. She came to her country's aid and organized this concert. Somehow Lou was involved. I assume that was how we got on the bill.

It was a cool gig. We got to hobnob with all the rock royalty, and the Stones were at the white-hot center. The movie industry and the music scene were starting to merge. More and more, actors mingled backstage at concerts and shows. Jack Nicholson, Lou's new best friend (they still sit next to each other at the Lakers games), was walking around with Warren Beatty and Anjelica Huston and Michelle Phillips.

It was great to work that big, wide stage in front of over sixteen thousand hometown fans. By this time, we had worked large audiences, having opened arenas for Alice Cooper, the Allman Brothers, and Bread (if you can believe it). The review in *Rolling Stone* said that we did a lot of pee-pee, ca-ca, and doo-doo jokes, displayed some very fine acting, and walked off to a thunderous standing ovation. Sounds accurate.

Our world was changing at light speed. Right about this time I hooked up with Rikki Jenny, who could have won the Farrah Fawcett look-alike contest. She was a waitress at the Rainbow Bar and Grill. I was there every night when I was in town, so eventually I wore down her resistance and she went out with me. After a few nights together, we decided that this was it and she moved in with me.

This momentous year ended with an invitation to Lou's annual, famous, Christmas party. It was attended by a who's who of showbiz. (Have to say this again for perspective: We were about a year away from picking up pop bottles on the street and now we were mingling with the Hollywood elite.) Anyway, Lou's front door opened and there in the foyer, right in front of us, was Ryan O'Neal making out with Ursula Andress, the stunning Swiss actress who walked out of the sea in a bikini in *Dr. No*, the first James Bond movie. She looked up, assessed that we were nobody, and went back to making out with Ryan.

There was nowhere to gawk at this party, because everybody there was somebody famous. We talked to Mick Jagger and couldn't understand a word he said. We just nodded and smiled. Rikki and I were just dazzled. (At another of Lou's Christmas parties, we ran into an extremely thin John Lennon, who was living in LA while he was separated from Yoko Ono for about a year and a half. He mumbled something and moved on.)

We drove to the party in a Nash Rambler station wagon. Tommy brought his parents. We were still new to all of it. I was surprised that nobody wanted us to get their car for them.

As our popularity and fame grew, three things happened with regularity during the following four years.

Number one: During Thanksgiving we were booked into Chicago for the whole week. That's the only way I knew that it was Thanksgiving—we were in Chicago. Every year, the venue got bigger, so that at the end we sold out the Arie Crown Theater in McCormick Place, capacity 4,249, for five straight days.

Number two: We would play the Troubadour the week between Christmas and New Year to sold-out audiences with the Persuasions, a fantastic a cappella group out of New York, opening for us. We had come full circle from our days at P.J.'s and performing alongside the best black musical acts in the country.

And each year our new album would get nominated for a Grammy, which we finally won in 1974 for *Los Cochinos*.

The Troubadour was an interesting deal. Doug Weston, the owner, made every act that played there sign a seven-option extension. So if an act got big and famous after playing the Troubadour, as Linda Ronstadt and Joni Mitchell did, they would still have to play the 275-seat Troubadour, if they wanted to play in LA—even if they could fill an arena.

It caused a lot of consternation among the managers of these acts.

But due to some oversight, or lack of interest, we were not signed to this extension. We could negotiate a new and very lucrative deal every time they wanted us to play there. And they wanted us to play there every Christmas.

The whirlwind of the road slowed down only when one of us would have to go in for some medical procedure, like a knee operation for me or some dental work for Tommy. We tried to schedule them at the same time. We called this period dry dock.

We had no sense of how successful we were, because we were on the road with no chance to spend money in any lavish way. We were very busy. The one change on the road was that we now could eat in any restaurant we wanted. Up to now, we had no real concept of dining out. Before we made the record, we either ate at Pioneer Chicken or made an inexpensive Chinese meal.

But when we were home, we had a chance to slow down and relax and take it all in. I remember one week from 1973 or so, we each got a check in the mail for $800,000. Two days later, we each got another check for $700,000. Record royalties.

That day, we both realized the same thing. We were making a shit-pot of money. But it didn't change us that much. Really. My main thought was *I better get a bank account.*

CHAPTER 21

Weeniegate

As the 1970s rolled on, the whole rock-and-roll, album-buying, concert-going audience was going apeshit. The baby boom generation was emerging all over the landscape. They had some money. And they needed product.

We grew out of the clubs pretty quickly. We were headlining our own concerts and had people opening for *us*. The next few years flew by like a tornado. Mostly you just remember the highlights.

Here are a few:

We played the biggest rock festival in the Midwest: Bull Island, Indiana. It was really just outside of Chicago, but the line dipped back to Indiana for a few miles...or some shit. The promoters hoped for fifty thousand; they got almost four hundred thousand. Funny. I don't remember our fee being multiplied by eight.

Needless to say, they were completely overwhelmed and reason ran out the door. It took us *eight hours* to drive through the crowd. Choppers weren't flying because of low visibility. The first act was supposed to go on at noon. By the time we got to the stage, it was midnight.

Scheduled to play: Joe Cocker, Black Sabbath, The Allman Brothers, Fleetwood Mac, the Eagles, Bob Seger, Santana, Ravi Shankar... and Cheech and Chong! And about twenty other big acts.

The first group to go on at midnight was an all-girl, hard rock band from Los Angeles named Birtha. Their T-shirt read BIRTHA HAS BALLS. I wore that shirt proudly for many years.

They played a hard-rocking set and were greeted with a big roar from the crowd that had timed its drugs for noon. The second they were finished, there was a big clap of thunder and a rain of *biblical proportions* started that I thought would wash away all of the people. It rained harder than I've ever seen and turned the whole place into a muddy swamp. Finally, after about fifteen minutes, it stopped.

Now these genius promoters, displaying more foresight, had hung a parachute over the stage. They wanted to protect the groups from the blistering sun…at noon. Obviously, they had not counted on the cloudburst any more than the extra 350,000 people.

So now, the parachute was full of water. About a swimming pool's worth of water was suspended right over the stage. The water was slowly rolling off the front edge of the chute, creating an intermittent waterfall. I thought I was at Trader Vic's.

All right, everybody! Let's welcome Cheech and Chong!

I walked out onstage and I couldn't see the end of the people. Far in the distance, they disappeared over a downslope and then into the fog. I looked down, from a very tall stage, at the people below. It looked like the evolution of man.

There were guys dressed in hides complete with wolf heads shaking totem spears. Three teenage hippie mothers, nursing babies. Other assorted hairy freaks. And they were all soaking wet, covered in mud, bouncing up and down and sort of chanting.

Tommy and I walked to the center of the stage to stand under the swimming pool. We looked at the audience and burst out laughing. To everybody but the cavemen under the stage, we were talking dots. This was long before big shows had video screens to accommodate a really big crowd. They hadn't even figured out the sound for that big a crowd. We had to keep saying, "We're moving over to this side of the stage now."

After a while, we gave in to the absurdity of the situation and I started doing disappearing coin tricks. For four hundred thousand people.

Hey... and it's gone! How does he do it?

Oddly enough, that was when the audience connected with us. We were on the same rain-drenched, 2:00 a.m., psychedelic, absurd cloud as they were. It took the laugh at least a minute to circulate through the crowd. We finished the show with "The Astronaut" to an ovation that we never heard the end of. It was too far away.

It was also a time of breaking barriers. We headlined in 1973 at Carnegie Hall in New York City, the mecca of classical music, where Vladimir Horowitz, Sergei Rachmaninoff, Maria Callas, and countless other classical artists played and sang.

And now it was Sha Na Na and Cheech and Chong!

Sha Na Na was introduced by Keith Moon, the drummer from the Who. In drag. Don't ask me, he's English. We played Carnegie one more time, with the Persuasions. One thing I noticed about some of these venerable old halls: The dressing rooms were barely hovels. And they were tiny. Were all those great classical artists midgets? I'd hit my head on beams all the time. And I'm Wilt the Stump, as you recall.

That same year, we sold out two shows in one day at the Kennedy Center in Washington, DC.

Time magazine interviewed us at the Kennedy Center. The reporter had no idea who we were. Which sort of pissed me off, because this was how a big, national magazine viewed us. She was unprepared and wondered how we were going to sell tickets or records. We told her about the ticket sales *for the event she was there to cover*, but she was still baffled. We were playing Carnegie Hall and the Kennedy Center, but this woman acted like we were still interlopers of some kind. I took it as an example of how the establishment didn't get us or what we were doing.

As Bob Dylan sang:

Something is happening here and you don't know what it is
Do you, Mr. Jones?

Anyway, we never had time to look down; we were moving too fast.

Another Grammy nomination and finally, as I said, a win for *Los Cochinos*, which literally means "the little pigs."

Yeah! Take that, society!

After recording four albums and touring behind them, I had a pretty clear picture of where we stood in show business.

As I mentioned, we were not like other comedy acts.

We were not exactly a musical act, either, but we had musical elements in our shows. But we also had number one singles and four straight albums at the top of the charts. Not even the Rolling Stones or Led Zeppelin was doing that.

People didn't know what to make of us, even after so much success. Many reviews, for years, included how the writer was "surprised" by what we did or how much he liked what we did. It was consistent, this feeling that people didn't get what we were or believe in it. There was never a sense of acceptance. Not quite a comedy act, not quite a musical act. We were always "other." And so, our success was somehow lesser because it was not achieved in a traditional way.

It was the same with movies. Massive hit after hit but critics were dumbfounded. How do they do this? No one considered that we were talented, worked hard and cared about what we did. After a few years, this success was not surprising to *us*.

That was why getting a good review from Pauline Kael in the *New Yorker* meant so much. She liked *Up in Smoke* and said so. She was not surprised. She saw what we were doing. But those moments were few.

Then suddenly, one day, might have been yesterday, we were "iconic."

Well, it wasn't always that way, pal.

I have no hard feelings about the journey. We've been successful and made a lot of people happy. I just wonder why we were so hard for people to see for so long. Not our fans, of course. But that woman from *Time* magazine and all her friends.

But fuck it. Time to go see if there's another check in the mail. I am proud of my roots and my family. I am a law-abiding citizen, the son of a thirty-year veteran of the Los Angeles Police Department. I have made a career, however, in comedy that is edgy, controversial, and more than a little antiestablishment. I try not to cause trouble, but it's an occupational hazard.

In 1973, we were playing Curtis Hixon Hall in Tampa, Florida. The Sunshine State was becoming infamous because it had been the site of a few recent rock-and-roll busts. Janis Joplin had been arrested at Hixon a few years before, for vulgar and indecent language.

What the fuck!

Jim Morrison of the Doors had been busted in Miami for whipping out his weenie. As it turned out, he really didn't whip out his weenie. But he was drunk and did refer to his weenie. The whole situation was big news for a while. Weeniegate.

All of this was the last thing on our minds when we arrived. The only thing on our minds was that we had just sold out two shows and Dr. John was opening for us. I love Dr. John. Gris-gris gumbo ya-ya.

In those days, once you got out of Miami, the rest of Florida was "the deep South." Tampa was no exception, and the good old boys ruled…especially the sheriff.

It was a very hot and sweaty summer night in the hall. The crowd was having a good time, and a haze of some kind hung over the audience. The first show had gone well, and we were just chilling and having dinner between shows. We noticed that a few more policemen were circulating backstage than had been at the first show. I didn't think much of it and went back to enjoying the fried chicken.

Once we got onstage for the second show, you could tell that the audience was a little more agitated, just a little more on edge. I think there had been some arrests in the audience during Dr. John's set.

What was different was that now there was a line of policemen in front of the stage with their backs to us, looking at the audience. Their heads were at stage level. In the middle of doing our bit "The Dogs," I crawled over, lifted my leg, and peed on a cop's head. The hot and sweaty and drunk/high crowd let it all out. I don't blame them. I thought I did a rather good pee that night.

We walked offstage and into our dressing room to find our road manager, Jimmy Root, darting around frantically, looking under everything for anything.

"Jimmy, what's up?" I said.

"You guys are getting busted."

"For what?"

"Obscenity, when you peed on the cop's head."

"You're kidding."

"No. I heard the cops talking about it when I came back here for a minute. They were arguing over who was going to take you to the station, because the one cop had both albums and he was pulling rank. You guys don't have anything on you, do you?"

Just then the cops came in and told us we were being arrested.

And could they get a picture?

On the way out, we shouted to the crowd, "Free the Jackson Five!"

We ended up being taken downtown in the paddy wagon, but not before it made its drunk rounds. It was sooo nice, riding around with three guys who had just thrown up on themselves and crapped their drawers.

Finally, we got to the station. They put us in a small holding cell that started to fill up rapidly. At this point, I was still having fun. I was trying to get the attention of the guard because this beige toilet paper simply wouldn't do.

Then they dragged in an unconscious guy who stayed that way the whole time we saw him. Right behind him was a hillbilly-looking guy who took out a handful of bullets from his front shirt pocket and said, "I guess I won't be needing these anymore," then threw the bullets in the corner of the cell. A Latino guy saw me from the corner and walked right over.

"Habla Espanol?"

"Un poco." A little.

He switched to English.

"Where you from?"

"LA."

"What you doing here?"

I hesitated and stumbled for a minute.

"Oh...you know."

"I get it."

I don't know what he got but he apparently got it.

"What are you in for?"

Again I stumbled, "Oh, you know."

"Drugs?" he said.

I agreed, just to get him off my back.

"Yeah, drugs."

"Oh, OK."

He started nodding his head. I thought he was trying to shake his brain awake. He looked up at me and went back into *Spanish.*

"OK, here's what you do. Tell the judge that you're not from this town…aaaand, you were walking in the park aaaand a guy came up and gave this package to you aaaand you didn't know what it was aaaand then the cops came.

"Now if the judge says, 'Which guy?' you say, 'Ahhh, it was a colored guy.'"

And there you have it, the classic "It was a colored guy" defense. Who needs Harvard Law School?

"Uh, Your Honor, I didn't know what I was doing. A colored guy sold it to me."

"Oh, OK. Case dismissed."

As I sat overnight in the cooler, I kept thinking about what was really happening. Were they just trying to harass hippies? It was a little late by now. There was something else bearing on this case. I wouldn't find out until the next day.

It seems that if the performer violates *any* of the statutes of the Hall, one of which is disrespect of authority, the Hall may withhold $5,000 from the *promoter's* purse. They waited for a sold-out house and then stole five grand, which was probably all the profits for the young promoter.

I flashed back to P.J.'s, from our club days in Hollywood. Some things never change.

In late 1974, after three number one albums in a row, three Grammy nominations and a zillion shows, we needed a rest. Right at the height of the recording and touring success, after the *Wedding Album*, we took a year off.

CHAPTER

Hooray for Hollywood

We had earned the time off. We needed to rest, recharge, and rejuvenate. Professionally and, as it turned out, personally.

Rikki and I had been living together for four years. One night after a gig in Northern California, we had the plane drop us off in Monterey. We told everyone we were going to spend the weekend. What we didn't tell them was that we were going to get married. The next day, just before sunset, we tied the knot on Pfeiffer Beach in Big Sur, with the pounding surf breaking in the background. Saying those vows, I felt like I was on acid.

I have been married three times, and if there's one thing I've learned it's that a happy marriage is predicated on the recitation of the following phrase: "Honey, I want to do whatever you want to do, that's what I want to do." It can get way, way more complicated than that, but if you start out from there, you'll save everybody, especially yourself, a lot of grief.

You may not entirely mean it when you say it, and your partner may know that you don't entirely mean it when you say it. But it is essential that you say it. It acknowledges that, all things being equal, you don't want to fight over trivial shit. And in the long run, most of it turns out to be trivial shit.

I like being married. I like having a relationship with one person I can count on who can also count on me. In a marriage with one person who is a celebrity, it's like having a third person in the union. The third person requires selfish attention and can intrude upon the intimacy of the couple, and it requires a great deal of patience and understanding to make it work. It is never easy.

I have learned over the years, sometimes in the very hardest way, to try to eliminate the battleground aspect of marriage. I have not always been successful, but I have always been happy when I succeeded… because, after all, "I want to do whatever you want to do" is the sine qua non of a happy marriage.

Back in LA, Rikki and I settled into a 1920s beach bungalow on El Matador State Beach in the most northern part of Malibu. We were almost the only ones out there. It was the first house I ever bought, and I would live there for the next forty years. Matador Beach has been voted the best beach in Los Angeles for as long as I can remember. You can see it twenty times a day on TV commercials, with its massive rocks on the beach. I took to the water immediately and either swam, body-surfed, or fished just about every day. I felt as if I could almost live off the land.

The first time I went out to see the house, nobody was home and it was locked up. I peeped in the windows and checked out the minimally furnished interior. In the living room, I saw an old black leather couch, sagging a bit, a pole lamp, and two Oscars on the mantel. The house had been rented for the previous five years by Conrad Hall and his wife, actress Katharine Ross. Conrad has been voted one of the ten best cinematographers in the history of film. He would eventually win three Academy Awards for cinematography, including one for *Butch Cassidy and the Sundance Kid*, the film on which he met Katharine.

Katharine Ross is, for my money, one of the most beautiful women ever to grace the silver screen. Besides *Butch Cassidy*, she also starred in the blockbuster film *The Graduate* and *The Stepford Wives*. The next time I went out to see the house, Katharine was standing at the kitchen sink washing the dishes. She had her hair pulled back and was the picture of effortless, natural beauty. I watched her through the window from afar for as long as was decent. We would become friends and my son Joey and her daughter Cleo would carpool to school together.

The house was a wooden bungalow that was originally purchased from the Army and then moved in three pieces from Zuma Beach to where it is now. It had no heat or gas when we moved in and depended on fireplaces and portable heaters. It was really a tear-down. I decided to make it an add-on. I recruited my friend Robert Gilbert to turn it into a handcrafted Hansel and Gretel–looking cottage. It seemed to fit the times. Robert went on to make similar, handcrafted houses for Bob Dylan and Don Henley of the Eagles.

Over the years, I made many lifelong friends in Malibu that I'm still close to today. One day, I was lying on the beach when I saw a guy coming down the hill from one of the neighboring houses. As he got closer I recognized him. It was Geraldo Rivera. Geraldo and I had met each other in New York when Cheech and Chong appeared on a telethon for his charity, One to One. He came jogging up to me with a big smile and said, "We should be friends." And we have been for almost forty-five years. Actually, we have been more like family. We have children the same ages who have grown up with each other on both coasts. We are bicoastal brown brothers.

"G-Man" is a world-class sailor, and we have had many aquatic adventures on his various sailboats around the world. He continues to be one of my best friends, even though he eats different colored beans . . . *and we have never ever smoked dope together, even when nobody was watching.*

Maybe a year after settling in, Rikki and I got the good news that the adoption of our daughter, Carmen, had been completed, and in four days we would hold a little fuzzy-headed girl in our arms. We named her Carmen after my maternal grandmother, who lived to be ninety-five. When she was little, Carmen held her arms upright, bent at the elbows, like she was getting ready to take off. So it was fitting that she became a Park City ski patrol member. She also became an EMT and eventually a nurse. But not before becoming a professional downhill mountain biker...and I lived through it. She and her husband, Mark, are now the parents of my three grandchildren, Randall, Katelyn, and Madelyn. I love them all, every day.

As I was saying before Malibu took over, Tommy and I both needed some rest. But we took the time off for another reason. We both realized that if Cheech and Chong was to continue we needed to go in another direction...and that direction was the movies.

All the great comedy teams of the past—Laurel and Hardy, Abbott and Costello, Martin and Lewis—did movies. We told Lou Adler that we were coming off the road but not going into the recording studio. We were going to concentrate on creating a movie. He took a big breath and said that he would try to get us a deal.

Chong and I were both living in Malibu, so getting together to write our first movie was easy. Figuring out what to do was the hard part. We had no idea how to begin or what to focus on.

One of my neighbors at the beach, two doors away, was the eminent screenwriter Waldo Salt. Waldo had won Oscars for writing *Midnight Cowboy* and *Coming Home*. He also wrote the screenplay for *Serpico* and was working on *The Day of the Locust* when I met him. In 1951, Waldo was blacklisted by the studios for refusing to testify before the House Un-American Activities Committee. For a clearer picture of what that McCarthy Era hysteria was like, look at the 2015 movie *Trumbo* starring Bryan Cranston.

Waldo liked to hang out and smoke dope. During one of our conversations, I asked him, "How do you write a movie?"

He took a big hit and said, "See that girl over there?"

He pointed to his secretary across the room.

"She follows me around all day and takes down everything I say... and that's how you do it."

I took a hit and said, "Can I borrow her?"

Waldo laughed and took another hit.

Chong and I finally got together and started. Our first idea was to do a greatest-hits movie. We would try to combine part of our stage show with some of our record bits into some kind of story. Adler was all for that idea, because it would involve the material on our records, in which he had a huge interest. As a matter of fact, when we finally started shooting, the temporary title was *Cheech and Chong's Greatest Hits*.

Just as we got going, a few random people joined the mix.

Chong has a lifelong habit of being influenced by the last person he spoke to. So our tai chi teacher Joel Laskin, an aspiring screenwriter, joined the conversation. I guess Tommy thought that he had a lot of experience, because he had something like twenty unproduced screenplays. They were unproduced for a reason.

Next came my cousin Louie, a writer as well, with a budding drinking problem. A few other people came and went, until we finally figured out that we had to do it ourselves. And by ourselves.

The biggest decision we faced was what or, more important, *who* was going to be the focus of the movie. We were used to doing a lot of different characters in our records and stage shows, but movies were different. They needed central characters to follow. "Pedro and Man" were the obvious choice. They were our most popular characters. So we started writing for them.

We wrote and we wrote and we wrote. Scene after scene. Finally, we handed Adler a giant stack of pages. He read them, and I suppose he showed them to some of his movie friends. The word came back that we needed more story. We took that to mean write more. So we wrote more.

We had no idea of standard structure. No sense or feel for first act, second act, third act, and so on. And it was a good thing that we didn't. We didn't fit in a standard structure. We didn't fit in a round hole or a square hole. We fit only in our own unique hole.

After almost a year, no deal had come together. The studios didn't understand us. They understood Hello Dolly! They didn't want to invest in us.

We had faced the same situation a few years earlier when they wanted us to do a network TV show. James Komack, an actor turned producer, got on to us and started following us around the country, watching our shows. He thought there was a great sitcom in there... somewhere.

NBC offered us a big deal, but they had no ideas on what they wanted us to do. To us, network TV was straight society, and we were in the middle of making records and doing concerts, which were the most happening things in entertainment. Why should we do some square-assed sitcom?

So we passed.

I thought Komack was going to have a heart attack. A big network deal was something he had really been chasing, and we just tossed it away.

So what he did was take the essence of two of our characters "the Old Man in the Park" and the Latino "Lowrider" and made *Chico and the Man*, which turned out to be a huge hit that launched Freddie Prinze. A couple of years later, we ran into Komack at some event and he told us rather sheepishly that he had created the show from our characters.

Duh, really?

We told him that it was all cool. He had done his own thing with it, and we didn't care because we didn't want to do TV at that point. He breathed a big sigh of relief, because I'm sure he thought we would sue him.

We had used other material and made it our own, so we held no grudge. *All comedians borrow* material and make it into their own thing. The good ones do, anyway. That's how they all start, doing their idols' jokes. Like Richard Pryor and Bill Cosby. You start out in a familiar place and then make it your own.

Things are obviously going to overlap if you are talking about the same subject. Komack took two characters, or types, that we had developed. But he took it from there. No harm.

After a year went by, there was still no deal in place to make a movie. We were not privy to any of the deal-making negotiations, so anything could have happened. We were totally in the dark. We had not had any revenue-producing jobs for a year, and we needed to get back to work.

Lou informed us that we had a unique job offer. The Aladdin Hotel in Las Vegas wanted to do an after-hours show with us, George Carlin, Lily Tomlin, and Gallagher. The idea was that once a month we would come in for three days and do some shows at 2:30 a.m., and the others would do the same on a rotating basis. This situation would go on for a year. I don't know about the others, but we had a ball.

We established a routine of getting up, working out, and then playing basketball at the Sporting House, which was a twenty-four-hour fitness facility that had weights, basketball, racquetball, swimming, and massage. The whole deal. You could go there at 3:00 p.m. and there would be twenty guys waiting to be next in basketball. I would then go and play poker, have dinner, and then go back to the hotel and sleep until 2:00 a.m. and then walk downstairs and do the show. And then go party after.

It was a nice routine, and a good time was had by all. The Aladdin paid three times what we had been getting per night on the road. So it was a pretty sweet deal to have while we waited for a movie to happen.

Finally, we got word from Adler that we had a deal from Paramount to do a movie. We always figured that if we did a movie it would be with Lou. He had been our guy from the beginning. We were so naïve that we didn't even have a lawyer representing us. We never had a lawyer for our record contract, either. We trusted that Lou would always give us a fair deal. He was a homeboy. We were to learn otherwise, and it would end our business relationship with Adler and take ten years to resolve in court.

Anyway, we were about to make our first movie. There is no more thrilling feeling (with your clothes on, anyway) than your first time in front of the camera. When I started seeing the first dailies, I *finally* fully connected with what I was doing as a movie actor.

When making a record, you only had your voice, and it took me a while to get used to hearing how I sounded.

Onstage you were using your body, too, but you couldn't see yourself.

Film was the whole package. It was like finding the perfect guitar to play. I was filled with an explosive energy that I had never felt before. Filming is a very energy-draining process, but I couldn't wait to get to the set every day. I felt like the Chicano Energizer Bunny.

We started right in using the same improvisational technique that we had used with records. The script, what there was of it, was mostly directions, like "Pedro walks out of the front door and gets in his car."

There was nothing describing the dance he does as he polishes his car, or the actions he goes through once he gets in the car and then drives off. Some of it was from what I did in the stage show, but most of it was made up for the first time on camera. I applied the same technique throughout the movie. Even bits that I had done a thousand times, like getting stoned in the car, had stuff that was seen for the first time in the movie. I was having the time of my life.

I couldn't say the same for Tommy. At first, he was uncomfortable in front of the camera and kept looking into the lens during a lot of the takes. Acting for the camera is pretending that the camera is not there. He eventually got better, but I think the thing that was really bothering him was that he was not the director. Lou Adler had usurped his position.

Since the beginning of his time in show business, Tommy had been the leader. He had started our group, just as he had started all his other bands. It was his natural position offstage, but onstage he was not the star performer. He always had a lead singer whose name was in the title. In Little Daddy and the Bachelors, he was a Bachelor. In Bobby Taylor and the Vancouvers, he was a Vancouver.

So when we began Cheech and Chong, he had his name in the title at last. And he was still the organizer of the group. (At the beginning, I followed his lead because he had much more legit showbiz experience and he was eight years older.)

When we started making records it was not a question of who was the leader; it was the process of coming up with funny stuff. We had many battles during the record years, but they were part of the standard creative process.

As we moved along in show business in those early years, people always assumed that we were best friends and had grown up together. That was how close our chemistry was. We were never "best friends." We were more like brothers. As brothers, we could love and hate with equal intensity, but we always had each other's backs...because we were brothers.

When Adler told us about the deal, he said that Paramount would do the deal only if he was the director. They knew him and they didn't know us. He said not to worry, because we would proceed as usual and direct ourselves. He would be there only to lend his expertise, as he had been involved in the production of *Brewster McCloud*, which was directed by Robert Altman, and *The Rocky Horror Picture Show*.

Sounded good. We just wanted to make a funny movie.

CHAPTER 23

Up in Smoke

On day one of *Up in Smoke* Adler was there calling the action, except that he didn't know that the director was supposed to *actually say* "Action!" for things to start. Lou Adler has many outstanding abilities; directing a film is not one of them. He told me later that he always wanted to direct and this was his chance. Oh.

Hey man, I would like to fly to the moon but that doesn't make me an astronaut!

Lou relied heavily on Lou Lombardo, our editor. Lombardo was Robert Altman's editor and had a lot of experience. We had no technical experience camerawise, but we knew how the scenes should go, and for us, that was where a real director would have helped us. After about three days, Tommy's frustration built up to the point where he just sulked off to his trailer and went to sleep.

The success of Cheech and Chong, whether on record or stage or in movies, depended on *the constant dialogue between Tommy and me*. It was really a dialogue that nobody else could have except the two of us. We had been together on the road with each other 24/7 for years. We didn't need an elaborately written script. We were not making a blueprint for somebody else to build. We were making it for ourselves and we knew what we were doing. If anybody got in between us, it was only a distraction, not a help.

Nothing was going to stop me from having a good time on my first movie, though, even if I had to go to his trailer and drag a pouting Chong onto the set. Which I did a few times.

Tommy and I each have unique and different comedy talents that complement each other so seamlessly that they appear to be one voice, one mind. It doesn't happen very often, and that's why good comedy teams are so rare. I was not going to let feuding egos spoil the party. Little by little an unspoken accommodation was reached between us, and we continued to make the movie. We would act and Lou, together with the cinematographer, would film it.

To people who were not used to improvisation, the rapid change could freak them out. We were blessed to have a crew and, especially, a cast that could handle quick change. None more so than Zane Buzby, the actress who played the groupie Jade East.

Zane was the first actress we auditioned for any role. We handed her three single-spaced pages of dialogue that was a Quaalude-soaked stream of consciousness. She blanched a little and asked if she could read it over for a minute. Then, without missing a beat, she launched into the character that you see in the film. She even improvised as she was reading it for the first time. We laughed our asses off during her audition and thanked her for coming. We had no idea how rare that performance was. She was the first one we had ever auditioned. We read more actresses for the role and none came within ten miles of her. One actress even burst out crying when we handed her the text.

We assembled a wonderful cast who were right there with us on the same wavelength. From the commitment of Strother Martin to the reemergence of Tom Skerritt as Cousin Strawberry. Edie Adams played Tommy's mom. The late June Fairchild as the Ajax Lady contributed a memorable bit. The great Stacy Keach as the immortal Sgt. Stadanko, and Mills Watson as Harry, his sidekick. Everybody was digging working on the movie. 'Cause anything could happen.

The whole crew was having lunch in the parking lot between the

the Roxy nightclub and the Rainbow Bar and Grill on Sunset Boulevard. Tommy and I were sitting at a table having lunch with Zane Buzby and Anne Wharton, who played Debbie in the movie. We were talking about weird roommates we all had and Zane launched into this story about a girl she roomed with who had a boyfriend named Alex. She had everybody rolling. Tommy said, "Let's shoot that!"

"When?"

"Now. Right after lunch. Here's the setup. I'll be inside the van with Zane and she starts to tell the story and I'm asleep. You're outside listening to the story and you think we're getting it on and you're trying to get a look…and everybody gets more and more excited."

It was the fastest scene we shot all day, and it gets one of the biggest laughs in the movie.

Oddly enough, our biggest deficiency became our biggest asset. Never having made a movie, we had no camera technique. We couldn't do camera wheelies or big swooping shots. We could just set up the camera and be funny in front of it. When we came up with a scene right after lunch we had no time to devise a complicated shot, nor did we need one. The biggest difference between comedies of the seventies and now is that the earlier films let the scenes play for the most part in master shots, and the current films edit the scenes heavily. This leads to a manufactured laugh instead of an organic one. I think that is why *Up in Smoke* has endured for so long. The essential humor of the scene *seeps in*, rather than having it *jammed in*.

The Adler-as-director situation kept festering with Tommy. But it was manageable, because we went right ahead and created our comedy the same way we always did. Adler, with Lou Lombardo's help, got the coverage we needed and on we went.

After we finished shooting, we were not prepared for how long the editing process would take. We were used to recording on one day and then the next day it's on the air. What I started to get a hint of during this process was that the filming part was just making "bricks." Now these "bricks" had to be assembled into a house, and that's where the film is *really made*. To get a movie to sustain different tempos over an hour and a half is a very difficult process. It is mostly done by trial and error. Tommy and I found out the hard way onstage every night.

If they don't laugh, it's not funny.

No matter how much you think it's funny or how much you want it to be funny.

If they don't laugh...

Finally, the day came when Adler had to show Paramount the first cut. Watching a first cut is one of the most painful experiences in moviemaking. There on the big screen, in living color, is *every shot you didn't get*. It's like going over a road full of potholes in a go-kart. You just sit there, shorten your neck, and cringe.

The film was shown before a small test audience in San Diego. It did not go well. There was no rhythm to the film. There were scenes that everyone laughed hard at but there was just no sustained laughter. We sat in the lobby as the audience filed out. We looked like the receiving line at a funeral.

Finally, Michael Eisner, the head of Paramount, came out. We braced for the worst. He said, "There's some good stuff in there, real laughs. Keep working. This is a unique movie. It's in there. Keep working."

Years later Chong would concoct this story about how Eisner had hated the movie and sold it back to Adler. Then when it started to get good previews, he had to buy it back for much more money. This story was such an egregious fabrication that when it finally reached the ears of Michael Eisner he was moved to issue a press release denying any such scenario. Paramount *always* owned the film. Over the years, Tommy has made several outrageous claims like this one, things I know not to be true. I don't know why he does this. Maybe he can't fully remember it all and just relates things as he wishes they were.

Adler tried his best to keep us out of the editing process, but we were like barbarians at the gate. We kept pressing to get in. Lou wanted it to be a Lou Adler film, and we knew it was a Cheech and Chong film. After a while, he would show us some reworked scenes and we would make our comments. At the next preview we would find out if they worked.

The film was starting to gather some rhythm. The biggest bone of contention was the ending. In Adler's version, it was all a dream. A cop, played by Stacy Keach, pulls us over and we roll down the window, smoke rolls out, and we see that it's Sergeant Stadanko. We imagined it all.

Nobody liked that version . . . least of all us.

The tension really started to rise between us and Lou over the ending until Lou Lombardo stepped in and said, "Lou, you have to go with the guys. They're the comedians."

A year later, we shot the ending you see in the film now. Simple scene: The guys are driving and discussing the show the night before and making big plans.

"We're going to be big but we need a manager. Hey, my cousin has a van. He could be our manager."

Man drops a burning joint in Pedro's lap and off they go, zigzagging down the highway. What we found out is that Cheech and Chong movies were about a day in the life of Cheech and Chong. These were cosmic characters living in the present, and their adventures were far more interesting and funny than plot. The plot of *Up in Smoke* (and there is one) is: Two guys meet and decide to form a band, but first they need to find a joint. Go. In some countries the film was entitled *Looking for a Joint.*

Finally, the film was ready and it was released in four theaters in Texas. Nobody was prepared for what happened. As I sat in a theater in Dallas, I couldn't believe the explosion of laughter. It was like nothing I've ever heard before. It kept up from the beginning to the end. Although there were some flat sections, the riotous ending sent the audience out laughing their heads off.

We had very little communication with Adler at this time because of the disagreement over the ending, so we didn't know officially how the film was doing. I put in a call to Frank Mancuso, the president of Paramount. I asked him how the film was doing. He started to read me off some figures.

"Are these good?" I asked. There was a slight pause and then he said, "Cheech, these are blockbuster numbers. You have a giant hit on your hands."

"Hmm. Good to know."

Up in Smoke exploded across the country in 1978, and they couldn't make prints fast enough to satisfy the demand. Just as our career was starting to slow down a tad, we made a movie and we went to a whole other level. *Up in Smoke* remains, to this day, a comedy classic. I can tell because I have received a big check every year for thirty years. For my money, *Up in Smoke* is one of the best comedies ever made. It was a worldwide hit that multiple generations have enjoyed and it identified a global stoner culture.

We were back on top!

CHAPTER 24

A lesson in show business

Around this time, we started to look more closely at the movie deal we had signed with Lou Adler. To our surprise, we had signed a deal that gave us 10 percent... and Adler 90 percent. Which can happen without the benefit of having a lawyer on your side.

At the *very least*, we felt it was a breach of the trust that we had built up over many years. He had acted in the capacity of our manager in every way. To us, it was in essence a breach of fiduciary duty. He can't represent his side *and* our side at the same time.

Here was a very knowledgeable businessman with many years of experience and all kinds of high-priced legal advice available to him doing an inequitable deal with two street comedians who were totally unrepresented by legal counsel. We never had a lawyer at any time in our dealings with Lou. We had no problem with the recording deal, because it was a standard first album deal. He even improved that deal once, unprompted.

That wasn't the case with the movie deal. We gave him every opportunity to rework this deal and make it fairer. We would all have a big payday and continue working together, but he refused. We went looking for a lawyer.

One of the other provisions of the contract was that we had apparently signed up to do our next five movies with Adler. We had this huge hit movie and we were stuck in this onerous contract. Maybe we *were* those two guys in the movie. We scrambled every way we could to find a way out. We went back out on the road and raised money for lawyers.

Finally, we were directed to Stan Coleman, who has been my lawyer ever since. I don't really know how he got us out of the deal. I don't want to know. But I heard rumors that it involved Polaroids with animals.

But seriously folks, I think the threat of an actual lawsuit in which Lou would have to testify was what brought this all to an end. We got out of the deal going forward, but there was no remedy found for improving our share of *Up in Smoke*.

Howard Brown was our manager briefly. Howard was introduced to us by our friend Marshall Blonstein, who was head of promotion for Ode Records, our label. I was never close with Howard. He was just too oily and crazy for me. He used to show up every day in a different costume. One day he was a cowboy with a giant ten-gallon hat and chaps. The next day he was "Manners" the Butler, with a derby hat, a pin-striped suit, and an umbrella over his arm. Then he was all in camouflage like some commando.

One night I drove up with my wife, Rikki, to our offices on the Columbia lot. I had left something at the office. It was about midnight. As we pulled up, Howard was exiting the office carrying a big box with all the office coffee supplies. Coffee, creamer, sugar, sweeteners, cups, spoons, and napkins. He put it in his car and waved good-bye.

In retrospect, he was perfect for Hollywood. He hung out with these studio heads and learned their hopes and fears. He realized that their biggest fear was in knowing that there is a very thin line between a "golden parachute" and a "golden shower."

With Howard representing us, we signed three movie deals before we had shot one foot of film. He set up one of the most astounding deals I have ever heard of. Despite his peculiarities, Howard did good work for us. And if you're just having a coffee, he's your man, too.

We had been working all day on preproduction for *Cheech and Chong's Next Movie*, which Howard had set up for us at Universal.

We were bushed, but we had to show up at the house of Frank Price, the head of Columbia Pictures. Howard had arranged for Frank to be joined by Sherry Lansing, vice president at Columbia, and Marvin Antonowsky, the legendarily tough head of business affairs.

Here was the drill. We had to tell them three stories and they would pick one. For the privilege of hearing our three stories, they had to hand us a check for $100,000 when we walked in the house.

On the walkway to the house, I turned to Tommy and said, "What stories do you want to tell them?"

"Let's tell them 'The Roadies.'"

We could riff for hours on rock-and-roll roadie adventures, but we really didn't have a story to tell.

"What else?"

"How about the story of you in the Canadian Rockies with the bears and shit?"

"OK, what else? We have to have three."

"We'll think of something. Just improvise."

The door opened and there stood the smiling trio. Sherry Lansing handed us a check for $100,000, which was ours to keep even if they didn't like any of the stories. We sat down in Frank's beautiful living room and proceeded to spin three stories that we made up as we went along. Whenever one of us would run out of story, the other one would pick it up and keep on going. They all nodded along and then excused themselves to another room.

We sat there in a daze looking around, dumbfounded that a major studio had paid us a hundred grand to pitch them stories. Even at that stage of our movie career, with almost no experience, we knew that this was exceptional.

Finally, they came back into the room. They commented on all the stories and in the end picked "The Roadies," at which point they handed us another check for $400,000, which meant that we had a "go" picture.

In the end we never made "The Roadies," but we did make a movie that made money (*Nice Dreams*, 1981), and everybody was happy. We were now back on the project treadmill making one movie after another. We were always in preproduction and postproduction at the same time for the next five years.

Commercial success in movies becomes almost a negotiable commodity. If you make a hit movie, you get offered everything, even if it doesn't make any sense.

Shortly after *Up in Smoke* was a bust-out winner, there was a big fire in Malibu. By some miracle, despite being right in the middle of it, my house was mostly spared. I only lost a barn and a garage, but the rest of the grounds were turned into a smoldering landscape.

As I was wandering around in a daze attempting to clean up, I saw a very tall, thin man walking down my driveway. I was on edge, as there were rumors of scavengers going around stealing anything they could. The man approached and I saw he had a script under his arm.

"Hi, you must be Cheech. My name is Tony Richardson, I'm a director."

I knew exactly who Tony Richardson was, because he had directed one of the great films of the 1960s and one of my all-time favorite movies: *Tom Jones*, with Albert Finney.

He looked around at the smoke rising from the ground.

"I suppose this is a bad time, but I have a script here for two guys. The characters are English, so you would have to act. But if you consent to do it, the studio will green-light it."

He arrived through the smoke like a mirage and he departed the same way.

This most unusual offer came from the very young producing-directing team of Brian Grazer and Ron Howard. They hadn't made a movie yet, but they were eager. I went to see them at Brian's house in Malibu. After lemonade and cookies, they got down to it. Ron did the pitching. Essentially it was this:

Cheech and Chong are raised by turtles. (Yes, *turtles*.)

They didn't know that they were *not* turtles because everyone in their world was...a turtle. I guess they never looked at each other. If they somehow found themselves on their backs, they couldn't right themselves because, well you see...they were turtles.

"We're thinking of calling it *The Turtle Boys*. What do you think?"

Now Ron and Brian have gone on to become a very successful, Academy Award–winning producing and directing team. I didn't see an Oscar in this story's future. I thanked them for the offer and quickly tried to get turtle images out of my head. And I never saw Tony Richardson again.

Motion pictures are *the* art form of the twentieth and twenty-first centuries. They are dreams caught on film and preserved in a collective memory for the rest of your life. They are shared and traded back and forth like myths around ancient campfires. And everybody wants to be in one.

The people who make them become stars and demigods.

They are also a business, so they have to make money. This dynamic makes everybody fucking crazy. It is very hard to go through the movie process on just about any level without it somehow tainting your personality. People are capable of being saints or sinners two seconds apart.

CHAPTER 25

You're slouching

We got out of the deal with Adler as I said, but it took two years. So in 1980, we went right to work.

Being movie stars took us to a whole new level. We were recognized a thousand times more than we were from records and stage. Exposure from live stage work pales in comparison to the worldwide reach of movies. Before, when we made records, hardly anyone knew who did what. We were just voices coming out of the speakers. Still, to this day people ask us who did which voices. With movies, there we were on the big screen. I was Pedro, and Chong was Man. Quickly, we even stopped calling them Pedro and Man and just called them Cheech and Chong.

The reaction to *Up in Smoke* was interesting in that I started getting a lot of attention as an actor. I got more than a few offers to act separate from Tommy. I turned them all down, because I had no thought of separating the act. We were just getting started. Tommy heard about some of the offers, and though he never said anything, I could tell that he was affected.

In order to make him feel more secure I threw him a big party at La Fonda, LA's most historic Mexican restaurant. We were celebrating his official designation as a movie director, a role our new contract gave him. I invited both our families and the key members of the crew. I bought him a director's chair, a megaphone, and a jacket with leather patches on the elbows to make him look like a "classic" director. We were ready to start *Cheech and Chong's Next Movie*.

I saw how not being designated the official "director" had affected Tommy, and I wanted to bypass that problem. I was really not interested in "titles"; I was interested in making a funny movie. I assumed that nothing would change and that we would continue working together as we always had, doing things together and making decisions together.

Little by little, however, that dynamic started to change. Chong finally found himself in the position he had always seen himself in.

But was he, really?

Though his name was now in the group's title, he was not the sole star performer.

Though he was the credited director, we both wrote and directed the movies together.

At some point, he decided that he would be the star director and that everything was his idea. It got to the point where I had to tell him that something was his idea or it wouldn't get done.

As we made the rest of our movies, he decided at some point that he had written everything and I was there just to help him fulfill his vision.

I guess I was just lucky to be in the room.

From the time I met him, Tommy always had a very big ego. That's fine. You need a big ego to succeed in showbiz. But now it had expanded into megalomania.

Like I said earlier, we were not best friends, we were brothers. He was the older brother and I was the younger brother.

However, there comes a time when the younger brother gets old enough. And with each film, I was learning more and more about how to make movies.

But now Chong increasingly wanted to be the boss and make all the decisions. We were improvisational artists, and when we were working at our peak, the ideas flowed back and forth like water. We were most assuredly equals when it came to creating our work.

But around our third or fourth movie, he didn't want me to write with him anymore. He said he was writing a script with his sister-in-law's stoner-artist boyfriend.

What fucking gall.

I told him, "Good luck getting me to do it." And I told his friend to get lost.

The great writing dynamic between Chong and me was that we could be honest when one of us was full of shit. He could tell me. I could tell him. We could also be honest with each other when one of us came up with an idea that was really great. We'd had a lot of success that proved this formula worked.

Now Tommy didn't want me—or anyone else, for that matter—to tell him he was full of shit and increasingly . . . he was full of shit.

The end came when we were about to make our final movie, *The Corsican Brothers*. I didn't especially want to make this movie because it was a period remake of an old Douglas Fairbanks Jr. movie. I thought we had more original things to say. I rationalized it by saying that Laurel and Hardy and Abbot and Costello had made period films, and I guess we could, too.

Tommy also presented this as a deal that *he alone* had worked out with the studio, which was news to me. He told me that he didn't want me to write this film with him or interfere with the direction. If I didn't want to do it on these terms, I should give back the money that I had accepted as an advance. He knew that I had already spent the advance on rebuilding my Malibu house.

I knew right then that we were making our last film together.

To make *The Corsican Brothers*, we moved to Paris in 1982, which would prove to be the agony and the ecstasy.

I wish that all young, adventurous people could spend a year of their lives in Paris. It is an enchanting, magical, romantic city. We had been spending more time in Europe as we had shot *Still Smokin* in Amsterdam, the dope-smoker capital of the world. What a cool city for Cheech and Chong.

Tommy and Shelby had decided to move to Paris on a long-term basis and even bought an apartment there. Rikki and I really lucked out. Through friends, we leased a luxurious, art-filled apartment on Avenue Foch in the sixteenth arrondissement, one of the most prestigious neighborhoods in the city.

The previous occupants had been Jerry Hall and Mick Jagger. Jerry called a couple of times and said, "Y'all seen anything of a big black book... It's got a black leather cover." That sentence seemed to take five minutes to say in her slow, sexy Texas drawl. The franc had gone to eight to one against the dollar. We were living "phat."

It should have been the happiest time of my life, and in many ways it was.

However, my partnership with Tommy was disintegrating and my marriage was coming apart at the same time. Rikki had gone to England to do horse training. She was trying to make the Olympic team in three-day eventing. It was a long shot, but if she didn't train for it, it was a no-shot at all. Believe me, we needed the time apart.

When I first arrived in Paris, I didn't enjoy it much. The weather was always gray and dreary. I didn't see the sun for months. I actually had dreams about lying on the beach in Malibu and having the California sun beat down on my back.

Eventually, the sun peeped through, and I started meeting new people who showed me around the city. Our publicist, Yanou Collart, represented movie stars and chefs. At least twice a week, we were taken to some three-star restaurant where the latest hot chef would make us special meals.

Tommy's daughter Robbie was one of the hot fashion models in Paris at the time, and she was walking in all the high-end designer shows like Issey Miyake, Kenzo, Jean Paul Gaultier. For a while, she was Karl Lagerfeld's muse. Through Robbie, we were introduced to the fashion world and its denizens. Like I said, it was an exciting and busy time.

Even the location for the movie was fabulous. We shot at the amazing and historic Chateau Dompierre just outside of Versailles. Every day we had lunch under a big white tent next to a beautiful lake filled with white swans . . . and always three kinds of wine. Ahh, the French.

Despite the rigid ground rules laid out by Chong, I wrote a couple of gags that appeared in the movie, like the scene with Rikki while I'm washing her horse. If you've seen the movie, you'll know which one it is.

I really stopped caring about the movie one day when we were shooting a big action scene in the courtyard with a hundred extras. Tommy and I were standing up high on the guillotine waiting for "Action!" when I heard from across the courtyard a high-pitched, feminine voice yelling, "Cut, cut." It was Shelby, who came walking across the yard and yelled at Chong to "Stand up straight. You're slouching." I think they had this idea that he was going for "handsome leading man" or something.

I remember thinking, *My dear fucking God, I have had enough.*

Eventually the movie wrapped, and I got out of there as fast as I could.

By this time, Rikki and our daughter Carmen had moved back to the United States to continue to train for the Olympics. Bruce Davidson, the world champion in three-day eventing, had a school in Unionville, Pennsylvania. I joined them there, but after about a week it was evident that our marriage was over.

I went back to Malibu with my tail between my legs and tried to figure out what was next.

Chong and Shelby and their three kids stayed in Paris after we made *The Corsican Brothers.* Over a year passed and finally the film came out in 1984. It didn't open well and then sank like a stone out of sight. It was our least successful film and was gone from theaters in two weeks. I think Tommy was very content to stay on the Left Bank and not have to come back to the United States and answer questions about the film.

Tommy and I weren't getting along at all. We hardly even spoke to each other after we made the movie.

Chong and I always had a love-hate relationship right from the start. We did both of those things with equal intensity. But the one undeniable thing we always had was comic chemistry. We had it in spades. We never had to think about it; it just was. We were lucky to not only have it but to recognize it and try not to get in its way.

We had developed it over the years through stage, records, and now movies, but our essential timing was there right from the beginning. As I have said, it was because we were both musicians. We viewed comedy as a type of music with its own distinctive rhythms and timing and inflections. We both knew exactly where to come in, or not come in, because we heard it as clearly as we heard a four/four beat. It was in our DNA. We were also each other's biggest fans when we weren't clashing over who was in control. I didn't necessarily want to be in control. I just didn't want to be controlled. And there was the rub.

At the beginning of our partnership, I usually deferred to his lead because he was older than I was and had a bit more experience. But I developed personally and was able to more than hold my own in our creative process. We had been doing this tug-of-war pretty much throughout our whole career. Most times, this friction was the irritant that produced the pearl. We could have all the heated arguments we wanted, and we had many, but in the end if something was funny we both knew it, because we'd be on the floor laughing our asses off. Those pearls invariably came out of an improvisation during recording when our egos were shut off and we listened to each other and didn't get in the way of our natural chemistry. The dynamic was manageable during the record and concert touring period, because nobody knew who did what on the records. And relatively few people saw us live onstage. Movies changed everything.

Now everybody saw who was the lowrider and who was the stoner, because we concentrated on those two characters for the movies. We did other characters in some movies, but Pedro and Man became Cheech and Chong and vice versa. The net effect of that was that people thought we were those characters.

I remember doing an interview with a major newspaper writer in LA, and after he asked his first question, I gave a long and involved answer after which he just stared at me.

"What? What's up, dude?" I asked.

After several more seconds of staring he said, "You don't speak with an accent."

I remember thinking, *Man, if this guy, who is a professional entertainment writer, thinks I'm Pedro, then what must everybody else think?*

It didn't bother me. In fact, I thought it was funny and I was getting so much positive feedback. What was there to complain about?

Increasingly, though, it seemed to bother Chong that everybody thought that he was the dim-witted Man character.

So, as we continued to make movies, a real struggle set in between us. Although Tommy was the credited director, we wrote and directed the movies together. Which he has often verified. We had never disagreed over who had done what before. Most of the time we didn't know who had done what, because we were in the moment of creativity doing improvs in the studio. I don't think our audience thought or even cared about who was the director and who was the writer. They thought of us as one unit: Cheech and Chong.

With movies there is a real division of duties. There are so many moving parts that have to come together to make the whole, and credit is a very jealously guarded asset. It shouldn't have been with us but Chong, as I have noted, increasingly wanted to be recognized as a director and more crucially as...the writer. His theory was that if he wrote down our ideas on paper, then he was the writer. I pointed out to him that that was stenography, not writing. We were having problems. More than once we split up during the movie years, always to get back together somehow and do another one.

All things have a shelf life. For film comedians, it's about six films, and that's if you're at the very top rung of the ladder. After that, you're into a generation different from the one who made you the biggest thing in the history of the world. The next generation wants their own comic heroes that capture the zeitgeist of their age group. There is nothing more Pop than a Pop comedian. They capture what's in the air right *now*. It's very mercurial. It's the definition of lightning in a bottle. It's not a hard-and-fast rule, but it pretty much holds true. That's why film comedians try to get into dramas, action films, animation, and so forth. Not only do they want to show other skills and ranges, but the returns start to dwindle if you're the comic voice of a generation for too long.

Cheech and Chong had reached their film use-by date around 1985. I think that was a big, underlying factor that fed into our discord.

More and more, I wanted Cheech and Chong to do other things than just the same old Sex, Drugs, and Rock and Roll. It would be very easy to turn our attention thirty degrees to other subjects like politics or other things happening in the world. We would have our own Cheech and Chong take on these new topics, but we needed a different beat.

But Tommy didn't want to stray from his image as the quintessential stoner, although he disdained it at the same time. It was typical of his personality. He was a true Gemini. I used to call him the World's Humblest Megalomaniac.

Our shrinking box office results also indicated that we needed a different direction.

Chong was, is, and always will be the world's best stoner. I knew we had come to the end of this particular journey. We had been together for seventeen years through clubs, records, concerts, and movies, and we were with each other virtually 24/7 for that whole time. Not only were we sick of each other and didn't want to hear anything the other guy had to say, we had pretty much run out of fresh things to say about the same old subjects. You know you're out of juice as the voice of your generation when you start doing remakes.

CHAPTER 26

You're into video, I'm into film

So I'm alone in Malibu playing the guitar, feeling sorry for myself and trying to stay in a marijuana-induced fog for as long as I could stand it. My comedy partnership was ending. My marriage was breaking up. And I had a big house payment due soon. So much fun. I wonder where my moon was during this period, astrologically speaking. Probably up Uranus.

One evening, Linda Livingston, one of my oldest and dearest friends, called me up and said, "You've got to get out of the house! Come on down to this show I'm working on."

Linda was always involved in a million projects and was good in all of them.

"It's a laser light show," Linda continued. "It's going to open the Olympics here in LA. They're going to run through the whole show. Come on! Have some fun."

OK, what the hell. Linda's right. I could do with a little fun.

When we got there, there was a nice mellow, hip-looking crowd milling about. The show started, and it was spectacular. It was a great example of the artistic possibilities for what a state-of-the-art laser show could do at that time.

As soon as the show was over, Linda grabbed me and said, "Come on, let's take some pictures!" She maneuvered me towards the photo pit. She pulled me over next to a beautiful young woman.

"Cheech, this is Patti. She works on the show. You met her before. I brought her in to show you some artwork." I vaguely remembered and just smiled and nodded.

"Here you guys, let's get a picture."

I said OK and put my arm around Patti's waist. *It was like I had grabbed an electric eel.* Everybody around us noticed it, too. I kind of walked away stunned.

The next morning, I woke up and called Linda and asked for Patti's number.

Patti Heid is from Appleton, Wisconsin. She is blonde, blue-eyed, beautiful, and funny…and an incredibly good, edgy artist. Our small talk, when we were getting our picture taken, had consisted of Patti saying that they were also celebrating her birthday, which was that day.

"Wow, really? My birthday was yesterday."

We looked into each other's eyes and we each knew what the other was thinking.

RUN! RUN! GET OUT OF THERE! DON'T LOOK BACK! RUN!!!

We didn't do that. Instead, we were married for twenty years. There were incredible highs and very low lows. Joey and Jasmine, my next two children, were born while we resided in Malibu. Joey developed a deep affinity for the ocean as I did. He was a member of the Junior Lifeguards from the ages of nine to eighteen. Jasmine, not so much so, but she really loves the beach part. Jasmine became more of the artist, like her mother, and graduated from The School of the Art Institute of Chicago, maybe the most prestigious art school in the nation or even the world. I love Joey and Jasmine with all my heart.

Well, Patti and I jumped into a hot and torrid relationship. She moved right in with me in Malibu as I tried to figure out what to do next.

And then one day I saw the future…MTV.

MTV has been around so long by now that they don't even play music anymore. But back when Music Television launched in 1981, it was pretty soon showing music videos 24/7, and the record-buying public was quickly glued to the channel. It was the hottest thing going, and that was all anybody in the industry talked about. Record sales (then soon compact disc sales) started to zoom.

Then in 1982, when Michael Jackson started releasing the videos from his legendary album *Thriller*, the whole thing took off into the stratosphere. I sat there and watched in amazement, just like everybody else. Jackson released seven singles, and seven videos, from that album over the course of about a year.

I was watching one of them in 1984 during my period of laying low and getting started with Patti. And then it hit me—this genre was perfect for Cheech and Chong!

We were musicians, filmmakers, and comedians. We could make video albums that were musical and funny and visual, just as we had made record albums. This was a godsend.

I called my friend Peter Lopez, a music industry lawyer who knew everybody and asked him if he knew where I could take my idea. He immediately mentioned Irving Azoff, then head of MCA Records. A quick meeting was set up. I pitched Irving the idea of a video album, and he bought it right there in the room.

I couldn't wait to tell Chong.

I had to wait for morning in Paris so in the meantime I started sketching out ideas for bits and songs that we could turn into videos. My head was buzzing with images.

Finally, I reached Tommy in France and started babbling about MTV and Irving Azoff and we could get a deal and make video albums and it would be great and...nothing.

He was, shall we say, underwhelmed.

Yes, he had heard of MTV. They had it in France, and he made it obvious that he wasn't as excited about the idea as I was. In the end he said, "You're into video, I'm into film. But if you want to go ahead, I'll come in and do a couple of bits."

Gee thanks, Chong.

I made the deal and started writing songs. By now, the idea had evolved into individual videos of the songs and a "mockumentary" about the making of the videos. I figured that I would direct the videos and Tommy would direct the mockumentary part. I had three songs sketched out in no time, and I waited for Tommy to show up.

A couple of weeks later Tommy came over from France and we worked on the songs and went into the studio to record them.

I then set about putting a cast and crew together. I still needed another song and waited for inspiration. I would not have to wait long.

One day I was sitting in my kitchen having my morning coffee and reading the newspaper when I came across an article about a young boy (I think he was twelve) who had been caught up in an immigration raid. Because he was mentally disabled, he wasn't able to communicate to the agents that he was an American citizen, and they mistook him for a Mexican illegal and deported him to Tijuana.

At the same time, the radio was playing Bruce Springsteen's song "Born in the U.S.A." I started laughing when I put the two together and began singing "Born in East L.A." The lyrics came out in a gush and I had my fourth song.

I had to get permission to parody Bruce's song. I figured that wouldn't be a problem since I'd become good friends with Springsteen's piano player, Roy Bittan. Also, the first time that Bruce Springsteen ever played with a band after releasing his first album was opening for Cheech and Chong sometime in the 1970s. Roy eventually joined the band, and I met him along the way. We hit it off immediately and are still pals today.

The funny thing was that I never knew what the original song was about. I just remember hearing the chorus "Born in the U.S.A." I had to rush out and get the CD to find out that the song was a protest about the treatment that the returning Vietnam War vets were getting. I was sure that Bruce would respond to my story of the unjust treatment by the immigration authorities...and he did. I got his permission, with Roy's help, and got ready to record "Born in East L.A."

The studio we'd be using was in an expanded trailer set up in Dennis Dragon's backyard in Malibu. Totally Cheech and Chong. Dennis was the founder of the Surf Punks band, but also a pretty good engineer. In his own studio, that is, where only he knew how everything worked. But it worked.

Dennis came from the musical Dragon family of Hollywood. Carmen Dragon, his father, was the conductor of the Hollywood Symphony Orchestra and did classical recordings. His brother, Daryl, was the Captain, of the Captain and Tennille.

(Fast forward: The first time I ever played "Born in East L.A." live onstage was at a benefit in Malibu with Dennis Dragon on keyboards and Eddie Van Halen on guitar. A rare, early performance for young Edward, who proceeded to drink copious amounts of alcohol despite having a second show to do. Good luck on that one.)

So there I was, a few weeks later, waiting in the trailer slash studio for Tommy Chong to show up. I had a feeling Tommy might pull something. He had been dragging his feet the whole project—that is, when I could get his feet in this country.

Finally, I could wait no longer and I called his house. I was surprised when he answered. He was still home.

"Hey Tommy, we're at the studio waiting for you. Did you forget?"

"No, it's your song, man, you do it."

His tone was flat and cold.

"We have to record the middle section with me and you going back and forth."

"Go ahead, man, it's your song, you record it."

"The middle section is for two guys—me and you."

"It's your song. You'll figure out something."

"So you're not coming in?"

"No."

"Wow...OK, see you later."

In all the years we had been together and all the projects we had done together, I had *never once* not been there for him. We may have argued back and forth, and sometimes it got very heated, but in the end we always worked it out. This was the first time I asked him to be there for me...and he refused. I sat there for a long time silently and took in what this meant. I wasn't so much mad as I was very sad.

Dennis Dragon broke my reverie. "So what are we doing?"

I thought for a few seconds and then said, "Set up a mike. We're finishing the song."

I went in and recorded both parts in one or two takes.

I put the crew together and began filming the videos. The mockumentary part was being filmed as it happened between the scenes. I tried to get Tommy to participate as much as possible, but he stayed true to his word when he'd said he would come in and do a few bits. And he'd already done that a few weeks before.

Chong was not on the song for "Born in East L.A.," so he wasn't in the video, either.

He went back to France to join his family and I guess to do "film."

The "Born in East L.A." video was released to MTV and became a sensation. It went to number one, and for a while it seemed to be on every time you turned on the TV. It was either "Money for Nothing" by Dire Straits or "Born in East L.A." The overall quality of the video was helped a lot by my in-house art director, Patti, who designed all the sets and half the costumes, all while being pregnant with Joey.

Roy Bittan told me that many times during Springsteen's concerts that year the crowd would sing "Born in East L.A." when they played "Born in the U.S.A."

From out of the blue, I got a call from Irving Azoff, who told me that he had shown a prerelease copy of the "Born in East L.A." video to Frank Price, who was now head of Universal Pictures. He said that Frank wanted to have a meeting. We had made two movies for Frank when he ran Columbia Pictures, so he was well acquainted with our work.

Frank got right to the point. "I think that there's a movie here," he said. "But it's for you by yourself. Let me know what you want to do but I'm ready to make a deal."

The moment of truth had arrived. I could continue to struggle along with Chong, which I didn't want to do. Or I could make a movie on my own.

I asked Tommy to come to my house for a meeting. He planned to pitch me an idea for a TV show.

Before he could get started, I told him that Frank Price had offered me a deal to do "Born in East L.A." as a solo project...and I was going to do it.

I could see that it shocked Chong to his core. He really thought that he had me completely under wraps.

"I still want to do movies with you," I told him. But I don't think he heard me as he turned his back on me and walked out to his car and drove away.

CHAPTER 27

Born in East L.A.

I had full confidence that I could pull this project off, because it was what I had been doing for several years, despite what those Cheech and Chong movie credits say. The credit didn't matter as much to me as the desire to make a good movie in a different direction.

Writing, starring in, and directing a motion picture is a grueling experience. There is some point during the process where you throw up your hands and scream, "I don't know what I'm doing!" but you get over it and continue.

I have to say that, even though it was grueling, I enjoyed every second of filming *Born in East L.A.* I was lucky enough to put together an outstanding cast with Daniel Stern, Tony Plana, Kamala Lopez, Paul Rodriguez, and Jan-Michael Vincent. Once again my long-time producer Peter Macgregor-Scott joined me, and I couldn't have done it without him. Peter worked on five Cheech and Chong movies, producing three of them, as well as most of the Steven Seagal action flicks and the Academy Award–winning movie *The Fugitive*.

Shooting most of the film in Tijuana, Mexico, was one of the most difficult aspects of the production. It wasn't that Tijuana itself was difficult; it was actually a cool place to be. And we needed it because we found an authenticity there that we couldn't have gotten anywhere else.

The problem was the bureaucracy in Mexico City that controlled everything. It was hard to get an answer that stuck. We finally realized in the end what ruled everything. *La Mordita*, or "the Bite," was the *unofficial tax* that was required in order for anything to move forward.

We had a ball shooting the film and every day was a new adventure. I was learning a lot under the tutelage of Alex Phillips Jr., the famed Mexican cinematographer.

I'll always remember the day we shot the stampede across the border with a hundred extras. There was a slight disturbance earlier in the week when Peter, my producer, was doing a radio interview on a local station trying to drum up a turnout for the scene. The announcer started berating him for coming down to Tijuana and ripping off the local extras and paying them nothing. I guess that was what they were used to. Peter told him that that was not the case, and we were paying them U.S. scale and providing lunch, transportation, and regular hours. The announcer ended up asking how he could be an extra and that he had a lot of friends who would like the work.

Little magical things happened all the time. When I was writing the scene where I teach the "Waas sappening" boys how to be *cholos*, I pictured a space between two buildings with turquoise wainscoting and clotheslines strung between the buildings. Our location scout took me to see a possible location. It was exactly what I had pictured in my mind's eye even down to the color of the walls.

We had a great time every day and were kind of sorry to have to come back to Los Angeles.

Eventually, we finished shooting and began the editing process. Then we were ready to show it to test audiences.

Test audiences are great if you have them come in and see the film. You hear where they laugh . . . or don't laugh, and you make your edits accordingly.

But having them fill out comment cards is a masochistic exercise that does nobody any good but makes the studio feel like it's doing something useful.

For example, one of the questions that the audience was asked was "What did you like best about the movie?"

One guy answered, "The girl in the green dress."

The next question was "What did you like least in the movie?"

The same guy answered, "When the girl in the green dress talks."

When given the opportunity, the audience turns into Siskel and Ebert. They rarely, if ever, give you anything on a comment card that you can use. The purest thing they can offer is what you hear when they see it. It doesn't just pertain to laughs. When there is a dramatic shift in the film you can hear it *and* feel it in the theater.

Finally, it was time to show it. The film wasn't so much released as it escaped. The studio put out a minimum of publicity. Between the start and end of production, Frank Price had been let go due to the failure of *Howard the Duck*, Universal's big-budget comedy of the year. The headline of *Variety* put it succinctly: DUCK COOKS PRICE'S GOOSE.

My film became an instant orphan with nobody to champion it. Incoming executives want nothing to do with their predecessors' films. It's almost as if they might catch something from them.

Born in East L.A. opened and was the second-highest grossing film in the nation that week. For the next four weeks in a row, it was the highest grossing film in the ten western states group. Nobody saw it coming. Tom Pollack, the incoming head of Universal, walked into his Monday morning staff meeting with a big smile on his face and said, *"Buenos días."*

The film even got great reviews. Kevin Thomas of the *Los Angeles Times* wrote "*Born in East L.A.* is an across-the-board winner, an exuberant crowd pleaser that marks its writer-director-star Cheech Marin's first effort apart from his long-time partner Tommy Chong. It has more energy and drive than *La Bamba*, which also examines Latino life, and it comes as a happy revelation to one who always found Cheech and Chong's pot humor puerile and tedious."

Shortly after *Born in East L.A.* was released in the United States,

I started experiencing a newfound respect in the Latino community. Not that they didn't love all things Cheech and Chong before—after all, they are Latino and have a certain relaxed attitude toward life—but now I started getting really respectful reviews in the establishment press for my first solo movie.

Writers recognized that I was handling a serious subject (the immigration fiasco) in a light but unflinching way. My theory about getting a message across in popular entertainment was to "slip it in their coffee." You get the message, but you don't choke on it. The proportion of message to entertainment is like the proportions of a hot air balloon. A big roomy balloon (laughter) is necessary to deliver a very small but important payload (message). It didn't hurt that *Born in East L.A.* was successful financially.

A few months after *Born in East L.A.* had finished its theatrical run, I got a call out of the blue asking if I would like to take the film to the Havana Film Festival as an official entrant. Of course I would, but the whole maneuver would be fraught with political hurdles.

The major hurdle was getting the studio, Universal, to approve the film physically going there. After all, the last thing they wanted was for the film to be seized in a foreign country, especially Cuba, where we had imposed a decades-long trade embargo. After a lot of backstage maneuvering, I was informed that I would be allowed to take the film to Havana. I had no idea what I was in for and what I was about to see.

Cuba had been closed to visits from ordinary U.S. citizens ever since Fidel Castro had taken over in 1959. There had also been many tense moments between the U.S. and Cuba: the Cuban Missile Crisis in the early sixties, the Bay of Pigs invasion, and an ongoing series of defections by refugees from this tightly controlled island that lay just ninety miles from our southern border. There had been no diplomatic relations between the two countries in almost thirty years…and yet there were ways to get in.

One way was to be invited, by Cuba, in a closely monitored cultural exchange. Their partnership with Russia meant that there would be plenty of Russian agents at the airport giving everybody the "Stalin stink eye." When we landed at José Martí Airport in Havana, it felt like we were landing in Moscow. But as soon as we left the airport, fact and fiction started to separate themselves.

The first thing I noticed was that there was very little military presence in the streets. In contrast, I had been promoting the film in the Dominican Republic and Venezuela some months before, and everywhere I had gone there were policemen and soldiers with automatic weapons standing guard waiting for something to happen. In Havana, there were no homeless, armless, eyeless beggars in the street. Whereas in the other countries, they crowded every intersection that we drove through. It made you wonder: Which was the democracy and which was the totalitarian state?

The very first thing that crosses your mind, though, when you drive into Havana is *Man, this place could use a coat of paint.*

Because of the embargo, all things were in short supply...and I mean *all* things. Havana has the biggest collection of fifties automobiles still running in the world. I can't even imagine what replacement parts are made of. Probably pig intestines or some shit.

Since all of the filmmakers were honored guests, we were given the best accommodations. We were put up at the Capri Hotel, a leftover from the Hyman Roth–style, Mafia-controlled Havana era. The most luxe hotel in the city had a giant pool of water in the hall right in front of the door to my room. It was there because of the crater-sized hole in the ceiling that leaked a steady stream of water. Getting in and out of the room was like running in a steeplechase over water jumps. The bellman must have done this a million times because, without comment, he opened the door, grabbed my bags, and leapt over the puddle like it was a crack in the cement. *Bienvenido a Cuba.*

After getting settled, I ventured down into the lobby to meet our guide from the festival. His name was Carlos, and his English was as good as my Spanish was bad. Like most Chicanos, I spoke some version of Spanglish. We stood there yakking for a few minutes until he looked up and saw a man enter the front door of the hotel. With a sly little smile on his face he said, "Come here, there's somebody I want you to meet."

"Hola Gabo!" he called out to the man striding across the lobby. They embraced like old buddies.

"Cheech, I would like you to meet Gabriel García Márquez."

I stood there frozen with my mouth as wide open as an airplane hangar. "Gabo" was the Nobel Prize-winning author of *One Hundred Years of Solitude,* one of the most important and influential novels ever written. He was the inventor of the genre known as Magical Realism. His books have been translated into more than thirty languages. I think I have read every word he has ever written. It was like meeting Shakespeare.

He smiled, shook my hand firmly and said *"mucho gusto,"* and then was gone. I was liking Cuba more and more as the day went on. We ventured out into the street to soak up the *sabor* of Havana.

I have traveled extensively all over Mexico, four countries in Central America—including six times in Costa Rica alone and, lately, Venezuela—Puerto Rico, and the Dominican Republic. I know the feeling of Latin American cities. Great wealth existing right next to dire poverty is not a shock to me. The vibe in Cuba was different from any other Latin American place I had been in before.

There was no great wealth, no ostentatious palaces, no Mercedes-Benz cars cruising the boulevards, not even one Colonel Sanders selling *Cuban pollo frito.* The people were definitely poor, but their cities were clean . . . but damn, they sure could have used some paint.

Cubans all had free universal health care, which was the best in the Latin American world, and free education all the way through college. They are the most educated people in the Latin American world. The literacy rate is almost 100 percent. In addition, they are the most sophisticated moviegoers. The average Cuban sees more than six movies a year, while the average American goes to the theater just under two times a year.

We also met two waiters who each had two doctorates, and there's the rub. No jobs that pay well and no place to go, since you can't leave the island. Communism sounds good in theory, but try to live in it. It will be very interesting to see what will happen once Castro is gone.

We spent the rest of the day walking around the historic streets of Havana trying to find the best place to buy cigars and Cuban rum, both of which I had promised to everybody back home. At the end of the day, we were taken to El Floradita, a historic bar and restaurant that Ernest Hemingway used to frequent back in the day. We all got drunk enough to stand on each others' shoulders and write our names high up on the wall beyond the reach of cultural revisionism.

Bright and early the next morning our little group gathered in the lobby: my producer, Peter Macgregor-Scott; my then wife, Patti; and our host, Sonia Levine from New York, whose Cuban-friendly group fostered cultural exchanges. Sonia, who maintained a residence in Havana and knew what was what, informed us that we were going to take a drive out in the country to check out the country's film school, where we would meet Tomás Gutiérrez Alea, Cuba's most famous film director. Alea had directed *Memories of Underdevelopment*, an international sensation, and was cofounder of the film school. I thought we would go by official tour bus, but instead Sonia said, "Naa! We'll just rent a car!" And we did.

The reason I'm noting this is that we were not under any kind of surveillance at all. Nobody followed us. We had no official caretaker. We just rented a car and away we went. I was actually more shocked that we could even rent a car in Cuba. We drove out into the countryside past fields and fields of sugar cane, corn, and rice, which contained very little farm machinery, but lots of oxen and farmers.

We arrived at the film school and were given an extensive tour. After a frugal lunch outdoors, we were introduced to Alea, who, like Gabo, shook our hands and then said hello and good-bye. I guess that's the official Commie deal. Whatever, we had fun and then we took our time and drove back to Havana.

We arrived back at the hotel in the late afternoon and went to the bar in the lobby to drink some cold Cuban beer. I guess there wasn't an embargo on beer, because they had all kinds. There's nothing like a cold beer in the tropics. Carlos joined us as he had finished his morning duties. Midway through our third beer, I was spotted by a couple of official-looking delegates from the festival. I knew they were delegates because they all had big-ass laminates that said "*Delegado Oficial.*" They waved in my direction and with big smiles on their faces shouted out in Spanish, "We loved your movie!"

"Really?" I said to Carlos. "How do they know the movie?"

"They're on the jury. They've just started showing the film."

As we sat there drinking, the same scene was repeated a couple more times. All were smiling and waving, but nobody came over to say hi. I asked Carlos about this.

"They're not allowed to mingle with the artists during the judging period. They might be influenced by bribes or something."

OK. I sure wouldn't want to do that.

"How much do you think it would take?" I joked. But Carlos gave me his sternest look.

"Don't even joke. This is the most serious film festival in Latin America."

"OK, I get it. No jokey con los judges."

You have to remember that Cheech and Chong films were, at this time, generally not shown in Latin American countries because of the drug content. We had much more coverage in the rest of the world than in places that spoke Spanish...that is, *all the drug-exporting countries*. Go figure.

As a consequence, I was virtually unknown in Cuba and with the delegates. To them, I was just another guy with a can of film under his arm, so it was really special when they shouted out to me. Carlos finished his beer and said that he would meet us back in the lobby in a couple of hours, because that night we were going to the most famous Cuban nightclub, the Tropicana.

To call the Tropicana a nightclub is a gross understatement. First of all, it's huge and it's outdoors under the stars. It holds over 1,500 patrons. Dinner and drinks are served, but it is the floor show that is the big attraction. There are at least fifty musicians in the orchestra and an even greater number of voluptuous showgirls on stage. There used to be two casinos, but after the revolution all that stopped. Sam Trafficante, the Florida-based mobster in charge, thought he could work a deal with Castro to keep gambling on the island. But Castro said, "Eh, no dice." And then hunted him down and put him in jail.

The Tropicana is the most lavish, tropical, sensual combination of music, dancing, and pulchritude in the world. When you experience the stage show you see exactly where Las Vegas got its start...but it is much more than that. It is also a theater production of Afro-Cuban music and dance. You see and hear exactly how Africa was brought to the New World along with Voodoo and Santeria. It is like a National Dance Theater with sequins and booty shaking. I have never seen anything like it since.

The next morning was a special day because we were to attend the first public screening of *Born in East L.A.* at the Yara Theater, a landmark historical theater (built in 1947) right in the heart of Havana. It was a large theater, holding over 1,600 people, and it was packed to the rafters. We all sat in the very back so we could see the whole audience reaction. There were giant laughs right from the start, even though the movie was subtitled in Spanish. The audience was with the film from the very first frame. At the most dramatic moment, when people are being stuffed into a truck to be smuggled across the border, you could hear sobbing all over the theater. It was something Cubans could personally relate to. I have experienced that same reaction from anyone who has gone through that immigrant experience whether they be Mexican, Cuban, Filipino, Iranian, Chinese, African. It doesn't matter. It is one of the most emotional life experiences for anyone to go through. In one of the closing scenes, where hundreds of people come over a hill and run unstopped into the United States, the audience rose to its feet and gave the film a standing ovation.

I was hustled out of the theater by the officials and into the blinding sun in front of the Yara. People quickly recognized me and reached out to hug me. They were laughing, they were crying. I was being mobbed. It was a total out-of-body experience. I will never forget that moment for as long as I live.

That night we were feted at a joyous party of dinner and dancing featuring Los Van Van, Cuba's most popular salsa group. The party lasted until the sun came up. At 9:00 a.m., we were driven, bleary-eyed, to the airport, to pass through the "Stalin stink eye" routine again. Three or four Russian agents roamed the waiting area with their hands clasped behind them looking over us with X-ray eyes. You were allowed to bring back four boxes of cigars and two quarts of rum, so I made sure everyone in our party had their limit of each. Even the KGB agents couldn't dampen the joy we felt from the week's activities.

We had come during the first week of the festival, so the attendance was relatively sparse compared to the second week, when the Hollywood contingent came with as much hoopla as Cuba could muster. Oliver Stone, Michael Douglas, and many other politically minded stars were given the red carpet treatment with event after event that filled their days with as many films, cigars, and bottles of rum as you could take. I tend to enjoy events that are not so organized so that you are left on your own, which is what happened to us.

I was still buzzing from Havana the whole week after we got back. I regaled all my friends with every detail until their eyes started to glaze over. Eventually I started to settle down…until late Saturday night at about 1:30 in the morning when the phone rang, waking me up from a sound sleep. It was Sonia Levine calling from Havana.

She screamed into the phone, "You won everything, you won everything!"

I could hardly hear her over the loud raucous party going on in the background.

"What, what are you talking about?"

"The Corals! The Corals! You won three!"

I quickly learned that the "Corales" were the trophies that they handed out for the various categories of the festival. They were named that because they were made out of black coral. I had forgotten that we were in the competition. Still yelling into the phone, Sonia informed me that *Born in East L.A.* had won the third-place Coral out of all the films entered in the competition. We also won a first-prize Coral for Art Direction, thanks to the "art broads" Rae Fox and Lynda Burbank.

Most meaningful, at least for me, was that I was awarded a first-prize Coral for best screenplay. If that weren't enough, we were presented with the Glauber Rocha Award, named in honor of Brazil's most famous director, which is presented to the picture voted Best Film by the Foreign Critics at the Festival. Wow! Try sleeping now.

I grabbed my bottle of Havana Club Cuban Rum, lit up a big fat Davidoff Cigar, and poured a toast to the Cine Festival de Havana.

One day during the next week I came home from town to find that I had a phone message on my machine. Absentmindedly I hit play while I was sorting through my mail and heard the following message:

"Hey Cheech, this is Richard Pryor. Hey man, I just saw your film Born in East L.A. *I went in not expecting much and was blown away. You did a great film. You should be proud. Catch you later."*

It doesn't get better than that.

CHAPTER **28**

Tito, Banzai, and Ramone

Now I had a big hit movie and I expected the gates to go flying open.

Universal (under that new leadership) said it loved what I was doing so I sent them my next script called *Born Again*. My character's face appears on a tortilla and all kind of miraculous things happen. I sent it in at the same time that they released Martin Scorsese's *The Last Temptation of Christ*. The movie caused an uproar of negative reaction among the religious community.

The upshot was that my script came flying back like a boomerang. They didn't want to have anything to do with anything even remotely religious. My script was not at all religious, but it didn't matter. They passed on my script, but they sent me a script about a policeman with a dog as a partner. I passed because I didn't want to do anything dog-oriented. Both reasons made about as much sense. I would soon have to eat my words.

As I waited around for something to happen with *Born Again*, I decided that maybe it was the title that was throwing them. I changed it to *Angel of Oxnard*. Still no green light.

Out of the blue, I got a call from my agent that Disney wanted me to audition for the role of Tito, a Chihuahua, in their new animated film, *Oliver and Company*. Jeffrey Katzenberg, the new head of animation at Disney, had been a driving force for *Up in Smoke* at

Paramount. The director was George Scribner, who had been raised in Panama and spoke Spanish.

I arrived at the recording studio and George handed me some pages and the direction that Tito was full of energy. Never having done animation before, I didn't know exactly what tone to set. I read the lines and everybody kind of smiled and thanked me for coming.

I got out into the parking lot and I thought, *That sucked!* I was pissed off at myself for what I thought was a blown opportunity. I couldn't remember the last time I had done an audition.

I marched right back into the studio and went right up to George and said, "I sucked. Can I do it again?"

George smiled and said, "Sure give it a go." Then he said, "Play it like Tito has one finger in an electrical socket."

That was all I needed, and I went for it full bore. Immediately, I could see everybody in the room light up. The writers started throwing out new lines and then writing more.

After half an hour, I couldn't talk, my voice was so worn out. But everybody was laughing and nodding their heads. George said, "We start recording in about a month. See you then!"

For the next year and a half, I recorded the voice of Tito. Every week the writers produced new scenes for Tito and Georgette, the French poodle voiced by Bette Midler. Finally, I had a romance in a movie, even though it was "doggie style."

My part kept growing and growing (get it?) until I was in the whole movie. I came out of every session worn to a frazzle, barely able to speak. When *Oliver and Company* was finally released, it was a huge success and I received glowing reviews. David Ansen wrote in *Newsweek*: "And best of all, Cheech Marin as the lecherous, jive Chihuahua named Tito. 'Check it ooouut!' advises the swaggering Tito, and you should, if only to see this hairless Hispanic mutt enter the Disney cartoon Hall of Fame."

Disney was just beginning an unprecedented string of animated movie triumphs that totally redefined what the art of animation was all about. After *Oliver and Company*, they released *The Little Mermaid, Beauty and the Beast, Aladdin, The Nightmare Before Christmas*, and the biggest one of all, *The Lion King*.

I was honored with a role in *The Lion King*, the part of Banzai, one of the three hyenas, along with Whoopi Goldberg and Jim Cummings. Three years earlier, while riding a ski lift with Jeff Katzenberg in Deer Valley, Utah, he told me, "I'm going to put you in this animated movie. Whoopi Goldberg's gonna do it. I'll let you know."

Three years later I'm in a studio in Burbank. Proud as hell to be there. Chong, so I'm told, turned down the part of the other hyena, because he didn't want to work for Disney and betray his ideals...or some fucking Tommy shit.

To be part of that process was one of the most pleasurable experiences of my life. I had a ringside seat at the construction of a movie classic. The animators would show me various drawings from studies they made drawing me while I was recording.

At first I thought, *OK, this is going to be cute*. But as I saw progressive drawings, I started to change my mind fast. When I saw video footage of how the animation would look, I was blown away. This was a whole new realm. It is extremely hard to make something that everybody loves. Everybody loves *The Lion King*. And for anyone that doesn't, your kids will make you love it, playing after playing after playing.

The promotional tour was once-in-a-lifetime material. The first time I saw the completed movie was in Washington, DC. When the musical number "Hakuna Matata" came on, I turned to Whoopi and asked who was singing.

Whoopi, who knew a lot about the world of Broadway actors, said it was Nathan Lane.

Nathan Lane is a force of nature in this movie. I am thoroughly entertained whenever Timon is on the screen.

I was in geek heaven when they did a rack focus on a safari shot in the plains. *Rack focus* is a camera term for when the focus of the lens is thrown from the foreground to the background...or vice versa. It is a very useful and fairly common technique but I had never seen it in an animated film. It was like some film barrier had been crossed and animators were gaining the respect that they so fully deserved.

The party that night was at the National Zoo. I don't know how they did it but they got the lions to roar pretty much throughout the night. If I was a dude in the jungle and I heard that sound, I would automatically think, *I am going to die.*

The next day we were at Radio City Music Hall in New York City. All my friends in New York came, and their kids went gaga over all the glam at the opening. I really felt that I was involved in something historic.

When we went to Orlando to do a big two-day international press tour, I took my young son Joey with me. We opened the door to our large two-bedroom suite to see three rooms filled with *Lion King* and other Disney merchandise. There were stuffed animals, video games, toys, candy, and everything else that Disney made, filling every corner of the suite. Joey found out that he could order any movie and had twenty-four-hour room service. He turned to me and said, "Dad, this is living."

To this day, there are multiple stage productions of *The Lion King* playing all over the world, and it has been a mainstay attraction on Broadway for many years. I was thrilled to be involved. For the young generations that don't know who I am, all I have to do is say, "We'll eat whatever's 'lioning' around!" and they instantly recognize my voice.

What I came to realize was that animation was what I was trained to do. Cheech and Chong records were animation without the animation.

I also realized that an animated voice has to be bigger than life. You are trying to match a large cartoon character, and a conversational voice will not cut it. You cannot go over the top because there is no top to go over. The bigger, the better.

Around this time, Pixar Animation Studio began to be a huge creative and commercial force with the release of *Toy Story*, directed by John Lasseter. In my opinion, it had by far the best script of 1995.

Eventually, Disney bought Pixar and merged it with Disney Animation Studios, and John Lasseter became the head of both companies. Anyway, I was overjoyed to be asked by John to voice the character Ramone, the 1958 Chevy Impala lowrider, in the megahit *Cars*. "Low and Slow" was his motto. *Cars*, of course, was a gigantic commercial and critical success and threw off more merchandising than any movie ever made. Ramone also appeared in *Cars 2* and *Cars 3*.

Another good memory from this period is from the making of *The Lion King* soundtrack. Whoopi and I went into a studio and said the line "Yeah, we'll be prepared!" in one or two takes. That line was added as background to a song on the soundtrack. We were paid the regular royalty rate. But since the soundtrack sold 15 million copies, that fifteen minutes of work earned me *mucho dinero*.

Animation has been berry, berry good to me.

CHAPTER 29

Ladies and gentlemen, Chet Pussy!!

By the 1990s, the Cheech and Chong legacy had grown enough to be a seminal influence on a new generation of filmmakers who had grown up watching them. Admittedly, they were young when they were watching the films, but time after time I heard the same story. They were turned on to Cheech and Chong films by their parents.

The same can be said for Cheech and Chong records. Whole families used to listen to them on cross-country trips. Big brothers used to let their little squirt brothers and sisters listen to *Big Bambu* while their parents were away. A lot of kids used to change album covers so that the Moody Blues albums contained Cheech and Chong records. Many families told me that they had a secret language based upon knowledge of certain movies.

Tommy and I once met this girl who told us that when her father *got out of prison* he found out that she was listening to our records. So he ran over them with his car in the driveway. He then yelled, "An' you tell 'em, 'Don't try to changes your names cause I'm hep to ya!'"

Well, you can't argue with that.

In a pretty short time, a lot of these kids started making films and records and doing stand-up. They had been listening to our records all along. But it was in film that we were most influential. It didn't matter if they were rappers or country singers or rockers or Latinos or whatever. We appealed to everybody right across the board. It didn't matter if they were stoners or not...but it didn't hurt, either.

What it had to do with was a sense of time. In our humor, time was malleable, it stretched and bended and took its time. The things that came out of it were juvenile and sophisticated at the same time. If we told corny jokes, they were the funniest corny jokes. If we got surreal, we made fun of the surreal. The studios didn't understand us. They just knew that we made money, so for the most part they left us alone. But the influence was there, and it was shared amongst the kids growing up.

About twenty-four years ago, I started hearing about this young filmmaker from Texas named Robert Rodriguez. He had made a feature film with very little money and a borrowed camera. That film, *El Mariachi*, was attracting a lot of attention on the festival circuit. It was a big winner at the Sundance Film Festival in 1993. Hollywood came a-calling.

I met Robert at a screening at the Directors Guild in Hollywood. We introduced ourselves, and he said he was a big fan and had grown up on us. He was dealing with the studios at the time, and they were giving him the same runaround that they give everybody.

The oddest thing about the studios is that no matter how much they want you, they need you, they've got to have you, as soon as you sign, you get thrown into the "swamp of development" where they try to get rid of everything that is unique about you. They constantly try to change you into something that they can understand but, more important, control. Robert was mired in that swamp at the time. I invited him and his wife, Elizabeth, who was his producer, out to my house in Malibu to relax and enjoy the beach.

(Coincidentally, that same night at the screening, I was introduced by my actor-friend Pepe Serna to a young actress he was working with. Not very many times in your life do you meet someone who you can tell right away is going to be a big star. This young woman was one of those people. There was just no doubt about it. The next morning, I told my friend and lawyer Stan Coleman that I had met this girl named Jennifer Lopez and that there was something special about her. It was an understatement, to say the least.)

Robert and Elizabeth came out to the beach and spent the weekend relaxing, eating, and bodysurfing the waves at Matador Beach. We all had a great time, and during the course of the weekend he showed me a short film he had made as a student at the University of Texas. It was called *Bedhead*, and it featured his two sisters and his little brother. Robert comes from a family of ten children, and family is very important to him, a feeling that translates over into those he works with as well. It was a family film that nobody really knows about, especially in the wake of the blood-and-guts features that followed.

Bedhead was hilarious, but what was most unique about it was its visual style. Robert was developing his own style of quick edits and zooming camera shots that really needed no dialogue. You understood the story immediately by the way that he presented it visually.

One of the unique things about Robert as a director is that he operates the camera at all times, so he is looking through the lens at you while talking to you. He's paying that much attention to how it *looks*. If you understand this as an actor, you start to pay attention to where the camera is and how close or far it is from you. You start to come up with things that need no dialogue, but still tell the inner workings of the character. That was how I developed my approach to my character and his toothpick in *Desperado*. The action of the toothpick told exactly how he was feeling; confident, nervous, afraid, sarcastic. I loved the interaction I developed with Robert. It was music to me, and it was exactly how I approached humor and acting.

When he *finally* got *Desperado*, his first feature, off the ground, he cast me in the part of Short Bartender. Typecasting, I guess. During this time, I started a routine with him that I continue to this day. When I knew he was making a new movie, I would call him periodically and ask him, "How's my part coming?" We would both laugh, but I've made seven movies with Robert. You take nothing for granted as an actor. I can't tell you how many times I've been assured that I have a part only to see it slip away. I really appreciate Robert's loyalty to me and all of the ways he has found for us to work together so often.

The making of *Desperado* was action-packed and intense. I was working with a group of fairly unknown but extremely talented actors who were about to become much bigger. Spanish heartthrob Antonio Banderas would become an internationally famous action star. Unknown Mexican *telenovela* actress Salma Hayek would burst onto the screen and become a worldwide object of desire. Steve Buscemi would go on to star in the big HBO hit *Boardwalk Empire*. Danny Trejo would be introduced as the ultimate bad guy whose face, body, and tattoos said it all. Quentin Tarantino was an up-and-coming director who had just made his first feature, *Reservoir Dogs*. He and Rodriguez had become buddies on the festival circuit, and Quentin would write the next feature that Robert would direct, *From Dusk Till Dawn*.

One afternoon, Robert called me and said that he was sending over the script for his new movie and to let him know what I thought. The script, by Tarantino, arrived and I settled in to read it. It was to star TV actor George Clooney in his feature film debut. George had a long TV résumé and had turned out more pilots than the Air Force Academy. Now he was starring in the mega-hit network drama *ER*, but oddly enough he had never starred in a movie.

The reading was going along just fine. It was a kidnap/escape story involving Harvey Keitel and Juliette Lewis as the victims and George Clooney and Quentin Tarantino as the bad guys. They were on the lam and decide to pull into a Mexican dive bar in the middle of the desert. Everything looks cool until everyone in the bar turns into vampires.

It was in the middle of the script around page fifty. I flipped back a couple of pages to see if I missed anything, but no, out of the blue... everybody turns into vampires. OK, whatever. I thought, *Either this is going to be a big cult movie or it's going to throw a big pail of cold water on everyone's career.* So buckle up and let's go.

A couple of days later Robert called again and said that they were having a reading of the script, and would I come in and read the part of Chet Pussy.

Hmmm, sounds Shakespearean.

So I show up and there's Robert, Quentin, and Harvey Keitel, and only a few more people at a very long table. Right away Rodriguez says that some people couldn't make the reading, and would I mind reading two other parts as well?

Sure, no problem.

I was having a ball switching accents and attitudes between the characters, but when I got to Chet Pussy, the dam burst. Chet was the barker outside the Titty Twister, the bar where all the action was to take place. He was a character I had seen live and in person every time I went down to Tijuana. He, or somebody like him, was at every bar along the strip in TJ. I could do this guy in my sleep, and so I went for it.

Robert and Quentin were laughing out loud but dramatic tough guy Harvey was laughing the most. I read two other characters that I really didn't pay too much attention to, then thanked everybody and split. By the time I got home, there was a message on my answering machine from Robert saying that he and Quentin wanted me to do all three parts.

Cool. Do I get paid three times?

When we finally got on the set, the first scene was the explosion of the bar that occurs at the end of the movie. So there we were in the middle of a dry lake bed out near Barstow. They had constructed an elaborate, three-story façade of the Titty Twister complete with flashing neon and twirling pasties. On "Action," we were all supposed to run for our lives out of the bar and then go to a certain mark and turn around to watch the bar explode. Robert had a crew with a big fire hose stationed just out of shot ready to douse the flames.

Robert called "Action," and we all ran out of the bar and hit our marks and turned around. As soon as we did, *boom*, there was this big explosion, and the front of the bar burst into flames.

"Cut, cut, cut!" yelled Robert. "OK, turn on the hoses."

The hoses got turned on and shot out a mighty stream of water that landed about ten feet short of the flames. Much shouting went on back and forth until everybody realized that the water would never reach the flames. A good half of the set got completely burned until somehow, using any means they had, including throwing dirt on the flames, they got the fire out.

Nice first shot.

We were all wandering around in the desert where the temperature had now climbed to over a hundred degrees, wondering what to do next. Suddenly, way off in the distance we saw a swirling dust cloud forming at the distant shore of the dry lake. Everybody was oddly fascinated until we realized that the cloud was building in size and speed... and was heading straight at us.

I wouldn't say that everybody panicked, but whatever you call the thing just below it, that was what they did. The camera crew did the quickest thinking as they grabbed their million-dollar cameras and ran for the nearest airtight shelter and wrapped their equipment in blankets. The dust storm was on us before we knew it, and the whole crew dove for cover wherever they could. It was like being stung by needles for five minutes. When the storm passed, Robert called for a time-out until they could figure out what to do next. What they figured out was that we would stop shooting for the day and start shooting again as soon as it was dark. I would take a movie crew into battle anytime, anywhere.

At this point, I was ready for anything, so it made sense that the first shot up was Chet Pussy in front of the Titty Twister yelling:

"Pussy, pussy, pussy! We have every kind of pussy! White pussy, black pussy, brown pussy, red pussy. Wet pussy, slippery pussy, apple pie pussy!"

That scene has become one of the most quoted of any I have ever done.

Needless to say, I had a lot of fun on that movie. I got to hang out with George Clooney, who turned out to be the coolest, most fun-loving guy... and was a big Cheech and Chong fan.

I would have paid to watch Salma Hayek dance seminaked with a big albino python around her neck. Instead I was being paid to watch her. I don't know how that many curves can fit into that petite a woman. I could have sold my seat at the end of the runway a thousand times over.

I spent a lot of time with Tito Larriva, who did much of the music. Tito was a mainstay of the LA punk scene, and he gave the picture an edgy sound that set it apart from anything else that was out there.

From Dusk Till Dawn was released and became a big hit, and it has remained a cult classic to this day. What really emerged after this movie and on into Robert's next movies was his use of a heavily Latino cast without calling specific attention to it. He cast these movies as they would occur in the everyday world of his native Texas. He really reflected the world as he saw it. Mexicans, Mexican-Americans, Chicanos, and Latinos were not *excluded* from his movies; they were specifically *included* because they represented reality. It was a major breakthrough in the film world.

It was the same mind-set we used in the Cheech and Chong films. From my point of view, *we* represented regular hippie street culture, and everybody agreed by making them huge hits. We put that mind-set out there, and many young filmmakers agreed by doing the same thing in their movies.

I kept on working with Robert Rodriguez and always had the best time, although I noticed a trend and pointed it out to him. I got killed in every one of his movies, as did a lot of other people. I started telling him, "Robert, you know when you kill me, your movie's over. So you might want to kill me later."

He would nod and laugh and then kill me again in his next movie.

At least the star power of the killer got raised when he had Johnny Depp kill me in *Once Upon a Time in Mexico*. It was a real treat working and hanging with Johnny Depp, who is the nicest and most gentlemanly actor I've ever worked with.

Finally, Robert listened to my advice when he cast me in *Machete* as Padre, the priest and brother of Machete.

Machete had the most bizarre path to the silver screen. It started out as a faux trailer that was inserted between two movies in *Grindhouse*, a collaboration between Robert Rodriguez and Quentin Tarantino...and then it went away.

But it didn't go away. It started picking up chatter on the Internet, and people wanted to see the movie and...what's up? It finally picked up enough steam and they made the movie.

I LOVE *Machete*. It horrifies me and cracks me up at the same time. Danny Trejo is given a shot as a romantic lead and he puts his head down and runs with it. It has convulsive energy.

So finally Robert killed me later (a crucifixion, as I recall). Nice touch...and he told me that he had discovered something. He said he learned the strength of introducing a new character halfway through a movie. Cool, Robert. How's my new part coming?

But if I had to pick my favorite Robert Rodriguez movie, it would have to be *Spy Kids*. It was *Bedhead* with a budget. That same rhythm, that same kid's point of view, that same sense of fun and silliness that he showed me out in Malibu had matured to major-league level. He hit that one out of the park. It has such great heart and true emotions. It was bravura filmmaking by Robert and has become a classic. It was a real pleasure to play Uncle Felix ("I'm not your uncle!") and to be in all the *Spy Kids* movies.

CHAPTER 30

Louie, Alex, and me

I was working on the set of *The Golden Palace* (more on that later) when I got word that they were doing the first-ever *Celebrity Jeopardy!* I immediately called my agent and said, "Get me on that show or you're fired."

It seemed like I had been preparing for this moment my whole life. Weird huh? Not really for me, because I had been playing some form of *Jeopardy!* with my cousins forever. We were anomalies. We were blue-collar, working-class, second-generation Chicano kids, who made themselves academics. My cousin, Louis Robles, was our leader.

Louie was the most brilliant kid I ever knew. He got a scholarship to every school he ever went to, from grammar school to the University of Tokyo. He was also very funny (I got my sense of humor from him), good-looking, and athletic. Louie was also a fantastic storyteller, which became his blessing and his curse. When we were little he used to make up scary stories to tell us at night, but only if we listened to them outside the covers of our beds. When we started whining, he would stop telling the story until we crawled out from under the covers and begged him to continue. He knew that being able to look us in the eye would heighten the scariness of the stories. He was also borderline sadistic.

The other members of the group were my cousin Rosalie (Louie's sister) and my other cousin Ray Gene Castro. We were all bright kids

212

that did well academically in Catholic school. Ray Gene, in fact, went on to become the first PhD in Chicano studies from Harvard University. I was always the runt of the litter, running as fast as I could to catch up.

The one TV program we got into watching early was the *GE College Bowl*, hosted by Allen Ludden. Whenever we could, we all watched it together, trying to be the one who got the most correct answers even though the questions were aimed at college kids and we were only ten or twelve. Of course, Louie always won. He was the oldest and had read more, but he was also the most naturally curious. He was our ringleader and set up his own version of the College Bowl for us. At various times, I represented Bryn Mawr, the Citadel, and even Gallaudet, a school for the deaf, where I had to write all my answers.

All of us were enrolled in Catholic school at this time. Now, some people love Catholic school and some people hate it. I was among the lovers. It was a great liberal arts education plus religion, which meant they could beat the shit out of you, which they did, a lot in my case. But between Catholic discipline and Louie's game playing, I developed what every student needs: the love of learning. Once you acquire it, every subject becomes interesting.

Granted, some subjects are easier or more interesting than others. For me, history was the engine that drove all other subjects. It provided a time line around which you could organize everything else. If you knew that the Magna Carta was signed in 1215, you could go forward or backward and place historical or literary or religious or scientific events in a relative chronology. Which came first: the Battle of Hastings (1066) or the War of the Roses (1455 to 1485)? What year did Martin Luther nail his ninety-five theses to the door of the Wittenberg Castle church (1517)? This history-based approach to learning gave me a strong foundation for that fateful day when I would walk onto the set of *Jeopardy!*

The other thing that *really* prepared me for *Jeopardy!* was the ability to answer fast. This is not a trait that comes easily or naturally. In my case, it was literally drilled into me by my cousin. Louie, being the brightest, always knew all the answers and got tired of waiting for us to finish thinking and come up with the correct answer. So his fix was to give us five seconds to answer, and if we didn't, he got to sock us in the arm. Remember, I said he was borderline sadistic. Get about four or five slow answers and it tends to speed up your thinking process.

Jeopardy! is a unique game in that you not only have to know the answer to the question, you have to know it first. When Alex (I just call him Al) Trebek is asking the question (actually, he just states information and your *reply* has to be in the form of a question), you pretty much have to know the answer halfway through his recitation. As soon as he finishes speaking, lights flash on both sides of the board, and only then can you hit your buzzer. If you buzz in too early, your buzzer shuts off for a second and a half...and too bad for you.

I play under the assumption that all the contestants know at least 90 percent of the answers, so the one who gets in first has the advantage. This is where a Catholic liberal arts education really comes in handy. It teaches you a lot about a lot of things. The saying goes that it teaches you "something about everything and everything about something." That "something" is religion. That subject goes really fast, because there are no questions. God tells them, they tell you. End of story.

It worked out well for me, because the history of Western civilization is to a great degree the history of the Catholic church. Up until almost the seventeenth century, all art was liturgical art. The only subject the Church lagged behind in was science, because for centuries it clung to the flat-earth model. A very funny comedian, Biff Rose, once said that "a Catholic education prepares you for anything that can possibly happen here in the twelfth century." True or not, it did set me up pretty nicely to be a contestant on *Jeopardy!*

There are two main theories about how to prepare for *Jeopardy!* One theory says to study everything you can. State capitals, presidents, Shakespeare's plays, dates of great inventions, wars, etc., etc. That is the long way around. The other theory says to study nothing, because a high percentage of the categories are things that you can't study for, like "Words with Three R's" or "Smells Like Teen Spirit" or that hoary chestnut, "Potpourri"... which could be anything. You just have to have a solid liberal arts education.

The other really interesting thing about *Jeopardy!* is that you do not have to necessarily know everything about the subject in question, but you have to know a little something about it. For instance, you do not have to have read *Huckleberry Finn*, but you must know that Mark Twain wrote it. But the more you know, the more it helps, in case Alex says, "Samuel Langhorne Clemens." (What was Mark Twain's real name?) You do not have to explain the Theory of Relativity, but you have to know that Albert Einstein conceived it.

I always counsel freshman college students who don't know what to major in to take a liberal arts approach because it will give them a well-rounded education, and somewhere along the path they will probably find something that will spark their interest and they can major in that. At the very least, it will teach them how to read and write and communicate to a much higher degree, even if they are writing with two thumbs on an iPhone. I can't tell you how many times people have been astounded that I know some bit of arcane trivia and they ask, "How did you know that?" I always answer, "I was awake when they taught it."

Which brings me to my next theory: All colleges teach the same basic information. Granted, I would much rather, as a door opener, have a bachelor's degree from Harvard than from some online university. But most of my heroes did not go to Harvard. They probably went to some lesser state university, if they went to college at all. But they were awake in class. And they had a love of learning.

So the first time I was on *Jeopardy!* I took the long way around. I tried to study everything. The only thing that frightened me was deciding where to start. Do you start at *A* for Aardvark or *K* for Knowledge? Fortunately, there is a primer put out by *Jeopardy!* that contains all the basic categories and information, but as I said, that only covers about half the categories. What I really needed was a technique for how to get faster.

I started studying with my cousin Louie. For a week, we crammed as many facts into my brain as we could without getting a cerebral hemorrhage. As I said, this is the long way around, but it was the only way I knew at the time. A very interesting dynamic started to emerge during these sessions.

All my life Louie had been my guru, my mentor, and the person I looked up to the most. But as we grew older, I began to enjoy some success and my cousin seemed to lag behind. I didn't notice it at first, because I was always on the road touring, but at family gatherings it became noticeable that Louie had a drinking problem. Eventually his life and family started to unravel. His marriage came apart, and he couldn't hold a steady job.

There was no way I could help him because he would not accept any help, especially from me. It was one of the great tragedies of my life to watch my idol crumble. As anyone who has ever dealt with alcoholism knows, the story line is never a straight road. There are many very deep lows and, if you're lucky, some highs at the end if you can beat the demon. Eventually, Louie gained sobriety, but the toll that the struggle exacted on his health led to his premature death.

As we started to study together, in our forties now, I noticed that our relationship had reversed itself, and now Louie was looking for my approval. He seemed to be delighted and amazed that his early training lessons had borne fruit. I even threatened to sock him in the arm if he didn't answer faster. He gave me a sad, painful smile but a smile nonetheless. He had long envisioned himself in the spot I was now in.

As the day for the taping arrived, we studied right up to the time we drove into the parking lot of the studio where the show was shot. I remember we were studying something about the states and their dates of admission to the Union.

Competing on *Jeopardy!* was the most nervous I'd ever been in show business. You can look like a real jackass if you give a stupid answer to a simple question. It's not like if you fuck up a joke in your live show and three drunks don't laugh. Millions and millions of people watch *Jeopardy!* and then millions more when they show the reruns.

I had been thinking of how I could possibly get an edge over my competitors, and then I remembered something one of my track coaches had shown me in high school. When he was timing runners, he used his index finger on his stopwatch instead of his thumb. "The reaction time is a little bit quicker," he said. *How much of a difference could it possibly make?* I thought to myself. I was about to find out.

The format was basic *Jeopardy!* Actors Alan Rachins and Steven Weber were my fellow contestants. I was competing against them as well as the other celebrities on the show all week. Whoever earned the most money won the title.

I started off the show great. I answered a couple of questions in a row and thought, *Hey, this is going to be a snap!*

Then I missed a couple of questions in a row, including a Daily Double, and just like that I was in the hole.

I started to feel a sense of dread, like looking down an elevator shaft. *Oh my God, after all these years of study and dedication and now I'm in the hole.* I took a deep breath, gathered myself, and started to come back.

At the end of the first round, I held a small lead. In Double Jeopardy, I started to pull away from the other two contestants, but it was not a runaway and they could possibly catch me on Final Jeopardy. The last question came up on the board, and we were asked to name the state that was admitted to the Union on Halloween in 18-something. I had just studied that stuff. I knew the answer was Arizona. I bet just enough to win although caution wasn't necessary, as I was the only one to get it right and become the first ever *Celebrity Jeopardy!* champion.

As the show ended and my family and everybody swarmed around to congratulate me, I looked over and saw Louie standing at the edge of the crowd. The look on his face was a cross between immense pride and bitter disappointment. I worked my way over to him and wrapped my arms around him in a big hug and said, "Thanks for getting me here." He didn't say anything and just nodded.

Before he could get a word out, two writers from the show came up to me and asked, "Are you a musician?"

"As a matter of fact I am. I've played guitar since I was eleven years old."

"We thought so."

"Why did you think that?"

"Because of your timing. You were right on the beat as soon as the lights went on. We also noticed that you used your index finger on the buzzer. Very few people know about that. Congratulations."

I had a lot of fun on *Jeopardy!* And there's a big lesson there. When someone is trying to teach you something, stay awake.

Winning *Jeopardy!* was a big deal to me. If I win an Oscar, it will not quite compare. It was something I had been doing all my life. It was satisfying, and I was glad to have Louie by my side for it.

A few years later, I participated in the first ever *Jeopardy! Million Dollar Celebrity Invitational.* There were three rounds but you had to win to advance. The winner got $1 million for his charity, second got $250,000, and third got $150,000.

In one of the early rounds, I faced Anderson Cooper and Aisha

Tyler. Anderson, a Yale graduate by the way, got way behind and lost the first game. Backstage, he walked around in shock. He'd won *Celebrity Jeopardy!* before. He couldn't believe what had happened. He came back out and played better for the second game but was too far behind. I advanced.

To his credit, he reported on his show that he'd been beaten by Cheech Marin, this stoner. He was very gracious about it, though I know he didn't like getting beat. Who does?

The same thing happened to me in the final against Jane Curtin and Michael McKean. I got way behind in the first game. Way behind. I won the second game, but it wasn't enough. I ended up third. McKean was a good player and had a great day. Hey, sometimes you get beat.

Over the years, I've become part of the *Jeopardy!* family. They come to me when they need a favor. One of the favors is to stay at home during *Celebrity Jeopardy!* week in case somebody doesn't show. But they pay me for my time, and I've taken a few $10,000 naps.

Much like animation, *Jeopardy!* been berry, berry good to me.

CHAPTER 31

Tin Cup

In any long career, I don't care if you're the Beatles, Elvis, or Frank Sinatra, there are going to be times when nothing is happening and you must reinvent yourself. It usually involves doing the opposite of what you have been doing.

After *Born in East L.A.*, I thought that my solo career as a writer-director would take off. I was ready to become the Chicano Woody Allen. For a variety of different reasons, that didn't happen and I experienced what every director faces: You start at square one with every project.

I got involved with several projects that took up a lot of time and energy and eventually wound up in a dead end. After enduring a lot of frustration, I accepted an acting job working on *The Golden Palace*, which was the *The Golden Girls* after Bea Arthur left. *The Golden Girls* was a giant middle-of-the-road commercial hit. I was happy to get the job that involved working with Betty White, one of my all-time favorites.

Betty White was the first person I remember seeing on TV when she was the dimple-cheeked teenaged cohostess of a daytime dance party show called *Al Jarvis' Make-Believe Ballroom*. It was a local LA TV show, and Betty was fresh out of high school. Even at the age of seven, I noticed one thing about Betty right away. She had the nicest-looking rack on television and always wore tight sweaters. When I

220

told her that, she smiled and batted her eyes, and with zero sincerity said, "Oh, they made me wear those."

Betty White is the mother of God as far as I am concerned.

The show was set in Miami and took place in a hotel that the "girls" (Betty White, Estelle Getty, and Rue McClanahan) had purchased and were running. The rest of the cast was Don Cheadle as the manager and yours truly as the cook. Don and I thought of ourselves as the "Afro-Cuban" rhythm section for the Lawrence Welk Band. The show lasted for one season, and then everyone went on their merry way.

There followed a very stagnant period in which I hustled as hard as I could but nothing seemed to come together.

Then one day, out of the blue, I got a call from Robert Rodriguez and started working on *Desperado*, as I've written about earlier.

Shortly after that, I got cast in *The Great White Hype*, directed by Reggie Hudlin and, more significant, written by Ron Shelton, who had written and directed *Bull Durham* with Kevin Costner. He also wrote and directed *White Men Can't Jump*, which was a big hit starring Wesley Snipes and Woody Harrelson.

I got called in to read for Ron for the part of Romeo in his new golf film called *Tin Cup*. I was the first actor he read for the role, and I gave it my all. Then they proceeded to read every Latino actor in Hollywood. I didn't hear from them for months. I would run into my fellow Latino actors around town and they all had been assured that they had the role locked up. Remember what I said about being an actor: You can take nothing for granted.

Finally, I got called back in to read with Kevin Costner and Ron. We read the script and acted out a lot of improvs. They seemed to be pleased, and I went home and waited.

In the meantime, I started working on *The Great White Hype*, a boxing movie that starred Samuel L. Jackson, Peter Berg, and Damon Wayans. It also featured Jamie Foxx and Jon Lovitz. I had a lot of fun hanging with everybody. One day I was talking with Samuel, who has remained a friend to this day. I told him I was waiting to hear from Ron Shelton about *Tin Cup*. Sam turned to me and very casually said, "Don't worry, you'll get it."

How did he know? Had he heard something?

The next day, I got a call from my agent who said I was to report to Tucson, Arizona, to start work on *Tin Cup* in a few days. I jumped out of my shoes, and I knew that this was my big shot.

Finally, I was costarring in a big budget studio film with a big fat movie star (Costner) and an A-list director in Ron Shelton. Of all the directors I've worked with, Ron is the most "Captain of the Ship" type of leader, and you feel safe and on course under his guidance. The rest of the cast was rounded out with the incredibly beautiful, internationally known model turned actress Rene Russo, and Linda Hart, a very talented veteran of stage and screen and a former member of the Harlettes, Bette Midler's backup singers. There was one part that was still left to cast, and that was the male antagonist to play across from Kevin.

Every day there were different rumors as to who it was going to be. One day it was Dennis Quaid. The next day it was Kurt Russell, and then finally we got the word that it was going to be Don Johnson.

I thought, *Hey, I know him.*

Don and I had met years earlier in our young careers. I was already known from Cheech and Chong, and Don had made a couple of independent movies, the most prominent being *A Boy and His Dog*, which I recommend everybody see. We were introduced by a group of girls that we both knew, including Pam Kath, whom I was dating. Don, right from the start, was very genial, had a great sense of humor, and exuded confidence. He was bound for glory. Very often we found each other at the same clubs at 2:00 a.m. looking for the same girls.

Years go by and I don't see him for a while. Then, out of the blue, he gets cast in *Miami Vice* and the rest is history. *Miami Vice* becomes a worldwide phenomenon and Donny becomes the most famous guy on the planet. His face is on every magazine cover in the world and Miami becomes a global destination because of his show.

It must have been like being in the Beatles with just one guy. The show set trends in fashion, music, how TV shows are shot, and anything else you want to name. You couldn't get more famous than Don Johnson on *Miami Vice*. You have to remember that TV is almost ten times bigger than movies as a medium, and *Miami Vice* was in over two hundred markets worldwide, all centered on Little Donnie Johnson from Flat Creek, Missouri.

After the show ended, he traded on his success in a lot of ways and made some movies, but nothing that compared to the fame he reached with *Miami Vice*. Don had always been vigilant, and he was looking around for a way to reintroduce himself. *Tin Cup* was perfect.

We all had the best time making *Tin Cup*, from beginning to end. I left the set on the last day with the whole crew chanting, "Cheech! Cheech! Cheech!"

This was where my love affair with golf started. The whole movie was shot on golf courses...and in strip bars. So I meeean...

Still, make no mistake. Making movies is a hard physical and mental test for long periods of time. You can lose your shit at any time during the process. The Pros don't. I consider myself a Pro.

Don arrived on the set, and we both gave each other a big hug and remembered the old days. The first scene we shot in the movie was the scene where Don drives up to Costner's trailer. He looks around at the dilapidated conditions and the plastic children's wading pool and says, "Is this your swimming pool, Roy?"

To which I ad-libbed, "No, it's a spa."

I could hear the crew trying to hold back their laughter. Shelton called "Cut" and everybody cracked up. From that point on we were off and running.

Lunch was called shortly thereafter, and everybody (except me) disappeared into their gigantic trailers. Right before lunch ended, Don emerged from his trailer with a script in his hand and walked right over to me. He handed me the script and said, "As soon as this movie ends, I'm starting a new television series for CBS called *Nash Bridges*. It's a cop show, and I want you to play my partner. It's written for an Irish guy named Donegan and he dies in the first episode but don't worry, we'll take care of that. I've just talked to all my producing partners and everybody is on board. You don't have to answer right away, tomorrow would be fine, but we have a twelve-episode commitment and we shoot in San Francisco. We'll have fun."

I didn't know what to say, so I called my agent. He didn't know what to say, either, because he wasn't getting a commission on this deal. The way it works is that if the agency, CAA in this instance, represented the producers, which they did, then they would get a package deal commission, so they couldn't double-dip and take a commission from the actors that they represented. I decided to take the offer and crossed my fingers.

Meanwhile back at the *Tin Cup* set, I was having the time of my life. My young son Joey, ten years old at the time, came out and stayed with me for a week and learned how to play golf. It is something we have enjoyed together ever since. Joey went on to become his Malibu High School team's most valuable player his senior year as well as a first-team All-League member.

I worked as hard as I could every day, because I was still insecure about my position on the movie. One night, I was waiting out in front of the hotel with Ron Shelton for a car to take us to dinner. He asked me how I was doing, and I said I just wanted to get two weeks' worth of film in the can so it would be harder to fire me. He looked at me with a strange smile on his face and said, "This is your movie. Go for it."

It was like he lit a fuse under me, and off I went.

Every day our Australian cinematographer, Russell Boyd, said to be sure to thank him when I receive my Oscar. I didn't get nominated, but I did get nominated for the American Comedy Awards as best supporting actor.

It was a golden opportunity to display my comedy and dramatic chops in the same movie. *Tin Cup* has gone on to be a classic, and is a favorite golf movie for golfers all over the world. I'm still very, very proud of that movie.

Finally, I had to say good-bye to Houston, where we went after Tucson, and say hello to San Francisco.

CHAPTER 32

Nash Bridges

If there is a city you have to own, San Francisco should be the one. It is one of the loveliest cities in the world. It has the Golden Gate Bridge and Golden Gate Park, and is as culturally diverse as any city in the country. San Francisco has been the incubator for most of the important cultural trends to come out of this country in the last hundred years. From the bohemians to the beatniks to the hippies, they all had their genesis in the City by the Bay. The dot-com culture and Silicon Valley started here and then took over. The organic food culture started here. The worldwide dominance of California wine started in nearby Napa.

And who can forget that the best weed is grown here in Northern California. Nice place to land.

I didn't know what to expect when I went to the set the first night. I learned very quickly that Don Johnson was completely in charge. We sat in Don's trailer schmoozing for a little while until they called us to set.

Don grabbed his drink and said, "OK. Time to show them how it goes."

I thought to myself, *What have I gotten into? Is this going to be a case of the star run amok?*

Don started talking to the director and the cinematographer and to the other department heads that were gathered around. Right away,

I realized that he knew what he was talking about. He knew as much about lighting as any cameraman I'd ever worked with. He was clearly versed in the subtleties of camera motion. We would make innovative camera moves all during our run. I shut my mouth, watched, and quickly saw that if this show was to succeed I could best serve it by having Donnie's back at all times.

When you start a show, you are usually trying to make a name for yourself. So you do everything you can for *you* to succeed. Don and I both already had names, so the most important thing for us was for *the show* to succeed. Neither of us ever tried to one-up or steal the spotlight from the other. In six years of working twelve to sixteen hours a day side by side, ten months a year, there was *never* a cross word between us...and believe me, Donnie could fly off the handle at people he thought were not doing their jobs.

Don could organize a city and a production like nobody I have ever seen. A year before we even started shooting, he had spent time with the mayor, Willie Brown, and made him part of our crew. Mayor Brown in turn introduced him to the fire and police chiefs and any other politico who could assist the production of the show. It was *essential* that we had the cooperation of a city where we would block off streets and tie up traffic for hours at a time. Sometimes we would film all night in upscale neighborhoods and be shooting machine guns at three in the morning. You need everyone's good will to pull that off.

Don also made friends of the high society set in the city, which was a very established milieu in San Francisco. People like the Gettys, author Danielle Steele, and socialite Denise Hale made introductions to countless important people in the city. All of these connections smoothed the way for the production of the show.

One day, Don came to work and said that last night at the opera he met the woman he was going to marry. Kelley Phleger was the daughter of one of the most prominent lawyers in the Bay area. His firm had put together some of the deals that got many tech companies in Silicon Valley up and running. A little over a year later, the beautiful Miss Phleger became the gorgeous Mrs. Johnson, and they now have three wonderful children.

Nash Bridges was network TV at its highest end. As a matter of fact, we became the most expensive hour-long show on TV at over $2 million an episode...and every bit of it was up on the screen. We had car chases and shoot-outs a-go-go. There was only one fly in the ointment for me. I could sign up for only three episodes at a time.

Technically, I was still under contract for a half-hour pilot I had shot earlier. For six months, I had to go to them to get permission to do any other TV work, even though the show didn't get picked up. They let me out to do three episodes of *Nash Bridges* and then I had to go back to them to do three more. At that point, they came up with the bright idea that since I was getting *so hot* they would rewrite the pilot they had passed on. I was now obligated to do six episodes of this new show.

Yikes! I didn't think so.

This new script had nothing to do with the original story I had signed up to do. Their argument was that this was just another episode of that original idea.

"I don't think so!"

"Fuck you!"

"Fuck you back!"

"See you in court."

So it was me, on my own dime, against the studio. Everybody wished me luck, but nobody stepped up to pay my legal fees. Finally, after several weeks, the case went to court...and I won.

Now, not only did I not have to do a show I didn't want to do, but I was now five episodes into a show that I was clearly costarring in... without a contract.

It will never happen in my life again. I had the network over a barrel. I told my lawyer, Stan Coleman, to tell them that "I am not greedy. And I am not stupid." I wanted to land somewhere in the middle.

In the end it was agreed that I could renegotiate my contract every year. Unheard-of for a network show. Generally, you sign a contract that binds you to a show for five to seven years with a small set increase every year. Which is total bullshit, because if you become an overnight star, the first thing you do is renegotiate. When it came time for the first renegotiation, they were happy to do so, because they viewed me as a very stable element in the show and they had an investment to protect.

Life is fucking lovely sometimes.

For the next six years, life was a joy. My family moved up from LA, and by another piece of luck we landed an incredible house right in the Seacliff neighborhood. It was right across the street from Robin Williams and down the block from Sharon Stone. From our back porch, which overlooked a cliff, you could hit the Golden Gate Bridge with a nine iron. We were right in between Baker Beach and China Beach. I learned that the narrow channel of water that connects the Pacific Ocean to the San Francisco Bay is called the Golden Gate, hence the name of the bridge. Our house was located right in the middle of the channel. If you wanted to take a postcard photo of the bridge, you would place the camera on my back porch. My two children were in good schools, and my wife, Patti, could do her art (she is a painter), and we started to gather a nice group of friends. I worked all day, every day.

I have never learned so much in one place as I learned on *Nash Bridges*. Through Don, I learned a ton about camera and lighting. I learned about developing a character day after day. I learned about working in an ensemble so that it became a band that played beautiful music together.

We had a great cast that included Don and me and Jodi Lyn

O'Keefe, Jeff Perry, Jaime Gomez, Annette O'Toole, James Gammon, Yasmine Bleeth, and my Swedish wife Inger, played by the talented Caroline Lagerfelt.

Right out of the box, we were a hit, and in the modern television landscape that is what you have to do. New shows no longer have the opportunity to grow and develop. You either grab an audience right away or you are gone.

Luckily, people wanted to see what we were doing. *Nash Bridges* was a very stylish show visually, from the wardrobe to the cars (we had four different Barracudas) to the incredible location we shot in every day. San Francisco never looked as good as it did week after week on *Nash Bridges*.

The thing that really set us apart from other shows in our genre was the camera style. We used a Steadicam all the time. We found new and innovative ways to use it. The best innovation of the show was the Steadicam on the back of a camera truck. The cameraman, Julian Chojnacki or Tommy Lohmann, would ride on the open tailgate or on a camera truck with a small crane which could swoop down to either side of the car. Don would then drive into the shot and then stay in the frame for the entire scene. This is *very hard* to do because he was not being towed. Don was driving live and he did it every time and only hit the truck once in six years. This method of filming was unique in series TV and set us apart in our own category.

When you are working on an hour-long TV show, it's really all that you do. You wake up in the morning and go to the set early and work for the next twelve to sixteen hours. The next day you start where you left off the previous day. Every day the call time gets later and the wrap time gets later, so that by the end of the week you are starting in the late afternoon and you are shooting all night. You do this for ten months straight, and by the end you are walking around like a zombie. The first month of vacation you do nothing but sleep. My family always returned to Malibu and enjoyed the summer weather.

Summers in San Francisco can be very cold. As somebody once said, "The coldest winter I ever spent was a summer in San Francisco."

Sometimes the season's work schedule would fall into a routine and other times it would be very chaotic. Don and I developed a tradition before the start of every season, before the production would overtake our lives. We would drive down to Pebble Beach on a Friday morning and play at the Pebble Beach Golf Links as soon as we got there. It was usually getting dark as we finished, so we would enjoy a nice dinner with friends and hit the hay. The next morning we would get up early and play Spyglass. After that we would enjoy a nice leisurely lunch, then play Cypress Point Club in the afternoon. Party a "little" at night, then the next morning play Pebble Beach again, then drive back home to beautiful San Francisco. Life was superb.

Every day I was in San Francisco, I felt like I was on vacation.

Some years, opportunities popped up that I was lucky to take advantage of. One year I was asked to be in the movie *Paulie* about a parrot that gets lost and tries to find his way back to the little girl that owns him. It was an underrated film when it was released, but over the years it has found its way into the hearts of children and adults everywhere. There is great love out there for *Paulie* and people tell me that everywhere I go. I only had to leave *Nash Bridges* for three days, but it was very much worth it.

CHAPTER 33

The Late Henry Moss

The late James Gammon, the actor who played Don's father on *Nash Bridges*, came to me on the set one day in 2000 with a script in his hand.

"I'm doing this play here in San Francisco and there's a great part for you if you want it."

"Tell me more," I said.

"Well the play is called *The Late Henry Moss*, and it's by Sam Shepard. He's doing it here in San Francisco where he did a lot of his early plays for the Magic Theatre. He's directing it and the cast is going to be me and Nick Nolte, Sean Penn, Woody Harrelson, Sheila Tousey, and you...if you want. T-Bone Burnett is going to do the music."

Sam Shepard is one of America's foremost playwrights. He's a winner of the Pulitzer Prize and eleven Obie Awards and has written some of the most iconic contemporary American plays like *True West*, *Buried Child*, and *Fool for Love*. He is also an actor and all my female friends think he's "dishy." He has starred as a leading man in many movies.

The script that Jimmy Gammon handed me had a handwritten message on the front: "Cheech, Here is a draft of where I'm at right now. Give it a read and I hope you join us, Sam."

How could you turn that down? It would mean that I would work all day on *Nash Bridges* and then do the play at night. We would rehearse for four weeks and then perform for six weeks. I didn't know what I was getting into, but I would live to tell.

The first day of rehearsal was before the whole cast and crew. Everybody from every department was there. We were all milling around and having coffee and getting to know each other. Nick Nolte walked in on crutches. He said he had injured his Achilles tendon on a weight machine. The weight machine and Nick Nolte did not seem to go together, but whatever. Nick was dressed in his usual hospital scrubs and a long, duster kind of coat. He had a fedora hat on with a rolled-up scarf around the band. He was carrying a large satchel.

Nick and I had known each other for more than a few years because we both lived in Malibu at the same time. His son Brawley and my son Joey played baseball together.

Originally, I moved from Hollywood to Malibu to get away from bad influences and helicopters. I moved to the farthest part of Malibu and who do I run into at the Trancas Bar but Nick Nolte, Gary Busey, and Jan-Michael Vincent. They were out there doing experiments. It was like going from the frying pan into the blast furnace. I tiptoed around the excess like I always do and still remained friends with all of them. So Nick and I knew each other.

Nick starts talking about how he's on this health kick and he's taking all these vitamins and so forth. While he's explaining, he reaches into his bag and pulls out a syringe and a vial.

"And you gotta put a little of this in," and he holds up the vial and extracts some of whatever is in there.

"And away you go."

With that he lets down the back of his scrubs and injects himself in the butt. Everybody's watching like *OK!*

"But the latest thing is this Human Growth Hormone."

He has another jar in his hand.

"It comes in this gel...and you just rub it on your balls."

Nick proceeds to stick his hands in his pants and rub it on his balls. Sam Shepard calls out, "Maybe we should start now."

Strictly speaking, this was my first play. And that's what I had them put in the *Playbill* that everybody gets when they walk in the theater. But in fact, because of Cheech and Chong, I had more live stage experience than everybody in the cast put together. I was eager to see how this thing was going to be put together.

The cast assembled again soon and grazed over the craft services. After a while it began to feel like we were starting way late. The stage manager came in and announced that we were being dismissed for the day. We would all be contacted about restart. The whole cast went *buzz, buzz, buzz, buzz, buzz.*

We soon learned that Sam had had a heart attack. We all held our breath, but three days later he was back on the stage. He looked a little grayer, but I could see that he was going to make it. Every day he got stronger and we started working.

In a Shepard play, the language and especially the cadence are very important. The language repeats itself with slight variations each time. It was like learning a weird-ass time signature in music. Like you were playing in 12/4. Once you get the meter down, you find out how to play with it. I must have looked like a mute for the first four days of rehearsal as I mumbled my way through the table reads. Even when we started to get it on its feet, I was still head down, mumbling, clutching the script. All the while I was trying to figure out who this guy was.

The one question I kept asking myself was *What must have gone on in this man's life to bring him out to the middle of the desert to be the "friend" of this abusive drunk, Henry Moss? What kind of self-esteem, if any, does he have?* It's the same question that his son, played by Nick Nolte, asks me in the play.

"Why do you take care of him? What's in it for you?"

And I answer, "It's like feeding cattle."

The line gets an enormous laugh, the biggest in the play, night after night without fail. It was not *meant* to be a funny line, but they were laughing, *so it was*. One night before one of the previews, Sam and I are standing backstage together. And he asks me, in disbelief, "Why do they laugh there?"

This is from the man who wrote the play. I answered him with what I had come up with on my own.

"First of all, because it's me saying it. I'm known as a comedian, so if there's any room for interpretation they're going to think it's meant to be funny. Also because it's the first time that Esteban has voiced an opinion about the whole situation. He indeed has an opinion and it's very perceptive."

It's like discovering that the gardener speaks perfect English. Everybody is surprised.

Sam and I got to be very friendly and had a mutual-admiration dynamic going on. That doesn't mean he didn't get on my case if I was late for a rehearsal or missed one because of my *Nash Bridges* schedule. One afternoon I came in late and he started getting on my case and I told him, "Sam, can you beat me on the front? Because they've been beating me on the back all day at *Nash*." He didn't laugh but he stopped.

I respected Sam to the nth degree, and it was amazing to see him work every day to keep carving and shaping the play. He would listen to the audience, listen to the actors, but most of all he would listen to his inner voice to tell him what was right or wrong or good or bad. At some point, it gets to be opening night and he has to give it over to the actors and wish them good luck.

The Late Henry Moss was a difficult play to get right. It was like driving a super tanker. You had to be very precise with how you steered it. It was a magnum opus and it dealt with all the familial themes that Shepard had been dealing with in several other plays like *True West*, *Buried Child*, and *Curse of the Starving Class*. Some nights it was unwieldy, and if it got off track it was going to be a long night. Other nights, everybody was right on it and it sang like classic opera. The play was in three acts with two intermissions and ran almost three hours. It required a commitment from the audience.

I looked at it like whittling, as I did in all those shows with Tommy. Every night I would carve a little more in different scenes. Sometimes I was louder, sometimes softer. Sometimes I walked different. Sometimes I didn't walk at all and played the scene from one spot. Every night I was looking for that one little thing that would give a clear focus as to who this guy was. After a while, a flower would bloom and the true meaning of the scene would appear. I had a ball during the whole process.

This production was a real event in San Francisco. People were flying in from all over the country to attend and especially from Hollywood. Producers, directors, studio heads, and other star actors were there every night. Backstage there was a blackboard and everybody's guests for the night were listed under their names. We would all gather around and see who was coming. Everybody would get excited at any big stars on the list.

Finally, I had a guest listed under my name. The cast moved in to see who it was. John Lasseter was the name.

Somebody said, "Who in the hell is John Lasseter?"

He was unknown to this group because he was an animation director. He had not yet achieved the enormous acclaim that would come his way as the director of *Toy Story* and *Cars* and the creative head of both Pixar and Disney studios. John had asked me to be in *Cars*. I had a sly smile on my face as I said, "John Lasseter is the name that will be appearing on a check that I will be getting for the next twenty years."

They were still befuddled.

John turned out to be a prince and one of the most good-natured, enthusiastic, and creative people I have ever met. I was deeply honored to be part of the Pixar family. John and his wife, Nancy, have treated me with the utmost kindness through the years, and I cherish their friendship.

It was a real mixed-barrel of monkeys that were acting in this play, and you never knew what might happen from one night to the next. Woody Harrelson and I occupied the two dressing rooms on the third floor and kept each other amused and focused every night. Woody was in the whole second act and then he was off. I came off in the middle of the third act and then would go to the third floor. Woody and I would get high and shoot the shit. Sometimes T-Bone would join us. We had a fun time. *The Late Henry Moss* made a big impression in San Francisco. The actors in the play had something in common offstage, too. All of our friends told us that we each were the best thing in the play. They were right.

The last year of *Nash Bridges* was in 2001. That sixth season had its ups and downs. Old cast members were leaving, and new ones were coming in. Some episodes took a little longer to deliver. CBS ordered a seventh season, but Paramount would not pay for it. They had already made their money. The show did 122 episodes and would be syndicated everywhere. So we ended our run.

I have to say that the six years I spent in San Francisco with Don Johnson and the cast and crew of *Nash Bridges* were among the most joyous, rewarding, hard-working, and hysterically funny hours I have spent on earth. Don Johnson is a world-class host, and he wants everybody to have a good time...himself included. That spirit drove the most hard-charging crew I have ever worked with. No matter how early you got there and how few hours of sleep you got the night before, the crew was always there first.

Don would take a few of us, mostly cast, out to lunch every day at the best restaurant in the area that we were shooting. So every day we got to eat at the best restaurants in a city known the world over for its restaurants. Thank you, Lord. And Don.

We even started our own four-star Vietnamese restaurant in

Ghirardelli Square, called Ana Mandara. It was the top of the food chain and the most beautiful restaurant I have ever been in. Don always wanted a hang in the city and now we had one. Under the direction and partnership of Chef Khai Duong, Ana Mandara was open for an inspiring twelve years in that highly competitive gastric strata. I had some of the best meals and best conversations of my life in that upstairs room.

On *Nash Bridges*, I learned to do action, drama, light comedy, more drama, and more action, and to build stamina by doing it every day. We got to shoot every part of this soulful city and beam it out to the rest of the universe. San Francisco will always have a special place in my heart.

One of the casualties of working so much for so long was that there was now a growing strain in my marriage. It was tough for Patti to be left alone with all the domestic responsibilities of house and kids while I was perceived to be living it up. The thing that saved me from participating excessively was that I always said, "Gotta go. Wife and kids."

CHAPTER 34

Chicano Art

One of the most fortuitous things to come out of *Nash Bridges* was that I was now gainfully employed and had discretionary income, which I used to start collecting Chicano art. I had been collecting this school of art since 1985 but San Francisco was where I really built the bulk of the collection.

I was self-educated in art history from a very early age. The group of cousins I described earlier had assigned me to learn about art and bring it back to the group. At age eleven, I started going to the library and checking out all the art books. In this fashion I learned about Rembrandt, Caravaggio, van Gogh, Picasso, Vermeer, and all the great giants of Western art. I kept going back to the library until there were no more books left to check out.

In addition, I started going to museums to see paintings live and up close. This was a whole different experience from seeing them reproduced in a book. Paintings must be seen in person. That is the only way you can really feel the texture of the paintings. It is the only way you can see the true colors that the artist intended. I fell in love with painting because of the lushness and luminosity and malleability of the medium. Hundreds of years later these paintings are still alive, and people can still feel the magnetism that drew people to these works of art in the first place.

The gap in my knowledge was contemporary art. I knew some

names, but not many. So with my wife, Patti, who was a painter, I started going around to Westside art galleries in Los Angeles. One of the first galleries I visited was the Robert Berman Gallery where I first saw Chicano artists. I recognized right away that these artists were special.

Chicano art began in the late sixties as the public face of the Chicano Civil Rights movement. They were the sign painters, poster makers, and the backdrop artists of a political force that was demanding equal rights for the Latino population in the country. So, in the beginning, Chicano art was political art. It was not Chicano art unless it had a Sacred Heart wrapped in barbed wire or clenched fists raised in protest or the black and red United Farm Workers flag with the Union Eagle in the center. Early on, it depicted scenes of protest and conflict as they occurred in the communities.

After a while, as some goals were met and the fervor of the movement cooled down, the artists started to develop their own artistic visions. They still depicted their communities from a myriad of different viewpoints. Whether it was political, social, historical, religious or gender-based or even abstract, the art reflected the taste, or *sabor*, of their communities. You could now see Chicano communities from Los Angeles to El Paso and from San Francisco to San Antonio depicted in all their multicultural glory.

The Chicano School was not a particular style of painting like the Impressionists or Expressionists. Chicano artists are for the most part university and/or art school trained. They are exposed to and influenced by virtually every style, old or new or international. Chicano art is a combination of traditional Mexican art and contemporary world art. What emerges is a third thing that has its own distinctive vision. It is an evolutionary form that keeps mutating while still maintaining a Latino element. It is the first truly American school of art in almost seventy years. It is right up there with the Hudson River School, the Ashcan School, and even Pop Art. It was the inspiration for what now has evolved into street art, which is the biggest worldwide movement in art today. I knew none of this when I first started collecting. I just knew that these artists were great painters because I had seen great painting all my life.

I have been an inveterate collector of *something* for as long as I can remember. Whether it was baseball cards, bottle caps, or matchbook covers, I had a passion for collecting the whole set. In the beginning of my collecting mania, I was just looking for something to put over the couch. As I went on, the addiction started to take hold. Sometimes I would do movies and get partially paid in paintings.

What became apparent to me very quickly was that this was a school that was unrecognized and underserved. Because of its political beginnings, Chicano art was pigeonholed as "Agit-Prop Folk Art" (Agitational-Propaganda) and was largely shut out of museums. Who wants a bunch of headband-wearing, dope-smoking, angry Chicanos picketing their museums because they were not in the show? Undaunted, these artists kept growing and developing their own special vision. And I kept collecting them.

Eventually, the friends that I had made in the art world started urging me to show the collection. I looked around for a way to do this. After a long search, I was introduced to Stacy King from San Antonio, Texas, in 1999. Stacy had a company that was doing large, educational museum shows on a national level. Soon, she would become the head of museum projects for Clear Channel Corporation. Stacy was the perfect person, because she was a Texan from San Antonio, the other major center of Chicano art besides Los Angeles. She understood the art and the environment from which it sprang. We went around and looked for corporate sponsorship. We did our little dog-and-pony show in every major corporate boardroom across America. Finally, we connected with Target Stores and the Hewlett-Packard Corporation, who put up the production money to get the show built.

From the time we first started planning the show to the time we signed up our last museum, ten years had gone by. Target continued supporting the show through seven years and fourteen major venues across the country, including the Smithsonian in Washington, DC, the De Young in San Francisco, the Museum of Contemporary Art in La Jolla, the National Hispanic Cultural Center in Albuquerque, the Weisman in Minneapolis, and the Los Angeles County Museum of Art (LACMA).

Thanks to the corporate sponsorship of Target, the tour was hugely successful and broke attendance records in every single museum that we played. Moreover, it identified large Latino populations previously unknown to museum officials in many of the cities that hosted the show. For many people, it was the first time they had ever been in *any* museum.

The "Chicano Visions" tour was the first of many, many exhibitions of different parts of the collection that I would do, and still continue to do, all over the world. I would not have been able to mount and coordinate any of these shows if it were not for the invaluable work of my collections manager, assistant, and general right-hand gal, Melissa Richardson Banks from Flour Bluff, Texas.

My mantra has always been "You can't love or hate Chicano art unless you see it." I realized at some point that that was the reason I was collecting, to share this wonderful school of art with the rest of the world. It has become a huge part of my life and I consider myself blessed to be in this position.

CHAPTER 35

The night Kate Middleton asked me to dance

There was fog on the moors and the hounds were baying the night I landed in Glasgow, Scotland, on October 17, 1997. Or maybe it was just the sound of the jet engines dying down and the fog of the three vodkas and the sleeping pill I took for the transatlantic flight from LA. Anyway it was foggy and I was hungry. I drove around looking for someplace to eat until I found a restaurant that looked like it had typical Scottish food. A giant yellow and red sign glowed up ahead: McDonald's. OK, sounds Scottish and they have a drive-thru. I like it already. It feels like home.

As I drove along, scared shitless, on the wrong side of the road wolfing down a typical Scottish Big Mac, I wondered to myself, *Am I the first Chicano ever to set foot in the land of* Braveheart? Would they look at me and ask, "What the hell are you?" Would they ask me to mow their lawn? I was kind of let down when I got off the plane and everybody wasn't wearing kilts and there were no bagpipes to greet us, but at least they all talked like Willie, the school janitor from *The Simpsons*. And while that was nice, I couldn't understand a damn word they were saying.

As I mentioned when I discussed living with Karen Dalton and her cast of junkies in Los Angeles, I had seen a Scottish movie once called *Trainspotting*, about some Scottish junkies and although the dialogue was in English, it was subtitled... in English. *Trainspotting* also had the funniest scene I've ever seen in a movie... ever. It was the scene where one of the junkies dove headfirst into a toilet to retrieve a heroin capsule he had stuffed up his butt after he forgot he had taken a laxative. I was still laughing three scenes later. I guess you had to be there.

Now which way to St. Andrews?

Oh, by the way, that was why I was here in the land of haggis; to play golf in the Dunhill Cup Pro-Am Golf Tournament at the historic Royal and Ancient Golf Club at St. Andrews, the birthplace of golf, a game I was still playing after extended exposure to it while working on *Tin Cup*.

As I pulled up in front of the St. Andrews Hotel, dawn was just breaking, throwing that magical early morning light across the golf course, which lay there like a sleeping virgin just outside the glass doors. While the concierge was getting my room ready and looking for a translator who spoke both American and Scottish, I wandered through the lobby and out the doors. There she was, St. Andrews, the most storied golf course in the whole world, softly bathed in day's first light with a gossamer haze clinging to her every curve, her bikini-waxed greens just begging for a hole-in-one. At that moment I had an epiphany: "Chicanos were meant to play here. Everybody wears plaid. It's like being in East LA, only with bad food and nobody speaks Spanish."

I had been invited, along with Don Johnson, my partner in *Nash Bridges*, and some other international celebrities to play alongside a handful of European sports stars and some of the best professional golfers in the world. It was like dying and going to golf heaven. We were to play the Old Course at St. Andrews, Kingsbarns, a relatively new course that was a cross between Pebble Beach and St. Andrews, and Carnoustie, a fabled old Scottish course that was over 150 years old. The weather at this time of year could range anywhere from blowing to sucking, but we lucked out and every day was sunny... except for the day we played Carnoustie when it rained sideways. It didn't matter; I was having the time of my life.

I teed the ball up on the first hole of St. Andrews. As luck would have it, I hit it straight down the middle of the fairway. "A blondie," my caddie cried out in his colorful gnarled brogue. I didn't want to show my ignorance by not knowing what a blondie was, so I just nodded my head and picked up my tee. It was only as we walked down the first fairway that I leaned into my caddie Ian and said, "Excuse me, what is a blondie?" He cocked his head to one side, and his face wrinkled into a lopsided smile as he said, "It's a fair crack up the middle, laddie." I love playing golf here; it's a great combination between exercise and a Rosetta Stone language lab.

One of the great things about a Celebrity Pro-Am is that you get to play right alongside the very best professional golfers in the world. In no other sport does this happen. You don't get to play point guard with Kobe Bryant when the Lakers play the Dallas Mavericks, but in golf you get to play in the same foursome with Lee Westwood and Phil Mickelson and others *while* they are competing for money. For the amateurs like myself, it's a thrill of a lifetime. For the professionals, it's like a bring-your-kids-to-work day; some have fun, and some don't. The only other obligation the celebrities have besides signing two hundred autographs per round is attending the social events in the evening. This is where the celebs earn their keep. It's surprising how many professional athletes and their families and friends are gaga over movie and music stars, and the reverse is true with entertainers and sports stars. So we all have a great time mingling with each other and trying not to get too drunk in case we have to get up and say something to the audience. Most everybody fails at this.

The second night of the tournament was the big gala event. Dunhill was the sponsor, and I guess they invited all their important clients. I'm still not sure if Dunhill makes cigarettes or tires. Maybe they make both. Maybe they make smoking-hot tires. At any rate, they have a lot of money, and the crowd was very well-heeled and well dressed. As Don and I mingled around hobnobbing with the riffraff, I noticed a very familiar face a few tables away. It was young Prince William, second in line to the British throne. He was attending St. Andrews University at the time, so it made sense that he would be there. He was laughing and yucking it up with his chums. That's English for "homeboys."

One of his circle recognized Don and me, or at least Don, and he leaned in and whispered in William's ear. His Princeness smiled and nodded and waved in our direction. In a flash, his buddy was right beside us and asked if it would be possible for William to meet us. I thought he just meant Don. After all, just a few years before he was on the cover of every magazine that had a cover. But then the prince's pal leaned into me and whispered, "Dave's not here, man"— the stoner password phrase. I wondered if I could score some royal weed from him.

We walked over to William's table and he immediately stood up and extended his hand. "So very nice to meet you."

I didn't know the proper etiquette so I shook his hand and said, "Charmed, I'm sure...Prince Charming?"

William couldn't have been nicer. He thanked us for being at the event, which I think benefited his late mother's charity. We made a little more small talk and then went back to our table to have dinner. Before we left, I noticed that there was a very attractive young lady sitting with him at his table, and I immediately recognized her as his girlfriend, Kate Middleton. They were both students at St. Andrews. Pictures of them had been all over the tabloids, as they had just started going out together publicly. Kate smiled demurely and nodded in our direction.

As I ate dinner, I couldn't help but think what it must be like to be a member of the "lucky sperm club." William and all his family hadn't been elected to any office, yet they were the rulers of the British Empire, but without any power, yet all of the responsibility. Sure they were rich...very rich...and that goes a long way. Now I've been rich and I've been poor and believe me...rich is better. The royal family is expected to act as the perfect representation of the British people. It's their gig; it's what they do. Now, if they fuck up too bad they are probably hauled up in front of Queen Elizabeth and given a royal reaming. She might even take away a couple of their castles and they would be down to ten apiece or so. That could really mess up their weekend. So for the most part the royals behave, at least in public. Image is everything, especially for the British—you know, stiff upper lip and all that. What! What!

William was not the first royalty I had ever met. When I lived in Paris, I had occasion to hang out with Prince Albert of Monaco quite a few times. His mother, Grace Kelly, was an American movie star before she married Prince Rainier and became Princess Grace of Monaco. Albert himself went to high school and college in the United States, so he was thoroughly Americanized. Albert was a cool guy and liked to have fun, but he also had responsibilities so he knew where to draw the line. His sister Princess Stephanie, on the other hand, was a real case. Eventually she ran away and joined the circus and became a lion tamer or something like that. Most royals don't go that far off the deep end. Most royals look at their options and go, "Let's see, ruler of the country...or unemployment? I'll go with ruler of the country."

What I did notice pretty consistently, though, was that the male royalty (the princes) put off getting married for as long as they possibly could...unless they were gay, in which case they got married as soon as possible. Go figure. If I were in their position (the straight princes), I would probably do the same thing. I mean, you can have any girl in the kingdom any time you want, hell, you could probably even have a harem if you kept it on the down-low, why tie yourself down? Even if your kingdom were Monaco, which is about the size of the Del Amo Fashion Center, you would have crazy choices. The answer is perpetuation of the lucky sperm club. The royal family needs royal heirs, preferably boys, although there are plenty of queens (of both sexes) out there. If they run out of heirs, the population might say to themselves, "Hey, what do we need these guys for, they're expensive and they don't do dick." Believe me, the royals know their history all too well. You start believing your own hype, and you end up standing in line for the guillotine.

All this is rumbling through my head as dinner is ending and I see a big band setting up for dancing. I'm just chilling as the band starts playing. Nobody is dancing yet and the first tune is coming to an end. The band starts up sort of a Glenn Miller swing tune, and I'm tapping my foot and eating my ice cream when I see this girl striding across the dance floor with a purpose, and she's heading right for my table. It's Kate Middleton, William's main squeeze.

I look up and watch her come toward me almost in slow motion, like Bo Derek in *10* when she's running down the beach. She gets about five feet from me and sticks out her hand. She wants me to dance. Her invitation is not a question nor is it a command, but there's no doubt that I should get up right now and dance with this beautiful young lady.

We dance a little swing dance and I twirl her around a couple of times and make small talk like "Are you a student here?" I'm sure she's thinking, "No dummy, I'm here on a work release program." She has a mission and she's accomplishing it with aplomb. The dance floor is full of people. Katie (my pet name for her now) and I have broken the ice and the floor is crowded with tweed-covered English jitterbugs. I resist every Chicano, two-drink-minimum urge to pull her in and dance close until I realize she's about my daughter's age and the tune comes to an end. As soon as the music stops, she takes my hand firmly and leads me back to my table and deposits me in my seat. I have just been the chick. She smiles and thanks me for the dance and she's off. Mission accomplished.

I'm sitting there in kind of a fog and Don leans in and chuckles and says, "Did you get her number?" I snap out of it and say, "No, I can't break her heart like that, she has a boyfriend. It would be too messy."

I remembered this when I watched William and Kate's royal wedding, which was seen by over two billion people. I thought, *She's better off. I hope she's happy...no, I really do.* And now a couple of years after that, she has had two children. She couldn't be doing a better job as princess, and the whole world loves her. I made the right decision. I raise a toast to their future and toss back a tequila. I feel like Bogey at the end of Casablanca.

CHAPTER 36

Endings, reunions, and new beginnings

After trying for a year to find another show that could be shot in San Francisco, I realized that it was not likely to happen. With great reluctance we pulled up stakes, took the kids out of school, and moved back to Malibu.

Tough life, huh? Actually 99 percent of all actors go from job to job, and those are the lucky ones. I was pretty fortunate to have that steady work for so long on *Nash Bridges*.

When we got back to Malibu, we knew our marriage had strained past the breaking point, and Patti and I parted ways. It was a sad time.

As I contemplated my future, the past returned via the telephone.

"Hi, Cheech! How are you? It's Lou."

As in Lou Adler.

His was a voice that I never thought I would ever hear on the phone again. Lou Adler, our longtime producer, the person we made all our gold records with, who owned our record company, and with whom we made our first movie, *Up in Smoke*, was calling me?

Tommy and I had been involved in an extremely acrimonious, ten-year-long lawsuit with Lou that ended up splitting us apart. The lawsuit stopped what had been a long winning streak between us that could have been even longer. There were a lot of bad feelings on both sides. It had been many years since I had spoken to Lou.

"I know it must be weird to hear from me," Lou continued. "Believe me, it's weird for me, too. But I have a project that I thought you might be interested in."

Lou explained that his wife, Paige, was involved in a project for underprivileged and handicapped kids at UCLA. She saw right away that a big percentage of the kids in the program were Latino. She also saw the project's materials had next to nothing to read, watch, or play with in Spanish. Certainly nothing fresh and new. Lou said he was starting a kids' record label. He wanted to know if I would like to do a kids' album in Spanish and English. No strings attached. I could approach it any way I wanted.

Lou is as proud a guy as I am. I know it took a lot for him to call me. Probably about as much as it took for me to take the call. He closed by saying, "You don't have to decide right away, but you can probably have some fun with this. Let me know."

I thought about it. And I thought about my long and tangled history with Lou. But I also recognized it was a very worthwhile project, so I decided to do it. I had an idea for a funny Tex-Mex bus driver who would sing Tex-Mex songs for kids that were funny and educational. A few days later, I told Lou I'd do it and went right to work.

I collaborated with my musician friend Peter Kaye, who had a studio in his apartment where we recorded all the tracks in both English and Spanish. My young son Joey played a character on the album. The record and the songs came together quickly and I had a ball doing it.

The title track was much-praised in 1992 and won some awards. In the song "Red, Blue, and Yellow Too," the chorus teaches kids to learn how to mix secondary colors from primary colors. I modeled it after the educational rhyme "Thirty Days Hath September," a creative way to teach children how many days are in each month. The song was adopted by the Los Angeles School System and has been used in their art curriculum. I am very, very proud of that album. *My Name Is Cheech, the School Bus Driver* is some of the best work I have ever created.

Parents come up to me all the time and say they listened to the music every day while taking their kids to school. They also tell me that if they hear "My Name Is Cheech, the School Bus Driver" first thing in the morning, the tune stays in their head all day. I don't know if this is good or bad.

While I was driving a school bus, Tommy got busted for selling bongs. John Ashcroft, the attorney general of the United States at that time, was a real right wing, conservative a-hole. He wanted to police the Internet and had decided to go after the marijuana paraphernalia industry first. Making it hard to order bongs online was surely on top of everyone's list. International terrorism could wait.

He organized a two-year sting operation that targeted over fifty vendors. Tommy's son and wife, Shelby, had started an art glass company that made bongs. Idaho and Pennsylvania were the only two states that would prosecute these cases. Chong Glass was very careful not to ship across those particular state lines. However, somebody embedded in their company took an order and sent out a shipment to Pennsylvania. As a consequence, their company was busted.

Chong Glass was by far the smallest defendant, but it had the biggest name and the government needed a face for their operation. Ashcroft said if Tommy didn't claim responsibility they would send his wife and son to prison. Tommy stood up and took the charge and was sentenced to nine months at the Taft Correctional Institution in Taft, California. It was a very bogus charge, but he couldn't fight the government. It would have broken him. I visited him once. He said that visit was enough, because every time I came to see him they would have to look up his butt. Aw, come on man, don't you want to have any fun?

Around this time, I got on the show *Judging Amy* as a continuing character for two years. I was paired opposite Tyne Daly as her love interest. It was such a pleasure acting with this lovely and supremely talented Emmy and Tony award-winning actress. We laughed and sang Broadway show tunes all day. Chong told me later that he and his fellow inmates laughed at our pairing. It must have been hilarious... in prison.

By 2000 or so, Tommy Chong and I had been broken up longer than we had been together. As you've read, the years that we were apart were great for me. I got to do other wonderful movies; act in, write, and direct *Born in East L.A.*; work on a hit television series with Don Johnson; act in the world premiere of a major play by Sam Shepard; do voice acting in classic animated films like *The Lion King* and *Cars*, and get involved in the Chicano art world. Best of all, I got to stay home and watch my children grow up.

So, while part of me missed being in Cheech and Chong, part of me did not miss it at all. And I wasn't exactly sitting on my couch all day.

Still, as you might guess, over the years people have asked me all the time: "When are you guys going to do another movie?"

I always answered, "Well, you never know."

In reality, we could never agree on who was going to do what regarding writing and directing, so any talks always led nowhere.

When we first broke up, Chong always thought that it was a temporary thing and I would come to my senses. He repeatedly told me that I would never be bigger than Cheech and Chong by myself. Maybe not, but that was not the point. I didn't want to be in a dysfunctional "marriage" anymore. I was much happier on my own.

He would call every once in a while and ask me if I wanted to get back together and my answer was always the same... no thanks. Sometimes he would call me live from onstage when he was doing stand-up and try to tease me with the audience. I went along with it a couple of times and then stopped answering his calls.

We weren't mortal enemies. I just preferred not working with him on a regular basis. He guest-starred on an episode of *Nash Bridges*. That was nice. See you around.

However, people would ask me *all the time*: When are you guys going to do something together? In the years since we broke up, our audience kept getting bigger and bigger because of the Internet. There were more generations of fourteen- to fifteen-year-old kids who were turned on to our movies and records. That drumbeat was always out there.

There were different people who were trying to get us back together to tour. Of course, first in line were our agents and managers, but Tommy's kids kept trying, too. His daughter Robbie tried her best to get us to write a movie together. Good luck with that one.

Then everybody focused on getting us to do a tour. Of all the things that we did together, stage work was the thing that we argued about the least. The reason was very simple. The audience either laughed or they didn't laugh. The results were immediate.

Next to try was Paris, Tommy's son. Paris is a great kid whom I like a whole lot. He was very calm and could manage his father. He never stopped trying. Finally, he got us to meet in person at my house. It turned out to be a disaster. It got heated and I told Chong exactly what I thought about him.

After hearing about that meeting from his father, Paris suggested that Tommy send me an e-mail. Paris thought that would be calmer. The e-mail that Tommy was going to send was not calmer, however. Paris rewrote it, and the message I received was reasonable. I started to think that maybe, just maybe, something was possible.

Over the years there were many times that I missed being on the road doing live shows. I missed going from city to city and feeling the pulse of the country. Now we were stuck, and neither one of us could access these riches that people were clamoring for all these years. It was like we each had half of a treasure map. We could not find the prize unless we put the two halves together.

When our agents and managers finally finished arguing and trying to outmaneuver each other, we signed a deal in 2008 with Live Nation to do a tour of the United States and Canada. Within a week it was sold out. Stranger things have happened, but I can't think of any right now.

Estranged bands like the Eagles can get back together and be fine, because all they have to do is play their instruments and sing. They don't even have to talk to each other...and they seldom do. On the other hand, we not only have to talk to each other, we have to do it with timing.

The ironic thing about our relationship was that no matter what dysfunction we were going through at any time, when we got on the stage, none of it mattered. We had this chemistry and harmony that was established almost against our wills. When we finally got onstage together, even without rehearsal, it was like we had been apart for twenty minutes, not twenty years.

We finished the tour and continued to do more dates and still do to this day. In 2015, Tommy was diagnosed with rectal cancer and went through chemo and radiation therapy. Thankfully he came through all right and continues to be healthy.

While I lived in San Francisco during the shooting of *Nash Bridges*, we rented out the Malibu beach house to a series of like-minded artists. Stewart Copeland, the drummer in the Police and a movie soundtrack composer, took the house for a summer while we stayed in San Francisco. Steve Zallian, one of today's preeminent screenwriters (*Schindler's List*, *The Girl with the Dragon Tattoo*, *American Gangster*) and his family lived in the house for over two years. He was very disappointed when I wouldn't sell it to him. He said that his family's happiest times were when they lived there.

Next, Danny Elfman, the musician and composer (the *Simpsons* theme and far too many big movies to mention), moved his whole studio in. He worked on movie after movie there and was reluctant to move out. I had to give him a deadline, because I wanted to move back in after my San Francisco days, and marriage, were over. I even extended the deadline twice.

But eventually I was back in. Kind of enjoying it but still kind of in shock from the marital changes in my life.

I wandered around. Things happen. Time goes by. I got an invite to a wine tasting. My friend Steve and I went. The road was narrow and winding, and we had to park way down the hill. We got out of the car at the same time as an obviously beautiful woman a few cars ahead of us. Steve asked me, "Which way do we go?"

I said, "I'm going wherever she goes."

Luckily, she was going to the same place and we were introduced to each other. Her name was Natasha Rubin. She was Russian, from St. Petersburg. She was a classical pianist and a graduate of St. Petersburg Conservatory. She was elegant and at the same time down to earth, especially with her Russian girlfriends. She switched languages frequently (she speaks four). I eavesdropped on some of her conversations. She was opinionated but with a sense of humor. She was exotic in a sophisticated way that only Russian women can be. In every way, Natasha was a knockout.

We started talking, and I found out that she did not know about Cheech and Chong—or even Cheech, for that matter—but *Tin Cup* was one of her mother's favorite movies. I thought it was a good sign. I asked her out, but before our first date she had to Google me. I couldn't wait to Google her back. I took her to see my friend George Lopez in concert at the Universal Amphitheater. Next, she invited me to see an opera. In a month, she learned all things Chicano, and I learned that operas are really long.

Our relationship developed rapidly, and before too long I asked her to move in with me in Malibu. Her family consisted of her mother, Natalia, who spoke only Russian (I would have fun with that later) and her young, talented, and very intelligent son, Max. Together, with my three children, we formed a new family unit.

After a few years we decided to get married and started planning our wedding. We would have it at the house and it would be attended by only our families and our closest friends. Natasha had even learned all the Chicano nicknames of everybody in the family, so I was pretty sure she was committed. Every day I thought about the approaching ceremony with a big smile, anticipating seeing everybody we loved in the world in the same place, at the same time.

We were married on the beach, in front of the house, with all of our children, Carmen, Joey, Jasmine, and Max, looking on. The ceremony was performed by the Mayor of Los Angeles, Antonio Villaraigosa. It was a fittingly grand climax to forty wonderful years in Malibu. We were in heaven and continue to be as we walk hand in hand into the sunset. Natasha is the best wife I could ever imagine. I'm a very lucky guy.

As I look ahead, I see good times and happiness in my personal life. I'm lucky to have such a wonderful family. As for work, I can only say that I'll do what I have always done: Be ready for whatever comes next.

THANKS

I'm used to working in teams. I have worked with teams of all kinds and all sizes. The ability of your team to work together will determine the success of your project. This has been a remarkably pleasant experience. For that rare occurrence I would like to thank the following teammates:

First and foremost I would like to thank Margret McBride, my literary agent. Margret first saw me give an art lecture in San Diego and immediately came up to me and said, "You should write a book." Sounds easy, but the work is very hard and constant, and she has proven to be a valiant warrior and a smooth diplomat. It was fun to see her switch into her secret identity of "Super-Agent" and slay all the dragons.

Faye Atchison, Margret's co-worker who always knew where everybody was and how to get ahold of them. Essential for getting the project completed.

John Hassan, my talented collaborator who came with a boatload of experience and some very sharp eyes and ears that always steered me away from the rocks and onto the shore. John is like a world-class jockey who knows when to let his horse run on its own and when to apply the crop. This book would not have been the same without his sage advice.

To all the people at Hachette, starting with the amazing Gretchen Young, vice president and executive editor, who from the outset tirelessly championed my book in-house through every phase of the publishing process and editorial assistant Katherine Stopa, who insured every detail was completed. No matter how many times I tried, I could not bullshit them. I think the world of you. Thank you very much.

Thanks

Thanks to Jamie Raab, my publisher, and Deb Futter, the editor-in-chief. I'm pretty sure they know what I'm doing.

To Brian Lemus for the outstanding cover that captures the essence of the story and you can see from across the airport.

Thanks to Melanie Gold (Managing Editorial), Jimmy Franco and Andrew Duncan (Publicity)—you can't have enough publicity—and John Pelosi (Legal), who just chuckled when I said, "Aw, they'll never notice."

Thanks to Yvette Shearer, my publicist, whose motto is "Don't worry; I'm on it."

And a huge thank-you to Melissa Richardson Banks, who has done everything for me for more years than I care to mention. It would take longer than the pages I have to list all the things she does for me. She knows when I'm about to freak out and just smiles and says, "I'll take care of it." My life would be very different without her unswerving support.

To Hugh M. Davies, who as director of the Museum of Contemporary Art San Diego (MCASD), opened doors and welcomed new voices in Chicano art.

Thank you to Stan Coleman, my best friend and lawyer (go figure), who has been there by my side protecting me for what seems like the last two hundred years.

To Tommy Chong, with whom by now I share certain DNA strains. We have shared enough scenarios to fill five more books.

To Linda Livingston, my oldest and dearest friend, who has been there from the very start and knows where all the bodies are buried, but more important, where all the photographs are, because she took them.

Thank you to Lou Adler for believing in us and me and for all the early guidance and the pictures along the way.

Most of all, thanks to my beautiful and talented wife, Natasha, who is always the first to read whatever I write. Somehow we have found each other, and I thank my lucky stars every day.